D1535137

The Language and Thought of the Child

'His theory of child development has influenced the way millions of schoolchildren have been taught.'
The Times Literary Supplement

'Piaget's imaginative and detailed studies of the development of thinking, from babyhood through infancy and adolescence, have inspired countless admiring followers and respectful critics. . . . Despite all the criticisms, there is a rich store of psychological insights and theoretical speculations, and a profusion of intriguing empirical observations and remarkably ingenious experiments, to be found in Piaget's pioneering work. Educational, developmental and cognitive psychology are all informed by his thought.'
Margaret Boden, author of The Creative Mind

'Piaget was a philosopher's psychologist who displayed an exceptional interdisciplinary expertise in making a major contribution to human knowledge.'
Leslie Smith, editor of Jean Piaget: Critical Assessments

Routledge Classics contains the very best of Routledge publishing over the past century or so, books that have, by popular consent, become established as classics in their field. Drawing on a fantastic heritage of innovative writing published by Routledge and its associated imprints, this series makes available in attractive, affordable form some of the most important works of modern times.

For a complete list of titles visit
www.routledgeclassics.com

Jean
Piaget

The Language and Thought of the Child

Third Edition

Translated by Marjorie and Ruth Gabain

London and New York

155.4
Pia

Le Language et la pensée chez l'enfant first published
1923 by Delachaux et Niestlé, Paris

English edition first published 1926
by Kegan Paul, Trench, Trubner & Co.
Second edition 1932
Third, revised and enlarged edition published 1959
by Routledge & Kegan Paul

First published in Routledge Classics 2002
by Routledge
2 Park Square, Milton Park, Abingdon, Oxon, OX14 4RN

Simultaneously published in the USA and Canada
by Routledge
270 Madison Avenue, New York, NY 10016

Reprinted 2006, 2007, 2008, 2009

Routledge is an imprint of the Taylor & Francis Group, an informa business

English Translation © 1959 Majorie and Ruth Gabain

Typeset in Joanna by RefineCatch Limited, Bungay, Suffolk
Printed and bound in Great Britain by the MPG Books Group

British Library Cataloguing in Publication Data
A catalogue record for this book is available from the British Library

Library of Congress Cataloging in Publication Data
A catalogue record for this book has been requested

ISBN 10: 0–415–26750–1
ISBN 13: 978–0–415–26750–2

Contents

indicate wherein consists the novelty of the studies which this volume inaugurates.

Up till now such enquiries as have been made into the intelligence and language of the child have been in the main analytic. All the different forms which reasoning and abstraction, the acquisition and formation of words and phrases may take in the child have been described, and a detailed and certainly serviceable catalogue has been made of the mistakes, errors and confusions of this undeveloped mentality, and of the accidents and deformities of the language which expresses it.

But this labour does not seem to have taught the psychologist exactly what he wanted to know, *viz.* why the child thinks and expresses himself in a certain manner; why his curiosity is so easily satisfied with any answer one may give or which he may give himself (testifying to that *n'importequisme* which Binet considered one of the chief characteristics of imbecile mentality); why he affirms and believes things so manifestly contrary to fact; whence comes his peculiar verbalism; and how and by what steps this incoherence is gradually superseded by the logic of adult thought. In a word, contemporary research has stated the problem clearly but has failed to give us the key for its solution. To the psychologist the mind of the child still gives an impression of appalling chaos. As M. Cramaussel once truly remarked: "Thought in a child is like a net-work of tangled threads, which may break at any moment if one tries to disentangle them."

Explanations have naturally been forthcoming to account for such striking facts. The weakness, the debility of the child's brain have been cited. But, I would ask, does this tell us anything? The blame has also been laid on the insufficiency of the experience acquired, on the lack of skill of the senses, on a too limited contingent of associations, on the accidents of imitation. . . . True as they may be, however, these statements lead us nowhere.

After all, the error has been, if I am not mistaken, that in examining child thought we have applied to it the mould and pattern of the adult mind; we have considered it from the point of view of the logician rather than of the psychologist. This method, excellent perhaps for establishing our first inventory, has yielded all it can yield, and ends only in a blind alley. It enables us to straighten out the skein but it does not teach us how to disentangle the threads.

M. Jean Piaget's studies offer us a completely new version of the child's mind.

M. Piaget is lucky enough to be still young. He was initiated into psychology at a time when the superficial associationism which had more or less intoxicated his seniors thirty or forty years back was dead and buried, and when vistas full of promise were opening out before our science. For James, Flournoy and Dewey it was the dynamic and pragmatic tendency that counted; for Freud, psycho-analysis; for Durkheim (no matter whether his doctrine was sound or not) the recognition of the rôle played by social life in the formation of the individual mind; for Hall, Groos, Binet and the rest, genetic psychology propped up by a biological conception of the child.

By a stroke of genius, M. Piaget having assimilated these new theories, or rather having extracted the good from each, has made them all converge on to an interpretation of the child's mentality. He has kindled a light which will help to disperse much of the obscurity which formerly baffled the student of child logic.

Do you know the little problem which consists in making four equal triangles with six matches? At first, while one thinks of it on the flat, it appears, and quite rightly so, to be insoluble; but as soon as one thinks of solving it in three-dimensional space, the difficulty vanishes. I hope I do not misrepresent M. Piaget's ideas in using this simple and somewhat crude example to illustrate the nature of his contributions to child psychology.

Up till now we were as helpless in the face of the problem presented by child mentality as before a puzzle from which several important pieces were missing, whilst other pieces seemed to have been borrowed from another game and were impossible to place. Now M. Piaget relieves our embarrassment by showing us that this problem of childish thought does not consist of one puzzle, but of at least two. In possession of this key we no longer try to arrange on the flat, pieces which in order to fit together require a space of three dimensions.

Our author shows us in fact that the child's mind is woven on two different looms, which are as it were placed one above the other. By far the most important during the first years is the work accomplished on the lower plane. This is the work done by the child himself, which attracts to him pell-mell and crystallizes round his wants all that is likely to satisfy these wants. It is the plane of subjectivity, of desires, games, and whims, of the Lustprinzip as Freud would say. The upper plane, on the contrary, is built up little by little by social environment, which presses more and more upon the child as time goes on. It is the plane of objectivity, speech, and logical ideas, in a word the plane of reality. As soon as one overloads it, it bends, creaks and collapses, and the elements of which it is composed fall on to the lower plane, and become mixed up with those that properly belong there. Other pieces remain half-way, suspended between Heaven and Earth. One can imagine that an observer whose point of view was such that he did not observe this duality of planes, and supposed the whole transition to be taking place on one plane, would have an impression of extreme confusion. Because each of these planes has a logic of its own which protests loudly at being coupled with that of the other. And M. Piaget, in suggesting to us with confirmatory proofs that thought in the child is intermediate between autistic thinking and the logical thought processes of the adult, gives us a general perspective of child mentality which will singularly facilitate the interpretation of its various functions.

This new conception to which M. Piaget leads us, whether in

tacit or explicit opposition to current opinion, could be stated (though always in very schematic and summary fashion) in yet another set of terms. Whereas, if I am not mistaken, the problem of child mentality has been thought of as one of quantity, M. Piaget has restated it as a problem of quality. Formerly, any progress made in the child's intelligence was regarded as the result of a certain number of additions and subtractions, such as increase of new experience and elimination of certain errors—all of them phenomena which it was the business of science to explain. Now, this progress is seen to depend first and foremost upon the fact that this intelligence undergoes a gradual change of character. If the child mind so often appears opaque to adult observation, it is not so much because there are elements added to or wanting in it, not so much because it is full of holes and excrescences as because it belongs to a *different kind* of thought—autistic or symbolic thought, which the adult has long since left behind him or suppressed.

The method which in M. Piaget's hands has proved to be so prolific is also one of great originality. Its author has christened it "the clinical method." It is, in fact, that method of observation, which consists in letting the child talk and in noticing the manner in which his thought unfolds itself. The novelty consists in not being content simply to record the answers given by the child to the questions which have been put to him, but letting him talk of his own accord.

If we follow up each of the child's answers, and then, allowing him to take the lead, induce him to talk more and more freely, we shall gradually establish for every department of intelligence a method of clinical analysis analogous to that which has been adopted by psychiatrists as a means of diagnosis[1]

[1] *Arch. de Psychol.*, XVIII., p. 276.

This clinical method, therefore, which is also an art, the art of questioning, does not confine itself to superficial observations, but aims at capturing what is hidden behind the immediate appearance of things. It analyses down to its ultimate constituents the least little remark made by the young subjects. It does not give up the struggle when the child gives incomprehensible or contradictory answers, but only follows closer in chase of the ever-receding thought, drives it from cover, pursues and tracks it down till it can seize it, dissect it and lay bare the secret of its composition.

But in order to bear fruit this method required to be completed by a judicious elaboration of the documents which it had served to collect. And this is where M. Piaget's qualities as a naturalist have intervened. All his readers will be impressed by the care with which he has set out his material, by the way in which he classified different types of conversation, different types of questions, different types of explanations; and they will admire the suggestive use to which he puts this classification. For M. Piaget is a first-class biologist. Before going in for psychology, he had already made his name in a special branch of the zoology of molluscs. As early as 1912 (he was then only fifteen) he published studies on the molluscs of the Neuchâtel Jura. A little later, he wrote a monograph on the molluscs of the Valais and Leman districts. The subject of his doctor's thesis in 1918 was the distribution of the different varieties of molluscs in the Valaisian Alps.

It must not be supposed, however, that in collecting psychological material in the place of snails, and in ordering and labelling it with so much care, M. Piaget has simply turned from one hobby to another. Far from it. His observations are not made for the pleasure of making them. Even in the days when he was collecting shells on the dry slopes of the Valais mountains, his only object was to discover whether there was any relation between the shape of those little animals and the altitude at which they live, between variation and adaptation. Still more is this so in his psychological work. His only aim in collecting, recording, and cataloguing all these different types of behaviour is to see the assembled materials in a clearer light, to facilitate the task of comparing and affiliating them one to another. Our author has a special talent for letting the material speak for itself, or rather for hearing it speak for itself. What strikes one in this first book of his is the natural way in which the general ideas have been suggested by the facts; the latter have not been forced to fit ready-made hypotheses.

It is in this sense that the book before us may be said to be the work of a naturalist. And this is all the more remarkable considering that M. Piaget is among the best informed of men on all philosophical questions. He knows every nook and cranny and is familiar with every pitfall of the old logic—the logic of the textbooks; he shares the hopes of the new logic, and is acquainted with the delicate problems of epistemology. But this thorough mastery of other spheres of knowledge, far from luring him into doubtful speculation, has on the contrary enabled him to draw the line very clearly between psychology and philosophy, and to remain rigorously on the side of the first. His work is purely scientific.

If then M. Piaget takes us so far into the fundamental structure of the intelligence of the child, is it not because the questions he set himself in the first instance were questions of function? The writer of these lines may perhaps be allowed to emphasize this idea of which he is a particular advocate. The functional question fertilizes the structural question, and states the problem better than any other way. It alone gives full significance to the details of mechanism, because it sees them in relation to the whole machine. So it may well be because he began with the questions: "Why does the child talk? What are the functions of language?" that M. Piaget has been led to such fertile observations and conclusions.

But we would never have done if we once began to point out all that is new and suggestive in this book. Why should we? The reader will discover it for himself by the perusal of its pages. I only wish in conclusion to address to my colleague a word of thanks in the name of the *Institut J. J. Rousseau*.

When we opened this Institute in 1912, it was hoped that the two main pillars upon which we intended to build the edifice— the scientific study of the child and the training of teachers— would not remain isolated, but be spanned and mutually reinforced by many a connecting arch. But the cares of organization, the unexpected developments of an undertaking which receives fresh impetus and grows faster than one had calculated, the requirements of daily teaching, to say nothing of the disturbances caused by the war—all these have prevented our scientific investigations from proceeding as we would have wished. The Institut Rousseau has, it is true, given birth to some remarkable works, such as *L'Instinct combatif* by M. Bovet, the director, such as the patient investigations made by Mlle Descœudres on child language; our students too have often collaborated in research, and have constantly taken part in experiments. It is only since M. Piaget's arrival, however, that a union closer than could ever have been hoped for has been achieved between the most rigorous scientific research and an initiation of the students to the psychology of the child.

Having therefore witnessed for two years the consummate skill with which my colleague has utilized and directed his developing powers in tracking down the quarry with which he has presented us in so masterly a fashion, I feel it both a privilege and a duty to express my sincere admiration for his work.

E. CLAPARÈDE.

primitive peoples, or worse still to the prejudices of the logical or epistemological system to which we unwittingly subscribe, try though we may to maintain a purely psychological attitude of mind. The logic of the text-books and the naïve realism of common sense are both in this respect fatal to any sane psychology of cognition, and the more so since in trying to avoid the one we are often thrown back upon the other.

For all these reasons I have abstained on principle from giving too systematic an account of our material, and *a posteriori* from making any generalizations outside the sphere of child psychology. All I have attempted has been to follow step by step the facts as given in experiments. We know well enough that experiment is always influenced by the hypothesis which occasioned it, but I have for the time being confined myself strictly to the discussion of facts.

Moreover, for teachers and all those whose work calls for an exact knowledge of the child's mind, facts take precedence over theory. I am convinced that the mark of theoretical fertility in a science is its capacity for practical application. This book is therefore addressed to teachers as much as to specialists in child psychology, and the writer will be only too pleased if the results he has accumulated are of service to the art of teaching, and if in return his own thesis finds practical confirmation in this way. He is convinced in this connexion that what he tries to prove in this work concerning the ego-centrism of child thought and the part played by social life in the development of reason, must admit of pedagogic application. If he personally has not attempted straight away to establish these consequences, it is because he prefers to let professional opinion have the first say.

Specialists in child logic will not, I hope, take me to task for the disjointed character of this book, which is, as I have said, simply a study of the facts of the case. I hope in a few years' time to produce a work dealing with child thought as a whole, in which I shall again take up the principal features of child logic, and state their relation to the biological factors of adaptation (imitation and assimilation). This is the subject which was dealt with in the lectures above referred to. Before publishing these in systematic form it will be necessary to give as minute and exhaustive a catalogue as possible of the material on which their conclusions are based. The present volume is the first of this series. I hope to follow it up with another, which will be entitled: *Judgment and Reasoning in the Child*. Together, these two will go to make up "Studies in Child Logic." In a second work I shall undertake to analyse causality and the function of reality in the child. Then only shall we be in a position to formulate a synthesis. If it were attempted any sooner, any such synthesis would be constantly interrupted by an exposition of the evidence, which in its turn would tend to be distorted in the process.

One last word in acknowledgment of my debt to those, without whose teaching this work could never have been undertaken. M. Claparède and M. Bovet of Geneva have consistently helped me by referring everything to the point of view of function and to that of instinct—two points of view without which one passes over the deepest springs of activity in the child. Dr Simon of Paris introduced me to the tradition of Binet. M. Janet, whose influence will often be traced in these pages, familiarized me with a psychology of conduct which offers a happy combination of genetic methods and clinical analysis. I have also been deeply influenced by the social psychology of M. C. Blondel and Professor J. M. Baldwin. It will likewise be apparent how much I owe to psycho-analysis, which in my opinion has revolutionized the psychology of primitive thought. Finally, I need hardly recall Flournoy's contribution to French psychology by his fusion of the results of psycho-analysis with those of ordinary psychology.

Outside the sphere of psychology I owe much to authorities who have not been quoted—or not sufficiently quoted—because of my desire to exclude all but strictly pædological

FOREWORD TO THE THIRD EDITION

This little book, written in 1923, was merely a collection of preliminary studies. In a foreword to its second edition, written in 1930, we stated that it would be followed by further studies on the child's ego-centric language and by what would have been entitled "Nouvelles Récherches sur la Logique de l'Enfant"—both were to be incorporated in one volume.

We have carried out the first of these intentions in this third edition by adding another chapter.[1] This new chapter uses the material collected by Mme A. Leuzinger-Schuler in which the child's speech with an adult is compared with speech between playmates. This study provides us with an opportunity for answering various questions which have been raised in connection with our hypotheses by D. Katz, Stern, Mrs. Isaacs, etc., and it will enable us once again to say what characterizes "intellectual ego-centrism," which has so often been given a meaning quite different from the one we attribute to this word (an

[1] Chapter 6

ill-chosen one, no doubt, but which is now generally accepted).

As to the "Nouvelles Récherches sur la Logique de l'Enfant" we confess to our shame that instead of appearing in one small volume as a supplement to this one and its complement *Judgment and Reasoning in the Child*, these studies have given rise to a series of independent works.

After having worked on *The Origin of Intelligence in the Child* and on *The Child's Construction of Reality*, two studies on the beginnings of intelligence, to which has since been added *La Formation du Symbole chez l'Enfant* (Delachaux et Niéstlé 1945), which is on the beginnings of representation, we returned to the problem of the child's sense of logic as regards number (*The Child's Conception of Number*), quantity (*Le Développement des Quantités chez l'Enfant*) and movement (*Les Notions de Mouvement et de Vitesse chez l'Enfant*). Finally, we have endeavoured to sum up all the results obtained in a logical synthesis (*Classes, Relations et Nombres*) and in a psychological synthesis (*The Psychology of Intelligence*).

JEAN PIAGET.

GENEVA.

weather is changing for the worse," "Bodies fall to the ground." At times, on the other hand, language expresses commands or desires, and serves to criticize or to threaten, in a word to arouse feelings and provoke action—"Let's go," "How horrible!" etc. If we knew approximately in the case of each individual the proportion of one type of speech to another, we should be in possession of psychological data of great interest. But another point arises. Is it certain that even adults always use language to communicate thoughts? To say nothing of internal speech, a large number of people, whether from the working classes or the more absent-minded of the *intelligentsia*, are in the habit of talking to themselves, of keeping up an audible soliloquy. This phenomenon points perhaps to a preparation for social language. The solitary talker invokes imaginary listeners, just as the child invokes imaginary playfellows. This is perhaps an example of that return shock of social habits which has been described by Baldwin; the individual repeats in relation to himself a form of behaviour which he originally adopted only in relation to others. In this case he would talk to himself in order to make himself work, simply because he has formed the habit of talking to others in order to work on them. Whichever explanation is adopted, it would seem that language has been side-tracked from its supposed function, for in talking to himself, the individual experiences sufficient pleasure and excitement to divert him from the desire to communicate his thoughts to other people. Finally, if the function of language were merely to "communicate," the phenomenon of verbalism would hardly admit of explanation. How could words, confined as they are by usage to certain precise meanings (precise, because their object is to be understood), eventually come to veil the confusion of thought, even to create obscurity by the multiplication of verbal entities, and actually to prevent thought from being communicable? This is not the place to raise the vexed question of the relation between thought and language, but we may note in passing that the very existence of such questions shows how complex are the functions of language, and how futile the attempt to reduce them all to one—that of communicating thought.

The functional problem therefore exists for the adult. How much more urgently will it present itself in the case of defective persons, primitive races and young children. Janet, Freud, Ferenczi, Jones, Spielrein, etc., have brought forward various theories on the language of savages, imbeciles, and young children, all of which are of the utmost significance for an investigation such as we propose to make of the child mind from the age of 6.

M. Janet, for example, considers that the earliest words are derived from cries with which animals and even savages accompany their action—threats, cries of anger in the fight, etc. In the earliest forms of social activity, for instance, the cry uttered by the chief as he enters into battle becomes the signal to attack. Hence the earliest words of all, which are words of command. Thus the word, originally bound up with the act of which it is an element, at a later stage suffices alone to release the act.[1] The psycho-analysts have given an analogous explanation of word magic. The word, they say, having originally formed part of the act, is able to evoke all the concrete emotional contents of the act. Love cries, for instance, which lead up to the sexual act are obviously among the most primitive words; henceforward these and all other words alluding to the act retain a definite emotional charge. Such facts as these explain the very wide-spread tendency of primitive thought to look upon the names of persons and objects, and upon the designation of events as pregnant with the qualities of these objects and events. Hence the belief that it is possible to work upon them by the mere evocation of words, the word being no longer a mere label, but a formidable reality

---

[1] British Journ. of Psych. (Med. Sect.), Vol. I, Part 2, 1921, p. 151.

partaking of the nature of the named object.[1] Mme Spielrein[2] has endeavoured to find the same phenomena in an analysis of the very earliest stages of child language. She has tried to prove that the baby syllables, *mama*, uttered in so many tongues to call the mother, are formed by labial sounds which indicate nothing more than a prolongation of the act of sucking. "Mama" would therefore be a cry of desire, and then a command given to the only being capable of satisfying this desire. But on the other hand, the mere cry of "mama" has in it a soothing element; in so far as it is the continuation of the act of sucking, it produces a kind of hallucinatory satisfaction. Command and immediate satisfaction are in this case therefore almost indistinguishable, and so intermingled are these two factors that one cannot tell when the word is being used as a real command and when it is playing its almost magical role.

Meumann and Stern have shown that the earliest substantives of child language are very far from denoting concepts, but rather express commands or desires; and there are strong reasons for presuming that primitive child language fulfils far more complicated functions than would at first appear to be the case. Even when due allowance is made for these theories in all their details, the fact remains that many expressions which for us have a purely conceptual meaning, retain for many years in the child mind a significance that is not only affective but also well-nigh magical, or at least connected with peculiar modes of behaviour which should be studied for themselves and quite apart from adult mentality.

It may therefore be of interest to state the functional problem in connexion with older children, and this is what we intend to

[1] See Jones, E, "A Linguistic Factor in English Characterology," *Intern. Journal of Psycho-Anal.*, Vol. I, Part 3, p. 256 (see quotations from Ferenczi and Freud, p. 257).

[2] See *Intern. Zeitschrift f. Psychoanal.*, Vol. VI, p. 401 (a report of the proceedings of the Psycho-analytical Conference at the Hague).

do as an introduction to the study of child logic, since logic and language are obviously interdependent. We may not find any traces of "primitive" phenomena. At any rate, we shall be very far removed from the common-sense view that the child makes use of language to communicate his thoughts.

We need not apologize for the introductory character of the questions dealt with in this work. We have simply thrown out certain feelers. We have aimed first and foremost at creating a method which could be applied to fresh observations and lead to a comparison of results. This method, which it was our only object to obtain, has already enabled us to establish certain facts. But as we have only worked on two children of six years old, and as we have taken down their talk—in its entirety, it is true—only for a month and during certain hours of the day, we advance our conclusions provisionally, pending their confirmation in the later chapters of the book.

I. THE MATERIAL

The method we have adopted is as follows. Two of us followed each a child (a boy) for about a month at the morning class at the *Maison des Petits de l'Institut Rousseau*, taking down in minute detail and in its context everything that was said by the child. In the class where our two subjects were observed the scholars draw or make whatever they like; they model and play at games of arithmetic and reading, etc. These activities take place in complete freedom; no check is put upon any desire that may manifest itself to talk or play together; no intervention takes place unless it is asked for. The children work individually or in groups, as they choose; the groups are formed and then break up again without any interference on the part of the adult; the children go from one room to another (modelling room, drawing room, etc.) just as they please without being asked to do any continuous work so long as they do not themselves feel any desire for it. In short, these school-rooms supply a first-class field of observation for everything connected with the study of the social life and of the language of childhood.[1]

We must anticipate at once any objection that may be advanced on the plea that since these children were used as subjects they were not observed in natural conditions. In the first place, the children, when they are in the play-room with their friends, talk just as much as they would at home, since they are allowed to talk all day long at school, and do not feel censured or constrained in any way whatsoever. In the second place, they do not talk any more at school than they would at home, since observation shows that up to a certain age, varying between 5 and 7½, children generally prefer to work individually rather than in groups even of two. Moreover, as we have taken down in its entirety the context of our two subjects' conversations, especially when it was addressed to an adult, it will be quite easy to eliminate from our statistics all that is not spontaneous talk on the part of the children, i.e., all that may have been said in answer to questions that were put to them.

Once the material was collected, we utilized it as follows. We began by numbering all the subjects' sentences. As a rule the child speaks in short sentences interspersed with long silences or with the talk of other children. Each sentence is numbered separately. Where the talk is a little prolonged, the reader must not be afraid of reckoning several consecutive sentences to one number, so long as to each sentence containing a definite idea only one number is affixed. In such cases, which are rare enough, the division is necessarily arbitrary, but this is of no importance for statistics dealing with hundreds of sentences.

Once the talk has been portioned out into numbered sentences, we endeavour to classify these into elementary functional

[1] Our grateful thanks are due to the ladies in charge of the *Maison des Petits*, Mlles Audemars and Lafandel, who gave us full freedom to work in their classes.

categories. It is this method of classification which we are now about to study.

§1. AN EXAMPLE OF THE TALK TAKEN DOWN.—Let us first of all give one complete example of the documents collected in this way, and let us examine it in all its complexity:

23. Pie (to Ez who is drawing a tram-car with carriages in tow): *But the trams that are hooked on behind don't have any flags.* (No answer.)

24. (Talking about his tram). *They don't have any carriages hooked on . . .* (He was addressing no one in particular. No one answers him.)

25. (To Béa), *'T'sa tram that hasn't got no carriages.* (No answer.)

26. (To Hei), *This tram hasn't got no carriages, Hei, look, it isn't red, d'you see . . .* (No answer.)

27. (Lev says out loud, "A funny gentleman" from a certain distance, and without addressing himself to Pie or to anyone else). Pie: *A funny gentleman!* (Goes on drawing his tram.)

28. *I'm leaving the tram white.*

29. (Ez who is drawing next to him says, "I'm doing it yellow"), *No, you mustn't do it all yellow.*

30. *I'm doing the stair-case, look.* (Béa answers, "I can't come this afternoon, I've got a Eurhythmic class.")

31. *What did you say?* (Béa repeats the same sentence.)

32. *What did you say?* (Béa does not answer. She has forgotten what she said, and gives Ro a push.)

33. (To Béa), *Leave him alone.*

34. (Mlle B. asks Ez if he would like to come with her), *Come here Ez, it isn't finished.* 34 bis. *Please teacher, Ez hasn't finished.*

35. (Without addressing himself to anyone,) *I'm doing some black stones . . .*

36. (Id), *Pretty . . . these stones.*

37. (To Ez), *Better than you, eh?* (No answer. Ez had not heard the previous remark.)

We have chosen this example from Pie (6½ years) because it is taken during the most sociable activity of which this child is capable: he is drawing at the same table as his bosom friend, Ez, and is talking to him the whole time. It would therefore be natural in a case of this kind if the sole function of speech were to communicate thought. But let us examine the matter a little more closely. It will be seen that from the social point of view the significance of these sentences or fragments of sentences is extremely varied. When Pie says: "*They don't have . . . etc.*" (24), or "*I'm doing . . . etc.*" (35) he is not speaking to anyone. He is thinking aloud over his own drawing, just as people of the working classes mutter to themselves over their work. Here, then, is a first category which should be singled out, and which in future we shall designate as *monologue*. When Pie says to Hei or to Béa: "*'T'sa tram . . . etc.*" (25) or "*This tram . . . etc.*" (26) he seems on this occasion to want to make himself understood; but on closer examination it will be seen that he cares very little who is listening to him (he turns from Béa to Hei to say exactly the same thing) and, furthermore, that he does not care whether the person he addresses has really heard him or not. He believes that someone is listening to him; that is all he wants. Similarly, when Béa gives him an answer devoid of any connexion with what he has just been saying (30), it is obvious that he does not seek to understand his friend's observation nor to make his own remark any clearer. Each one sticks to his own idea and is perfectly satisfied (30–32). The audience is there simply as a stimulus. Pie talks about himself just as he does when he soliloquizes, but with the added pleasure of feeling himself an object of interest to other people. Here then is a new category which we shall call the *collective monologue*. It is to be distinguished from the preceding category and also from those in which thoughts are actually exchanged or information given. This last case constitutes a separate category which we shall call *adapted information*, and to which we can relegate sentences 23 and 34b. In this case the child talks, not at random, but to specified persons, and with the object of making them listen and understand. In addition to these practical and objective forms of information, we can distinguish others of a more subjective character consisting of commands (33), expressions of derision or criticism, or assertions of personal superiority, etc. (37). Finally, we may distinguish mere senseless repetitions, questions and answers.

Let us now establish the criteria of these various categories.

§ 2. THE FUNCTIONS OF CHILD LANGUAGE CLASSIFIED.—The talk of our two subjects may be divided into two large groups— the *ego-centric* and the *socialized*. When a child utters phrases belonging to the first group, he does not bother to know to whom he is speaking nor whether he is being listened to. He talks either for himself or for the pleasure of associating anyone who happens to be there with the activity of the moment. This talk is ego-centric, partly because the child speaks only about himself, but chiefly because he does not attempt to place himself at the point of view of his hearer. Anyone who happens to be there will serve as an audience. The child asks for no more than an apparent interest, though he has the illusion (except perhaps in pure soliloquy if even then) of being heard and understood. He feels no desire to influence his hearer nor to tell him anything; not unlike a certain type of drawing-room conversation where every one talks about himself and no one listens.

Ego-centric speech may be divided into three categories:

1° *Repetition (echolalia)*: We shall deal only with the repetition of words and syllables. The child repeats them for the pleasure of talking, with no thought of talking to anyone, nor even at times of saying words that will make sense. This is a remnant of baby prattle, obviously devoid of any social character.

2° *Monologue:* The child talks to himself as though he were thinking aloud. He does not address anyone.

3° *Dual or collective monologue:* The contradiction contained in the phrase recalls the paradox of those conversations between children which we were discussing, where an outsider is always associated with the action or thought of the moment, but is expected neither to attend nor to understand. The point of view of the other person is never taken into account; his presence serves only as a stimulus.

In *Socialized speech* we can distinguish:

4° *Adapted information:* Here the child really exchanges his thoughts with others, either by telling his hearer something that will interest him and influence his actions, or by an actual interchange of ideas by argument or even by collaboration in pursuit of a common aim.

Adapted information takes place when the child adopts the point of view of his hearer, and when the latter is not chosen at random. Collective monologues, on the other hand, take place when the child talks only about himself, regardless of his hearers' point of view, and very often without making sure whether he is being attended to or understood. We shall examine this criterion in more detail later on.

5° *Criticism:* This group includes all remarks made about the work or behaviour of others, but having the same character as adapted information; in other words, remarks specified in relation to a given audience. But these are more affective than intellectual, i.e., they assert the superiority of the self and depreciate others. One might be tempted in view of this to place this group among the ego-centric categories. But "ego-centric" is to be taken in an intellectual, not in an ethical sense, and there can be no doubt that in the cases under consideration one child acts upon another in a way that may give rise to arguments, quarrels, and emulation, whereas the utterances of the collective monologue are without any effect upon the person to whom they are addressed. The shades of distinction, moreover, between adapted information and criticism are often extremely subtle and can only be established by the context.

6° *Commands, requests* and *threats:* In all of these there is definite interaction between one child and another.

7° *Questions:* Most questions asked by children among themselves call for an answer and can therefore be classed as socialized speech, with certain reservations to which we shall draw attention later on.

8° *Answers:* By these are meant answers to real questions (with interrogation mark) and to commands. They are not to be compared to those answers given in the course of conversation (categ. 4), to remarks which are not questions but belong to "information."

These, then, are the eight fundamental categories of speech. It goes without saying that this classification, like any other, is open to the charge of artificiality. What is more important, however, is that it should stand the test of practical application, i.e., that any reader who has made himself familiar with our criteria should place the same phrases more or less in the same categories. Four people have been engaged in classifying the material in hand, including that which is dealt with in the next chapter, and the results of their respective enquiries were found to coincide within 2 or 3 per cent.

Let us now return to one of these categories in order to establish the constants of our statistical results.

§ 3. REPETITION (ECHOLALIA).—Everyone knows how, in the first years of his life, a child loves to repeat the words he hears, to imitate syllables and sounds, even those of which he hardly understands the meaning. It is not easy to define the function of this imitation in a single formula. From the point of view of behaviour, imitation is, according to Claparède, an ideomotor adaptation by means of which the child reproduces and then simulates the movements and ideas of those around him. But from the point of view of personality and from the social point of view, imitation would seem to be, as Janet and Baldwin maintain, a confusion between the I and the not-I, between the activity of one's own body and that of other people's bodies. At his most imitative stage, the child mimics with his whole being, identifying himself with his model. But this game, though it seems to imply an essentially social attitude, really indicates one that is essentially ego-centric. The copied movements and behaviour have nothing in them to interest the child, there is no adaptation of the I to anyone else; there is a confusion by which the child does not know that he is imitating, but plays his game as though it were his own creation. This is why children up to the age of 6 or 7, when they have had something explained to them and are asked to do it immediately afterwards, invariably imagine that they have discovered by themselves what in reality they are only repeating from a model. In such cases imitation is completely unconscious, as we have often had occasion to observe.

This mental disposition constitutes a fringe on the child's activity, which persists throughout different ages, changing in content but always identical in function. At the ages of our two children, many of the remarks collected partake of the nature of pure repetition or echolalia. The part played by this echolalia is simply that of a game; the child enjoys repeating the words for their own sake, for the pleasure they give him, without any external adaptation and without an audience. Here are a few typical examples:

> (Mlle E. teaches My the word "celluloid") Lev, busy with his drawing at another table: "*Luloïd . . . le le le loid . . .* " etc.
> (Before an aquarium Pie stands outside the group and takes no interest in what is being shown. Somebody says the word "triton".) Pie: "*Triton . . . triton.*" Lev (after hearing the clock strike "coucou"): "*Coucou . . . coucou.*"

These pure repetitions, rare enough at the age of Pie and Lev, have no interest for us. Their sudden appearance in the midst of ordinary conversation is more illuminating.

> Jac says to Ez: "Look, Ez, your pants are showing." Pie, who is in another part of the room immediately repeats: *"Look, my pants are showing, and my shirt, too."*

Now there is not a word of truth in all this. It is simply the joy of repeating for its own sake that makes Pie talk in this way, i.e., the pleasure of using words not for the sake of adapting oneself to the conversation, but for the sake of playing with them.

> We have seen on page 7 the example of Pie hearing Lev say: "A funny gentleman," and repeating this remark for his own amusement although he is busy drawing a tram-car (27). This shows how little repetition distracts Pie from his class-work. (Ez says: "I want to ride on the train up there"), Pie: *"I want to ride on the train up there."*

There is no need to multiply examples. The process is always the same. The children are occupied with drawing or playing; they all talk intermittently without listening very much to each other; but words thrown out are caught on the bounce, like balls. Sometimes they are repeated as they are, like the remarks of the present category, sometimes they set in action those dual monologues of which we shall speak later on.

The frequency of repetition is about 2% and 1% for Pie and Lev respectively. If the talk be divided into sections of 100 sentences, then in each hundred will be found repetitions in the proportion of 1%, 4%, 0%, 5%, 3%, etc.

§ 4. MONOLOGUE.—Janet and the psycho-analysts have shown us how close in their opinion is the bond which originally connected word and action, words being so packed with concrete significance that the mere fact of uttering them, even without any reference to action, could be looked upon as the factor in initiating the action in question.

Now, independently of the question of origins, it is a matter of common observation that for the child words are much nearer to action and movement than for us. This leads us to two results which are of considerable importance in the study of child language in general and of the monologue in particular.

1° The child is impelled, even when he is alone, to speak as he acts, to accompany his movements with a play of shouts and words. True, there are silences, and very curious ones at that, when children work together as in the *Maison des Petits*. But, alongside of these silences, how many a soliloquy must take place when a child is alone in a room, or when children speak without addressing themselves to anyone.

2° If the child talks even when he is alone as an accompaniment to his action, he can reverse the process and use words to bring about what the action of itself is powerless to do. Hence the habit of romancing or inventing, which consists in creating reality by words and magical language, in working on things by means of words alone, apart from any contact either with them or with persons.

These two varieties belong to the same category, that of the monologue. It is worth noting that the monologue still plays an important part between the ages of 6 and 7. At this age the child soliloquizes even in the society of other children, as in the classrooms where our work has been carried on. We have sometimes seen as many as ten children seated at separate tables or in groups of two or three, each talking to himself without taking any notice of his neighbour.

Here are a few examples of simple monologue (the first variety) where the child simply accompanies his action with sentences spoken aloud.

Lev sits down at his table alone: "*I want to do that drawing, there . . . I want to draw something, I do. I shall need a big piece of paper to do that.*"

Lev knocks over a game: "*There! everything's fallen down.*"

Lev has just finished his drawing: "*Now I want to do something else.*"

Lev is a little fellow who is very much wrapped up in himself. He is always telling every one else what he is doing at the moment. In his case, therefore, monologue tends in the direction of collective monologue, where every one talks about himself without listening to the others. All the same, when he is alone he goes on announcing what he is going to do, with no other audience than himself. It is in these circumstances that we have the true monologue.

In the case of Pie, the monologue is rarer, but more true to type; the child will often talk with the sole aim of marking the rhythm of his action, without exhibiting a shade of self-satisfaction in the process. Here is one of Pie's conversations with context, where monologue is interspersed with other forms of talk:

53. Pie takes his arithmetic copy-book and turns the pages: *1, 2 . . . 3, 4, 5, 6, 7 . . . 8 . . . 8, 8, 8, 8 and 8 . . . 9. Number 9, number 9, number 9* (singing) *I want number 9.* (This is the number he is going to represent by a drawing).

54. (Looking at Béa who is standing by the counting-frame but without speaking to him): *Now I'm going to do 9, 9, I'm doing 9, I'm doing 9.* (He draws).

55. (Mlle. L. passes by his table without saying anything). *Look, teacher, 9,9,9 . . . number 9.*

56. (He goes to the frame to see what colour to choose for his number so that it should correspond to the 9th row in the frame). *Pink chalk, it will have to be 9.* (He sings).

57. (To Ez as he passes): *I'm doing 9, I am*—(Ez) What are you going to do?—*Little rounds.*

58. (Accident to the pencil) *Ow, ow!*

59. *Now I've got to 9.*

The whole of this monologue has no further aim than to accompany the action as it takes place. There are only two diversions. Pie would like to inform someone about his plans (sentences 55 and 57). But in spite of this the monologue runs on uninterrupted as though Pie were alone in the room. Speech in this case functions only as a stimulus, and in nowise as a means of communication. Pie no doubt enjoys the feeling of being in a room full of people, but if he were alone, his remarks would be substantially the same.

At the same time it is obvious that this stimulus contains a certain danger. Although in some cases it accelerates action, it also runs the risk of supplanting it. "When the distance between two points has to be traversed, a man can actually walk it with his legs, but he can also stand still and shout: "On, on! . . . " like an opera singer."[1] Hence the second variety of child soliloquy where speech serves not so much to accompany and accelerate action as to replace it by an illusory satisfaction. To this last group belong certain cases of word magic; but these, frequent as they are, occur only in the strictest solitude.[2] What is more usual is that the child takes so much pleasure in soliloquizing that he forgets his activity and does nothing but talk. The word then becomes a command to the external world. Here is an example of pure and of collective monologue (cf. next chapter) where the child gradually works himself up into issuing a command to physical objects and to animals:

---

[1] P. Janet, *loc. cit.*, p. 150.

[2] These cases will be dealt with elsewhere.

> "*Now then, it's coming* (a tortoise). *It's coming, it's coming, its coming. Get out of the way, Da, it's coming, it's coming, it's coming . . . Come along, tortoise!*"
>
> A little later, after having watched the aquarium, soliloquizing all the time: "*Oh, isn't it* (a salamander) *surprised at the great big giant* (a fish)," he exclaims, "*Salamander, you must eat up the fishes!*"

In short we have here the mechanism of solitary games, where, after thinking out his action aloud, the child, under the influence of verbal excitement as much as of any voluntary illusion, comes to command both animate and inanimate beings.

In conclusion, the general characteristic of monologues of this category is that the words have no social function. In such cases speech does not communicate the thoughts of the speaker, it serves to accompany, to reinforce, or to supplement his action. It may be said that this is simply a side-tracking of the original function of language, and that the child commands himself and external things just as he has learned to command and speak to others. There can be no doubt that without originally imitating others and without the desire to call his parents and to influence them, the child would probably never learn to talk; in a sense, then, the monologue is due only to a return shock of words acquired in relation to other people. It should be remembered, however, that throughout the time when he is learning to speak, the child is constantly the victim of a confusion between his own point of view and that of other people. For one thing, he does not know that he is imitating. For another, he talks as much to himself as to others, as much for the pleasure of prattling or of perpetuating some past state of being as for the sake of giving orders. It is therefore impossible to say that the monologue is either prior to or later than the more socialized forms of language; both spring from that undifferentiated state where cries and words accompany action, and then tend to prolong it; and both react one upon the other at the very outset of their development.

But as we pass from early childhood to the adult stage, we shall naturally see the gradual disappearance of the monologue, for it is a primitive and infantile function of language. It is remarkable in this connexion that in the cases of Pie and Lev this form should still constitute about 5% and 15% respectively of their total conversation. This percentage is considerable when the conditions in which the material was collected are taken into account. The difference in the percentages, however, corresponds to a marked difference in temperament, Pie being of a more practical disposition than Lev, better adapted to reality and therefore to the society of other children. When he speaks, it is therefore generally in order to make himself heard. It is true, as we saw, that when Pie does talk to himself his monologue is on the whole more genuine than Lev's, but Pie does not produce in such abundance those rather self-satisfied remarks in which a child is continually announcing his plans to himself, and which are the obvious sign of a certain imaginative exuberance.

§ 5. COLLECTIVE MONOLOGUE.—This form is the most social of the ego-centric varieties of child language, since to the pleasure of talking it adds that of soliloquizing before others and of interesting, or thinking to interest, them in one's own action and one's own thoughts. But as we have already pointed out, the child who acts in this manner does not succeed in making his audience listen, because, as a matter of fact, he is not really addressing himself to it. He is not speaking to anyone. He talks aloud to himself in front of others. This way of behaving reappears in certain men and women of a puerile disposition (certain hysterical subjects, if hysteria be described as the survival of infantile characteristics) who are in the habit of thinking aloud as though they were talking to themselves, but are also conscious of their audience. Suppress the slightly theatrical element in this attitude, and you have the equivalent of the collective monologue in normal children.

The examples of §1 should now be re-read if we wish to realize how socially ineffectual is this form of language, i.e., how little impression it makes upon the person spoken to. Pie makes the same remark to two different persons (25 and 26), and is in nowise astonished when he is neither listened to nor answered by either of them. Later on he asks Béa twice, "What did you say?" (31 and 32), but without listening to her. He busies himself with his own idea and his drawing, and talks only about himself.

Here are a few more examples which show how little a child is concerned with speaking to anyone in particular, or even with making himself heard:

> Mlle L. tells a group of children that owls cannot see by day. Lev: "*Well, I know quite well that it can't.*"
>
> Lev (at a table where a group is at work): "*I've already done "moon" so I'll have to change it.*"
>
> Lev picks up some barley-sugar crumbs: "*I say, I've got a lovely pile of eye-glasses.*"
>
> Lev: "*I say, I've got a gun to kill him with. I say, I am the captain on horseback. I say, I've got a horse and a gun as well.*"

The opening phrase, "I say, I" which occurs in most of these sentences is significant. Every one is supposed to be listening. This is what distinguishes this type of remark from pure monologue. But with regard to its contents it is the exact equivalent of the monologue. The child is simply thinking out his actions aloud, with no desire to give anyone any information about it.

We shall find in the next chapter examples of collective monologues no longer isolated or chosen from the talk of two children only, but taken down verbatim from all-round conversations. This particular category need not therefore occupy us any longer.

The collective monologue represents about 23% of Lev's and 30% of Pie's entire conversation. But we have seen that it is harder to distinguish the pure from the collective monologue in Lev's case than in Pie's. Taking therefore the two types of monologue together, we may say that with Lev they represent 38%, and with Pie 35% of the subject's sum of conversation.

§ 6. ADAPTED INFORMATION.—The criterion of adapted information, as opposed to the pseudo-information contained in the collective monologue, is that it is successful. The child actually makes his hearer listen, and contrives to influence him, i.e., to tell him something. This time the child speaks from the point of view of his audience. The function of language is no longer merely to excite the speaker to action, but actually to communicate his thoughts to other people. These criteria, however, are difficult of application, and we shall try to discover some that admit of greater precision.

It is adapted information, moreover, that gives rise to dialogue. The dialogues of children deserve to be made the object of a special and very searching investigation, for it is probably through the habit of arguing that, as Janet and Baldwin have insisted, we first become conscious of the rules of logic and the forms of deductive reasoning. We shall therefore attempt in the next chapter to give a rough outline of the different stages of conversation as it takes place between children. In the meantime we shall content ourselves with examining adapted information (whether it takes place in dialogue or not) in relation to the main body of talk indulged in by our two subjects, and with noting how small is the part played by this form of language in comparison to the ego-centric forms and those socialized forms of speech such as commands, threats, criticisms, etc., which are not connected with mere statement of fact.

The form in which adapted information first presents itself

to us, is that of simple information. Here are a few clear examples:

> Lev is helping Geo to play Lotto: "*I think that goes here.*" Geo points to a duplicate card. Lev: "*If you lose one, there will still be one left.*" Then: "*You've got three of the same,*" or: "*You all see what you have to do.*"
> Mlle R. calls Ar "Roger." Pie: "*He isn't called Roger.*"

Such remarks as these are clearly very different from dual monologues. The child's object is definitely to convey something to his hearer. It is from the latter's point of view that the subject speaks, and no longer from his own. Henceforward the child lays claim to be understood, and presses his claim if he does not gain his point; whereas in the collective monologue words were thrown out at random, and it little mattered where they fell.

In adapted information the child can naturally talk about himself as about any other subject of conversation. All that is needed is that his remarks should be "adapted" as in the following examples:

> Ez and Pie: "I shall have one to-morrow (a season-ticket on the tramway)—*I shall have mine this afternoon.*"
> Ez and Pie are building a church with bricks: "*We could do that with parallels too. I want to put the parallels on.*"

We are now in a position to define more closely the distinction between the collective monologue and adapted information. The collective monologue takes place whenever the child talks about himself, except in those cases where he does so during collaboration with his hearer (as in the example just given of the church building game), and except in cases of dialogue. Dialogue, in our view, occurs when the child who has been spoken to in a proposition, answers by talking about something that was treated of in this proposition (as in the example of the tramway season-ticket), and does not start off on some cock-and-bull story as so often happens in collective monologue.[1]

In conclusion, as soon as the child informs his hearer about anything but himself, or as soon as in speaking of himself, he enters into collaboration or simply into dialogue with his hearer, there is adapted information. So long as the child talks about himself without collaborating with his audience or without evoking a dialogue, there is only collective monologue.

These definitions and the inability of collective monologue to draw others into the speaker's sphere of action render it all the more remarkable that with Pie and Lev adapted information numbers only half as many remarks as collective monologue. Before establishing the exact proportion we must find out what sort of things our two subjects tell each other, and what they argue about on those rare occasions when we can talk of arguments taking place between children.

On the first point we may note the complete absence between the children of anything in the nature of explanation, if by this word we mean causal explanation, i.e., an answer of the form "for such a reason" to the question "why?" All the observed cases of information which might be thought to resemble explanation are statements of fact or descriptions, and are free from any desire to explain the causes of phenomena.

Here are examples of information which simply state or describe:

> Lev and Pie: "*That's 420.*" "*It isn't 10 o'clock.*" "*A roof doesn't look like that*" (talking of a drawing). "*This is a village, a great big village,*" etc.

[1] For such cock-and-bull stories, see page 7, sentence 30.

Even when they talk about natural phenomena, the information they give each other never touches on causality.

> Lev: "Thunder rolls—*No, it doesn't roll*—It's water—*No it doesn't roll*—What is thunder?—*Thunder is . . .* " (He doesn't go on.)

This absence of causal explanations is remarkable, especially in the case of machines, motors, bicycles, etc., which the subjects occasionally discuss, but always from what we may call the factual point of view.

> Lev: "*It's on the same rail. Funny sort of cart, a motor cart—A bicycle for two men.*"

Now each of these children taken separately is able to explain the mechanism of a bicycle. Pie does so imperfectly, but Lev does so quite well. Each has a number of ideas on mechanics, but they never discuss them together. Causal relations remain unexpressed and are thought about only by the individual, probably because, to the child mind they are represented by images rather than by words. Only the underlying factual element finds expression.

This peculiarity comes out very clearly when children collaborate in a game.

> Here for instance are Pie and Ez occupied in drawing a house together. Pie: "*You must have a little button there for the light, a little button for the light . . . Now I'm doing the 'lectric light . . . There are two 'lectric lights. Look we'll have two 'lectric lights. These are all squares of 'lectric lights.*"

We shall have occasion in later chapters to confirm our hypothesis that the causal "why" hardly enters into child conversation. We shall see, particularly in chapter 3, that the explanations elicited from one child by another between the ages of 6 and 8 are for the most part imperfectly understood in so far as they seem to express any sort of causal relation. Questions of causality are therefore confined to conversations between children and adults, or to those between younger and older children. Which is the same thing as saying that most of these questions are kept hidden away by the child in the fastness of his intimate and unformulated thought.

Here are those of the remarks exchanged by Lev and Pie which approach most nearly to causal explanation. It will be seen that they are almost entirely descriptive:

> Lev: "*We ought to have a little water. This green paint is so very hard, most awfully hard*" . . . "*In cardboard, don't you know? You don't know how to, but it is rather difficult for you, it is for every one.*"

Childish arguments, it is curious to note, present exactly the same features. Just as our two subjects never communicate their thoughts on the why and wherefore of phenomena, so in arguing they never support their statements with the "because" and "since" of logic. For them, with two exceptions only, arguing consists simply in a clash of affirmations, without any attempt at logical justification. It belongs to the type which we shall denote as "primitive argument" in our essay in the following chapter on the different stages of child conversation, and which we shall characterize by just this lack of motivation.

The example given on page 23 (the argument between Lev and a child of the same age about thunder) proves this very clearly. Here are three more examples, the first two quite definite, the third of a more intermediate character.

> Ez to Pie: "You're going to marry me—Pie: *No, I won't marry you*—Oh yes you'll marry me—*No*—Yes . . . etc."

"Look how lovely my 6 is going to be—Lev: *Yes it's a 6 but really and truly it's a 9*—No, it's a 6, Nought—*You said nought, and it's not true, it's a 9. Really it is*—No—*Yes*—It was done like that already—*Oh no, that's a lie. You silly.*"

Lev looks to see what Hei is doing: "*Two moons*—No, two suns.—*Suns aren't like that, with a mouth. They're like this, suns up there*—They're round—*Yes they're quite round, but they haven't got eyes and a mouth.*—Yes they have, they can see—*No they can't. It's only God who can see.*"

In the first two examples the argument is simply a clash of contrary affirmations, without mutual concessions and without motivation. The last is more complex. When Lev says "*It's only God who can see*" or "*They are like this,*" he does seem at the first glance to be justifying his remarks, to be doing something more than merely stating facts. But there is no explicit justification, no attempt to demonstrate. Hei asserts and Lev denies. Hei makes no effort to give any reasons for believing that the sun has eyes, he does not say that he has seen pictures which have led him to such an idea, etc. Lev for his part does not attempt to get at Hei's point of view, and gives no explicit reason for defending his own. In the main then there is still only a clash of assertions, different enough from the two following little arguments, one of which, by the way, takes place between a child and an adult.

These indeed are the only examples we have found where the child tries to prove his assertions. They should be carefully examined, considering how seldom the fact occurs before the age of 7 or 8.

Lev talking to Mlle G.: "*You've been eating paint*—No, I haven't, which?—*White paint*—No—*Oh, yes you have 'cos there's some on your mouth.*"

The reader will note the correct use made of "because" at the age of 6½. In the three lists of complete vocabularies given by Mlle Descœudres[1] "because" is used by the seven-year-old but not by the five-year-old child.

> Here is another instance, again of Lev: "*That is 420—But it's not the number of the house—Why not?—The number of the house is on the door.*"

Note here the use of "why" in the sense of "for what reason" (cf. chapter 5). The reader will see how superior these two arguments are to the preceding examples.

We can draw the following conclusions from these various facts:

1° Adapted information, together with most of the questions and answers which we shall examine later, constitute the only categories of child language whose function, in contrast to the diverse functions of the ego-centric categories, is to communicate intellectual processes.

2° The frequency of adapted information is only 13% for Lev and 14% for Pie, a remarkable fact, and one which shows how little the intellectual enquiry of a child can be said to be social. These figures are all the more striking when we remember that collective monologue constitutes respectively 23% and 30% of the sum of the remarks made by the same subjects.

3° These informations conveyed from one child to another are factual in the sense that they do not point to any causal relations, even when they deal with the material used by the children in their work and with the numerous objects, natural or artificial, which they like to draw or build (animals, stars, motor-cars, bicycles, etc.).

4° The arguments between the two children are, with two

---

[1] A. Descœudres, "Le development de l'enfant de deux à sept ans," *Coll. Actual. Ped.*, 1922, p. 190.

exceptions only, of a low type, inasmuch as they consist merely of a clash of contrary assertions without any explicit demonstration.

§ 7. CRITICISM AND DERISION.—If we set aside questions and answers, the socialized language of the child in its non-intellectual aspect may be divided into two easily distinguishable categories: on the one hand commands, on the other criticism and derision. There is nothing peculiar about these categories in children; only their percentage is interesting.

Here are a few examples of criticisms, taunts, *Schadenfreude*, etc., which at the first glance one might be tempted to place under information and dialogue, but which it will perhaps be found useful to class apart. Their function is not to convey thoughts, but to satisfy non-intellectual instincts such as pugnacity, pride, emulation, etc.:

> Lev: *"You're not putting it in the middle"* (a plate on the table).
> *"That's not fair." "Pooh! that's no good." "We made that house, it isn't theirs." "That's not like an owl. Look, Pie, what he's done." "Well, I know that he can't." "It's much prettier than ours." "I've got a much bigger pencil than you." "Well, I'm the strongest all the same,"* etc.

All these remarks have this in common with adapted information that they are addressed to a specified person whom they influence, rouse to emulation and provoke to retort and even to quarrelling. This is what obliges us to class as socialized language such remarks as those towards the end, beginning: "Well, I," which in other respects resemble collective monologue. What, on the other hand, distinguishes these phrases from information proper, is that with the child even apparently objective criticisms contain judgments of value which retain a strongly subjective flavour. They are not mere statements of fact. They contain elements of derision, of combativeness, and of the desire to assert personal superiority. They therefore justify the creation of a separate category.

The percentage of this group is low: 3% for Lev, and 7% for Pie. This may be a question of individual types, and if this category is too weakly represented in subsequent research, we may have to assimilate it to one of the preceding ones.

§ 8. COMMANDS, REQUESTS, THREATS.—Why is the ratio of adapted information so low in comparison to that of the ego-centric forms of speech, particularly in comparison to collective monologue? The reason is quite simple. The child does not in the first instance communicate with his fellow-beings in order to share thoughts and reflexions; he does so in order to play. The result is that the part played by intellectual interchange is reduced to the strictly necessary minimum. The rest of language will only assist action, and will consist of commands, etc.

Commands and threats, then, like criticisms, deserve a category to themselves. They are, moreover, very easy to recognize:

> Lev (outside a shop): "*Mustn't come in here without paying. I shall tell Gé*" (if you come). "*Come here Mr Passport.*" "*Give me the blue one.*" "*You must make a flag.*" "*Come along, Ro. Look . . . you shall be the cart,*" etc.
>
> Pie: "*Ez, come and see the salamander.*" "*Get out of the way, I shan't be able to see,*" etc. (About a roof): "*No, take it away, take it away 'cos I want to put on mine,*" etc.

We need not labour the point. The only distinction calling for delicate discrimination is that between requests which tend imperceptably to become commands, and questions which contain an implicit request. All requests which are not expressed in interrogative form we shall agree to call "entreaties," and shall include in the present category; while for interrogative requests a place will be reserved in our next category. Here are some examples of entreaty:

Lev: "*The yellow paint, please.*" "*I should like some water,*" etc.

Pie: "*The india-rubber, teacher, I want the india-rubber.*"

Under requests, on the other hand, we shall classify such sentences as: "Ez, do you mind helping me?" "May I look at it?" etc. This distinction is certainly artificial. But between an interrogative request and a question bearing on immediate action there are many intermediate types. And since it is desirable to distinguish between questions and commands, we must not be afraid of facing the artificiality of our classification. So long as we are agreed upon the conventions adopted, and do not take the statistics too literally, the rest need not detain us. It is not, moreover, the ratio of commands to orders that will be of most use to us, but the ratio of the bulk of socialized language to the bulk of ego-centric language. It is easy enough to agree upon these fundamental distinctions.

The percentage of the present category is 10% for Lev and 15% for Pie. Dialogue and information were for the same subjects respectively, 12% and 14%.

§ 9. QUESTIONS AND ANSWERS.—A preliminary difficulty presents itself in connexion with these two categories which we propose to treat of together: do they both belong to socialized language? As far as answers are concerned, we need be in no doubt. Indeed, we shall describe as an "answer" the adapted words used by the person spoken to, after he has heard and understood a question. For instance:

"What colour is that?—(Lev) *Brownish yellow.*" "What are you doing, Lev?—*The boat,*" etc.

To answers we shall assimilate refusals and acceptances, which are answers given not to questions of fact but to commands and requests:

"Will you give it back to me? (the ticket).—*No, I don't need it. I'm in the boat*" (Lev).

These two groups, which together constitute answers, obviously belong to socialized language. If we place them in a separate category instead of assimilating them to adapted information, it is chiefly because answers do not belong to the spontaneous speech of the child. It would be sufficient for his neighbours to interrupt him and for adults to question him all the time, to raise a child's socialized language to a much higher percentage. We shall therefore eliminate answers from our calculations in the following paragraph. All remarks provoked by adults will thus be done away with. Answers, moreover, constitute only 18% of Lev's language and 14% of Pie's.

The psychological contents of answers are highly interesting, and would alone suffice to render the category distinct from information. It is of course closely connected to the contents of the question, and we shall therefore deal simultaneously with the two problems.

And the questions which children ask one another—do they too belong to socialized language? Curiously enough the point is one that can be raised, for many remarks are made by children in an interrogative form without being in any way questions addressed to anyone. The proof of this is that the child does not listen to the answer, and does not even expect it. He supplies it himself. This happens frequently between the ages of 3 and 5. At the age of our two subjects it is rarer. When such pseudo-questions do occur, we have classed them as monologue or information (e.g. "*Please teacher is half right? Yes, look*" Lev). For the present we shall therefore deal only with questions proper.

Questions make up 17% of Lev's language and 13% of Pie's. Their importance is therefore equal and even superior to that of information, and since a question is a spontaneous search for information, we shall now be able to check the accuracy of our assertions concerning this last category. Two of its characteristics were particularly striking: the absence of intellectual intercourse among the children on the subject of causality, and the absence of proof and logical justification in their discussions. If we jump to the conclusion that children keep such thoughts to themselves and do not socialize them, we may be met with the counter assertion that children simply do not have such thoughts, in which case there would be no question of their socializing them! This is partly the case as regards logical demonstration. With regard to causal explanation, however—and by this we mean not only the appeal to mechanical causality such as is made only after the ages of 7 or 8 (see chapter 5, § 3), but also the appeal to final, or as we shall call it, to pre-causality, i.e., that which is invoked in the child's "whys" between the ages of 3 and 7 to 8—as regards this type of explanation, then, there are two things to be noted. In the first place, the children of the *Maison des Petits* deal in their drawings and free compositions with animals, physical objects (stars, sky, rain, etc.), with machines and manufactured objects (trains, motors, boats, houses, bicycles, etc.). These might therefore give rise to questions of origin and causality. In the second place, "whys" play an important part in all questions asked of grown-ups by children under 7 (cf. p. 289 where out of three groups of 250 spontaneous questions we noted respectively 91, 53 and 41 "whys"). Now among these "whys" a large number are "whys of explanation," meaning "for what reason" or "for what object." Explanation supplies about 18% of the subject-matter dealt with in the questions of the child of 6 or 7, such as we shall study it in chapter 5. If, therefore, there are few questions of explanation in the talk of our two present subjects, this is strongly in favour of the interpretation we have given of information and dialogue between children in general. Intellectual intercourse between children is still factual or descriptive, i.e., little concerned with causality, which remains

"*Do you know that gentleman?*" "*How shall I paint the house?*"
"*How does this go?*" (a ball in the counting-frame).

Pie: "*Are you coming this afternoon, Béa?*" "*I say, have you
finished yet?*" etc.

This enormous numerical difference between the questions
bearing upon children's activity as such, and those dealing with
causal explanation is very remarkable. It proves how individualistic the child of 6 still shows himself to be in his intellectual
activity, and how restricted in consequence is the interchange of
ideas that takes place between children.

A second category of questions, made up of 27 of Lev's and
41 of Pie's, deals with facts and events, time and place (questions
of "reality" treated of in chapter 5).

Facts: "*Is your drum closed?*" "*Is there some paper, too?*" "*Are
there snails in there?*" (Pie.)

Place: "*Where is the blue, Ez?*" "*Where is she?*" (the
tortoise).

Time: "*Please teacher, is it late?*" "*How old are you?*" (Pie.)

It will be seen that these questions do not touch upon
causality, but are all about matters of fact. Questions of place
predominate in this category, 29 for Pie and 13 for Lev.

Another numerous category (51 for Pie, 48 for Lev) is made
up of questions purely concerning matters of fact, questions of
nomenclature, classification and evaluation.

Nomenclature: "*What does "behind" mean?*" "*What is he
called?*" (a cook) (Lev).

Classification: "*What ever is that?*" "*Is that yellow?*" (Lev).

Evaluation: "*Is it pretty?*" (Lev, Pie).

We may add a few questions about number (five by Lev, one
by Pie):

"Isn't all that enough for 2fr.50?" "And how much for 11?" (Lev).

Finally, mention should be made of two questions by Pie and one by Lev about rules (writing, etc.).

"You put it on this side, don't you?" (the figure 3) (Lev).

The following table completely summarizes the questions asked by Lev and Pie, including their "whys."

		LEV		PIE	
Questions of causal explanation	. . .	2		0	
			2		0
Questions of Reality { Facts and events	. . .	7		8	
Time	. . . .	7		4	
Place	. . . .	13		29	
			27		41
Actions and intentions	. . . . .	. . .	141	. . .	78
Rules	. . . .	. . .	1	. . .	2
Questions of Classification { Nomenclature	. . .	7		0	
Classification and evaluation		41		51	
			48		51
Number	. . . . . .	. . .	5	. . .	7
TOTAL	. . . .		224		173

We shall not dwell upon the criteria of the different categories nor upon their functional interest; these problems form the subject-matter of a later chapter on "A child's questions" (chapter 5). It will be enough if we conclude from this table that questions from one child to another (questions from children to adults play only a negligible part in this group), bear first and foremost upon actual psychological activity (actions and intentions). Otherwise, when they concern objects and not persons, they bear upon the factual aspect of reality, and not upon causal relations. These conclusions are markedly different from the results supplied by Del (chapter 5: Questions of a child to an adult). Before drawing any conclusions, however, from the difference between questions from child to child and questions from child to adult, we should have to solve a big preliminary problem: how far do the questions which Lev and Pie ask adults out of school hours resemble those of Del (whys of explanation, etc.)? At the first glance, Del, although he has worked like the others during school hours, seems to approximate much more closely to what we know of the ordinary questioning child of 6. But Lev and Pie are perhaps special types, more prone to statement and less to explanation. All we can do, therefore, is to extend the work of research as carried out in this chapter and in chapter 5.

II. CONCLUSIONS

Having defined, so far as was possible the various categories of the language used by our two children, it now remains for us to see whether it is not possible to establish certain numerical constants from the material before us. We wish to emphasize at the very outset the artificial character of such abstractions. The number of unclassifiable remarks, indeed, weighs heavily in the statistics. In any case, a perusal of the list of Lev's first 50 remarks, which we shall give as an example for those who wish to make use of our method, should give a fair idea of the degree of objectivity belonging to our classification.[1] But these difficulties are immaterial. If among our results some are definitely

---

[1] See Appendix.

more constant than others, then we shall feel justified in attributing to these a certain objective value.

§ 10. THE MEASURE OF EGO-CENTRISM.—Among the data we have obtained there is one, incidentally of the greatest interest for the study of child logic, which seems to supply the necessary guarantee of objectivity: we mean the proportion of ego-centric language to the sum of the child's spontaneous conversation. Ego-centric language is, as we have seen, the group made up by the first three of the categories we have enumerated—*repetition, monologue* and *collective monologue*. All three have this in common that they consist of remarks that are not addressed to anyone, or not to anyone in particular, and that they evoke no reaction adapted to them on the part of anyone to whom they may chance to be addressed. Spontaneous language is therefore made up of the first seven categories, i.e., of all except *answers*. It is therefore the sum total of all remarks, *minus* those which are made as an answer to a question asked by an adult or a child. We have eliminated this heading as being subject to chance circumstances; it is sufficient for a child to have come in contact with many adults or with some talkative companion, to undergo a marked change in the percentage of his answers. Answers given, not to definite questions (with interrogation mark) or commands, but in the course of the dialogue, i.e., propositions answering to other propositions, have naturally been classed under the heading *information and dialogue,* so that there is nothing artificial about the omission of questions from the statistics which we shall give. The child's language *minus* his answers constitutes a complete whole in which intelligence is represented at every stage of its development.

The proportion of ego-centric to other spontaneous forms of language is represented by the following fractions:

$$\frac{Eg.\ L}{Sp.\ L} = 0.47 \text{ for Lev,} \quad \frac{Eg.\ L}{Sp.\ L} = 0.43 \text{ for Pie.}$$

(The proportion of ego-centric language to the sum total of the subject's speech, including answers, is 39% for Lev and 37% for Pie.) The similarity of result for Lev and Pie is a propitious sign, especially as what difference there is corresponds to a marked difference of temperament. (Lev is certainly more ego-centric than Pie.) But the value of the result is vouched for in yet another way.

If we divide the 1,400 remarks made by Lev during the month in which his talk was being studied into sections of 100 sentences, and seek to establish for each section the ratio $\dfrac{Eg.\ L.}{Sp.\ L.}$, the fraction will be found to vary only from 0.40 to 0.57, which indicates only a small maximum deviation. On the contrary, the *mean variation*, i.e., the average of the deviations between each value and the arithmetical average of these values, is only 0.04, which is really very little.

If Pie's 1,500 remarks are submitted to the same treatment, the proportions will be found to vary between 0.31 and 0.59, with an average variation of 0.06. This greater variability is just what we should expect from what we know of Pie's character, which at first sight seems more practical, better adapted than Lev's, more inclined to collaboration (particularly with his bosom friend Ez). But Pie every now and then indulges in fantasies which isolate him for several hours, and during which he soliloquizes without ceasing.

We shall see in the next chapter, moreover, that these two coefficients do actually represent the average for children between the ages of 7 and 8. The same calculation based on some 1,500 remarks in quite another class-room yielded the result of 0.45 (a. v. = 0.05).

This constancy in the proportion of ego-centric language is the more remarkable in view of the fact that we have found nothing of the kind in connexion with the other coefficients which we have sought to establish. We have, it is true, determined the proportion of socialized factual language (*information* and *questions*) to socialized non-factual language (*criticism, commands*, and *requests*). But this proportion fluctuates from 0.72 to 2.23 with a mean variation 0.71 for Lev (as compared with 0.04 and 0.06 as the coefficients of ego-centrism), and between 0.43 and 2.33 with a mean variation of 0.42 for Pie. Similarly, the relation of ego-centric to socialized factual language yields no coefficient of any constancy.

Of all this calculation let us bear only this in mind, that our two subjects of 6½ have each an ego-centric language which amounts to nearly half of their total spontaneous speech.

The following table summarizes the functions of the language used by both these children:

		Pie	Lev
1	Repetition	2	1
2	Monologue	5	15
3	Collective Monologue	30	23
4	Adapted Information	14	13
5	Criticism	7	3
6	Commands	15	10
7	Requests	13	17
8	Answers	14	18
	Ego-centric Language	37	39
	Spontaneous Socialized Language	49	43
	Sum of Socialized Language	63	61
	Coefficient of Ego-centrism	0.43 ∓ 0.06	0.47 ∓ 0.04

We must once more emphasize the fact that in all these calculations the number of remarks made by children to adults is negligible. By omitting them we raise the coefficient of ego-centrism to about 0.02, which is within the allowed limits of deviation. In future, however, we shall have completely to eliminate such remarks from our calculations, even if it means making a separate class for them. We shall, moreover, observe this rule in the next chapter where the coefficient of ego-centrism has been calculated solely on the basis of remarks made between children.

§ 11. CONCLUSION.—What are the conclusions we can draw from these facts? It would seem that up to a certain age we may safely admit that children think and act more ego-centrically than adults, that they share each other's intellectual life less than we do. True, when they are together they seem to talk to each other a great deal more than we do about what they are doing, but for the most part they are only talking to themselves. We, on the contrary, keep silent far longer about our action, but our talk is almost always socialized.

Such assertions may seem paradoxical. In observing children between the ages of 4 and 7 at work together in the classes of the *Maison des Petits*, one is certainly struck by silences, which are, we repeat, in no way imposed nor even suggested by the adults. One would expect, not indeed the formation of working groups, since children are slow to awake to social life, but a hubbub caused by all the children talking at once. This is not what happens. All the same, it is obvious that a child between the ages of 4 and 7, placed in the conditions of spontaneous work provided by the educational games of the *Maison des Petits*, breaks silence far oftener than does the adult at work, and seems at first sight to be continuously communicating his thoughts to those around him.

Ego-centrism must not be confused with secrecy. Reflexion in the child does not admit of privacy. Apart from thinking by images or autistic symbols which cannot be directly communicated, the child up to an age, as yet undetermined but probably somewhere about 7, is incapable of keeping to himself the thoughts which enter his mind. He says everything. He has no verbal continence. Does this mean that he socializes his thought more than we do? That is the whole question, and it is for us to see to whom the child really speaks. It may be to others. We think on the contrary that, as the preceding study shows, it is first and foremost to himself, and that speech, before it can be used to socialize thought, serves to accompany and reinforce individual activity. Let us try to examine more closely the difference between thought which is socialized but capable of secrecy, and infantile thought which is ego-centric but incapable of secrecy.

The adult, even in his most personal and private occupation, even when he is engaged on an enquiry which is incomprehensible to his fellow-beings, thinks socially, has continually in his mind's eye his collaborators or opponents, actual or eventual, at any rate members of his own profession to whom sooner or later he will announce the result of his labours. This mental picture pursues him throughout his task. The task itself is henceforth socialized at almost every stage of its development. Invention eludes this process, but the need for checking and demonstrating calls into being an inner speech addressed throughout to a hypothetical opponent, whom the imagination often pictures as one of flesh and blood. When, therefore, the adult is brought face to face with his fellow-beings, what he announces to them is something already socially elaborated and therefore roughly adapted to his audience, i.e., it is comprehensible. Indeed, the further a man has advanced in his own line of thought, the better able is he to see things from the point of view of others and to make himself understood by them.

The child, on the other hand, placed in the conditions which we have described, seems to talk far more than the adult. Almost everything he does is to the tune of remarks such as "I'm drawing a hat," "I'm doing it better than you," etc. Child thought, therefore, seems more social, less capable of sustained and solitary research. This is so only in appearance. The child has less verbal continence simply because he does not know what it is to keep a thing to himself. Although he talks almost incessantly to his neighbours, he rarely places himself at their point of view. He speaks to them for the most part as if he were alone, and as if he were thinking aloud. He speaks, therefore, in a language which disregards the precise shade of meaning in things and ignores the particular angle from which they are viewed, and which above all is always making assertions, even in argument, instead of justifying them. Nothing could be harder to understand than the note-books which we have filled with the conversation of Pie and Lev. Without full commentaries, taken down at the same time as the children's remarks, they would be incomprehensible. Everything is indicated by allusion, by pronouns and demonstrative articles—"he, she, the, mine, him, etc."—which can mean anything in turn, regardless of the demands of clarity or even of intelligibility. (The examination of this style must not detain us now; it will appear again in chapter 3 in connexion with verbal explanation between one child and another.) In a word, the child hardly ever even asks himself whether he has been understood. For him, that goes without saying, for he does not think about others when he talks. He utters a "collective monologue." His language only begins to resemble that of adults when he is directly interested in making himself understood; when he gives orders or asks questions. To put it quite simply, we may say that the adult thinks socially, even when he is alone, and that the child under 7 thinks ego-centrically, even in the society of others.

What is the reason for this? It is, in our opinion, twofold. It is due, in the first place, to the absence of any sustained social intercourse between the children of less than 7 or 8, and in the second place to the fact that the language used in the fundamental activity of the child—play—is one of gestures, movement and mimicry as much as of words. There is, as we have said, no real social life between children of less than 7 or 8 years. The type of children's society represented in a class-room of the *Maison des Petits* is obviously of a fragmentary character, in which consequently sequently there is neither division of work, centralization of effort, nor unity of conversation. We may go further, and say that it is a society in which, strictly speaking, individual and social life are not differentiated. An adult is at once far more highly individualized and far more highly socialized than a child forming part of such a society. He is more individualized, since he can work in private without perpetually announcing what he is doing, and without imitating his neighbours. He is more socialized for the reasons which have just been given. The child is neither individualized, since he cannot keep a single thought secret, and since everything done by one member of the group is repeated through a sort of imitative repercussion by almost every other member, nor is he socialized, since this imitation is not accompanied by what may properly be called an interchange of thought, about half the remarks made by children being ego-centric in character. If, as Baldwin and Janet maintain, imitation is accompanied by a sort of confusion between one's own action and that of others, then we may find in this fragmentary type of society based on imitation some sort of explanation of the paradoxical character of the conversation of children who, while they are continually announcing their doings, yet talk only for themselves, without listening to anyone else.

Social life at the *Maison des Petits* passes, according to the observations of Mlles Audemars and Lafendel, through three stages. Up till the age of about 5, the child almost always works alone. From 5 to about 7½, little groups of two are formed, like that of Pie and Ez (cf. the remarks taken down under the heading "adapted information.") These groups are transitory and irregular. Finally, between 7 and 8 the desire manifests itself to work with others. Now it is in our opinion just at this age that ego-centric talk loses some of its importance, and it is at this age, as we shall see in the next chapter, that we shall place the higher stages of conversation properly so-called as it takes place between children. It is also at this age, (cf. chapter 3) that children begin to understand each other in spoken explanations, as opposed to explanations in which gestures play as important a part as words.

A simple way of verifying these hypotheses is to re-examine children between 7 and 8 whose ego-centrism at an earlier stage has been ascertained. This is the task which Mlle. Berguer undertook with Lev. She took down under the same conditions as previously some 600 remarks made by Lev at the age of 7 and a few months. The co-efficient of ego-centricism was reduced to 0.27.[1]

These stages of social development naturally concern only the child's intellectual activity (drawings, constructive games, arithmetic, etc.). It goes without saying that in outdoor games the problem is a completely different one; but these games touch only on a tiny portion of the thought and language of the child.

If language in the child of about 6½ is still so far from being socialized, and if the part played in it by the ego-centric forms is so considerable in comparison to information and dialogue etc., the reason for this lies in the fact that childish language includes two distinct varieties, one made up of gestures, movements, mimicry etc., which accompany or even completely supplant the use of words, and the other consisting solely of the spoken word. Now, gesture cannot express everything. Intellectual processes, therefore, will remain ego-centric, whereas commands etc., all the language that is bound up with action, with handicraft, and especially with play, will tend to become more socialized. We shall come across this essential distinction again in chapter 3. It will then be seen that verbal understanding between children is less adequate than between adults, but this does not mean that in their games and in their manual occupations they do not understand each other fairly well; this understanding, however, is not yet altogether verbal.

§ 12. RESULTS AND HYPOTHESES.—Psycho-analysts have been led to distinguish two fundamentally different modes of thinking: *directed* or *intelligent thought*, and *undirected* or, as Bleuler proposes to call it, *autistic thought*. Directed thought is conscious, i.e., it pursues an aim which is present to the mind of the thinker; it is

---

[1] We are at the moment collecting similar data from various children between the ages of 3 and 7, in such a way as to establish a graph of development. These results will probably appear in the *Archives de Psychologie*.

intelligent, which means that it is adapted to reality and tries to influence it; it admits of being true or false (empirically or logically true), and it can be communicated by language. Autistic thought is subconscious, which means that the aims it pursues and the problems it tries to solve are not present in consciousness; it is not adapted to reality, but creates for itself a dream world of imagination; it tends, not to establish truths, but so to satisfy desires, and it remains strictly individual and incommunicable as such by means of language. On the contrary, it works chiefly by images, and in order to express itself, has recourse to indirect methods, evoking by means of symbols and myths the feeling by which it is led.

Here, then, are two fundamental modes of thought which, though separated neither at their origin nor in the course of their functioning are subject, nevertheless, to two diverging sets of logical laws.[1] Directed thought, as it develops, is controlled more and more by the laws of experience and of logic in the stricter sense. Autistic thought, on the other hand, obeys a whole system of special laws (laws of symbolism and of immediate satisfaction) which we need not elaborate here. Let us consider, for instance, the completely different lines of thought pursued from the point of view of intelligence and from that of autism when we think of such an object as, say, water.

To intelligence, water is a natural substance whose origin we know, or whose formation we can at least empirically observe; its behaviour and motions are subject to certain laws which can be studied, and it has from the dawn of history been the object of technical experiment (for purposes of irrigation, etc.). To the autistic attitude, on the other hand, water is interesting only in connexion with the satisfaction of organic wants. It can be drunk. But as such, as well as simply

[1] There is interaction between these two modes of thought. Autism undoubtedly calls into being and enriches many inventions which are subsequently clarified and demonstrated by intelligence.

in virtue of its external appearance, it has come to represent in folk and child fantasies, and in those of adult sub-consciousness, themes of a purely organic character. It has in fact been identified with the liquid substances which issue from the human body, and has come, in this way, to symbolize birth itself, as is proved by so many myths (birth of Aphrodite, etc.), rites (baptism the symbol of a new birth), dreams[1] and stories told by children.[2] Thus in the one case thought adapts itself to water as part of the external world, in the other, thought uses the idea of water not in order to adapt itself to it, but in order to assimilate it to those more or less conscious images connected with fecundation and the idea of birth.

Now these two forms of thought, whose characteristics diverge so profoundly, differ chiefly as to their origin, the one being socialized and guided by the increasing adaptation of individuals one to another, whereas the other remains individual and uncommunicated. Furthermore—and this is of the very first importance for the understanding of child thought—this divergence is due in large part to the following fact. Intelligence, just because it undergoes a gradual process of socialization, is enabled through the bond established by language between thoughts and words to make an increasing use of concepts; whereas autism, just because it remains individual, is still tied to imagery, to organic activity, and even to organic movements. The mere fact, then, of telling one's thought, of telling it to others, or of keeping silence and telling it only to oneself must be of enormous importance to the fundamental structure and functioning of thought in general, and of child logic in

[1] See Flournoy, H. "Quelques rêves au sujet de la signification symbolique de l'eau et du feu." *Intern. Zeitschr. f. Psychoan.*, Vol. VI. p. 398 (cf. pp. 329 and 330).
[2] We have published the case of Vo of a child of 9, who regards humanity as descended from a baby who issued from a worm which came out of the sea. Cf. Piaget, "La pensée symbolique et la pensée de l'enfant. *Arch. Psych.*, Vol. XVIII, 1923.

particular. Now between autism and intelligence there are many degrees, varying with their capacity for being communicated. These intermediate varieties must therefore be subject to a special logic, intermediate too between the logic of autism and that of intelligence. The chief of those intermediate forms, i.e., the type of thought which like that exhibited by our children seeks to adapt itself to reality, but does not communicate itself as such, we propose to call *Ego-centric thought*. This gives us the following table:

	Non-communicable thought	Communicable thought
Undirected thought	*Autistic thought*	*(Mythological thought)*
Directed thought	*Ego-centric thought*	*Communicated intelligence*

We shall quickly realize the full importance of ego-centrism if we consider a certain familiar experience of daily life. We are looking, say, for the solution of some problem, when suddenly everything seems quite clear; we have understood, and we experience that *sui generis* feeling of intellectual satisfaction. But as soon as we try to explain to others what it is we have understood, difficulties come thick and fast. These difficulties do not arise merely because of the effort of attention needed to hold in a single grasp the links in the chain of argument; they are attributable also to our judging faculty itself. Conclusions which we deemed positive no longer seem so; between certain propositions whole series of intermediate links are now seen to be lacking in order to fill the gaps of which we were previously not even conscious; arguments which seemed convincing because they were connected with some schema of visual imagery or based on some sort of analogy, lose all their potency from the moment we feel the need to appeal to these schemas, and find that they are incommunicable; doubt is cast on propositions connected with judgments of value, as soon as we realize the personal nature of such judgments. If such, then, is the difference between personal understanding and spoken explanation, how much more marked will be the characteristics of personal understanding when the individual has for a long time been bottling up his own thoughts, when he has not even formed the habit of thinking in terms of other people, and of communicating his thoughts to them. We need only recall the inextricable chaos of adolescent thought to realize the truth of this distinction.

Ego-centric thought and intelligence therefore represent two different forms of reasoning, and we may even say, without paradox, two different logics. By logic is meant here the sum of the habits which the mind adopts in the general conduct of its operations—in the general conduct of a game of chess, in contrast, as Poincaré says, to the special rules which govern each separate proposition, each particular move in the game. Ego-centric logic and communicable logic will therefore differ less in their conclusions (except with the child where ego-centric logic often functions) than in the way they work. The points of divergence are as follows:

1° Ego-centric logic is more intuitive, more "syncretistic" than deductive, i.e., its reasoning is not made explicit. The mind leaps from premise to conclusion at a single bound, without stopping on the way. 2° Little value is attached to proving, or even checking propositions. The vision of the whole brings about a state of belief and a feeling of security far more rapidly than if each step in the argument were made explicit. 3° Personal schemas of analogy are made use of, likewise memories of earlier reasoning, which control the present course of reasoning without openly manifesting their influence. 4° Visual schemas also play an important part, and can even take the place of proof in supporting the deduction that is made. 5° Finally, judgments of value have far more influence on ego-centric than on communicable thought.

In communicated intelligence, on the other hand, we find 1° far more deductive, more of an attempt to render explicit the relations between propositions by such expressions as *therefore*, if . . . then, etc. 2° Greater emphasis is laid on proof. Indeed, the whole exposition is framed in view of the proof, i.e., in view of the necessity of convincing someone else, and (as a corollary) of convincing oneself whenever one's personal certainty may have been shaken by the process of deductive reasoning. 3° Schemas of analogy tend to be eliminated, and to be replaced by deduction proper. 4° Visual schemas are also done away with, first as incommunicable, and later as useless for purposes of demonstration. 5° Finally personal judgments of value are eliminated in favour of collective judgments of value, these being more in keeping with ordinary reason.

If then the difference between thought that can be communicated and what remains of ego-centric thought in the adult or the adolescent is such as we have described it, how much more emphasis shall we be justified in laying on the ego-centric nature of thought in the child. It is chiefly in connexion with children between 3 to 7 and, to a lesser degree, with those between 7 to 11 that we have endeavoured to distinguish ego-centric thought. In the child between 3 and 7 the five characteristics which have just been enumerated actually go to make up a kind of special logic which we shall have occasion to mention throughout this volume and the next. Between 7 and 11 this ego-centric logic no longer influences what Binet and Simon call the "perceptual intelligence" of the child, but it is found in its entirety in his "verbal intelligence." In the following chapters we shall study a large number of phenomena due to ego-centrism, which, after having influenced the perceptual intelligence of children between the ages of 3 and 7, influence their verbal intelligence between the ages of 7 and 11. We are now therefore in a position to realize that the fact of being or of not being communicable is not an attribute which can be added to thought from the outside, but is a constitutive feature of profound significance for the shape and structure which reasoning may assume.

The question of communicability has thus proved itself to be one of those preliminary problems which must be solved as an introduction to the study of child logic. There are other such problems, all of which can be classed under two main headings.

A. *Communicability*: (1) To what extent do children of the same age think by themselves, and to what extent do they communicate with each other? (2) Same question as between older and younger children, (a) of the same family; (b) of different families. (3) Same question as between children and parents.

B. *Understanding*: (1) To what extent do children of the same age understand each other? (2) Same question as between older and younger children (of the same and of different families). (3) Same question as between children and parents.

The problems of the second group will be dealt with in a subsequent chapter. As to group A, we think that we have supplied a partial solution to the first of its problems. If it be granted that the first three categories of child language as we have laid them down are ego-centric, then the thought of the child of 6½ is in its spoken manifestation ego-centric in the proportion of 44 to 47%. What is socialized by language, moreover, belongs only to the factual categories of thought. At this age, causality and the faculty for explanation are still unexpressed. Does the period between 6 and 7 mark a turning point in this respect? We still lack the material to make a sufficient number of comparisons, but judging from what seems to be the rule at the *Maison des Petits*, we believe that the age at which the child begins to communicate his thought (the age when ego-centric language is 25%) is probably somewhere between 7 and 8. This does not mean that from the age of 7 or 8 children can immediately understand each other—we shall see later on that this is far from being the case—it simply means that from this age onwards they try to improve upon their methods of interchanging ideas and upon their mutual understanding of one another.

2

TYPES AND STAGES IN THE CONVERSATION OF CHILDREN BETWEEN THE AGES OF FOUR AND SEVEN[1]

This chapter continues the preceding one and also completes it. Our aim has simply been 1° to check the statistical data obtained from observations made on Pie and Lev, 2° to establish a certain number of types of conversation held between children of the same age; these being on a wider scale than the types of simple propositions examined in the last chapter, and capable eventually of representing the successive stages of childish conversation between the ages of 4 and 7.

The conclusions of chapter 1 may well appear presumptuous, based as they were on observation of two children only, i.e., of two psychological types at the outside. The same experiment

[1] With the collaboration of Mme Valentine Jean Piaget. We also wish to thank Mlle G. Guex who helped us to collect our materials.

needed to be carried out on a whole group of children, and thus reach the greatest possible variety of psychological types. It is such an experiment as this which will be described in the present chapter. The subject of analysis will now be the verbatim report of conversations held, not by one or two specified children, but by the inmates of a whole room, in which they move about from one place to another and which they enter and leave at will. What has been taken down is really the outcome of observations made from a fixed place upon some twenty children on the move. In the *Maison des Petits*, where all these observations have been made, the children between the ages of 4 and 7 occupy a whole floor of five rooms (arithmetic room, building room, modelling room, etc.), and they move about just as they please from one room to another, without being compelled to do any consecutive work. It is in one of these rooms that the data were collected which will form the subject of our present enquiry.

§ 1. CHECK OF THE COEFFICIENT OF EGO-CENTRISM.—One of the first results of these verbatim reports was to show that the talk taken down could be classed in the same categories as those which had been used for Lev and Pie. The language of our 20 subjects, while it reflects differences of temperament, remains the outcome of the same functional needs. In the domineering child there will be an increase of orders, threats, criticisms, and arguments, while the more dreamily inclined will indulge in a greater number of monologues. The proportions will differ, but in each child all the categories will be represented. The difference will be one of quantity not of quality.

Now in Lev and Pie, who represent fairly different types, the coefficients of ego-centrism are very close (0.47 and 0.43). Can we infer from this that the average coefficient between 4 and 7 will be 0.45 or somewhere near? The calculation was made on the sum total of the remarks made by our 20 subjects (boys and girls differing in race and upbringing). The same procedure was adopted as before of taking successive sections of 100 sentences each. These 100 consecutive sentences are thus no longer the successive remarks of one child, but the general conversation in a given room where there are always three or four children talking together. There is therefore every chance that the calculation will yield objectively valid results. Now the average coefficient of ego-centrism which was reached in this way was of 0.45 ± 0.05, representing the proportion of the ego-centric categories to the total language minus answers. As the average age of the children is 6, this is an interesting confirmation of the conclusions of the last chapter.

§ 2. TYPES OF CONVERSATION BETWEEN CHILDREN.—In the first chapter we established a certain number of types of childish talk, but this was done according to type, and not according to the stage of development reached, i.e., without regard to the problem of the development of these types in relation to one another, and of conversation in general among children. This is the problem which we must now approach. We had, moreover, been entirely concerned with isolated remarks, viewed of course in relation to their context, but numbered and classified sentence by sentence. We shall now have to find types, not of isolated, but of general conversation, and these will be partly independent of the earlier types, partly related to them in a manner which we shall specify later on.

When, in the first place, can conversation properly be said to take place between children? Whenever—to fix an arbitrary minimum—three consecutive remarks about the same subject are made by at least two interlocutors. Here are two of the simpler possible schemas of conversation:

I (1) Remark by A.
   (2) Remark by B adapted
       to (1).
   (3) Remark by A adapted
       to (2).

II (1) Remark by A.
   (2) Remark by B adapted
       to (1).
   (3) Remark by C adapted
       to (1) or (2).

After this, all conversation will consist of the language which we have described as socialized. A's remarks may be informations, criticisms, orders, or questions. The remarks made by B and C may belong to those same four groups, or come under answers. But, as we have said, types of conversation will be on a wider scale than types of remarks, and will be independent of these. Thus information, questions, commands, etc., may all appear as constituents of a single conversational type X. The questions we have to answer may therefore be stated as follows: 1° What are the types of conversation between children? 2° Are these types contemporaneous, or do they represent different stages of development? 3° If they constitute stages, what is their genesis? Are they derived from ego-centric language? If so, what is the process of evolution by which a child passes from ego-centric language to the higher types of conversation?

Now it seems to us possible to establish certain stages from a point which has not yet reached the level of conversation, but is represented by the collective monologue. This leads us to the following table. We offer it with due reservation, and chiefly with the object of ordering and schematizating our classifications.

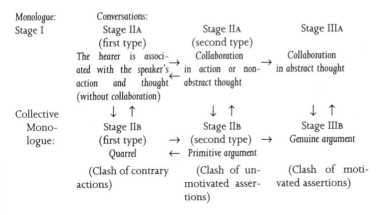

Monologue:	Conversations:		
Stage I	Stage IIA (first type)	Stage IIA (second type)	Stage IIIA
	The hearer is associated with the speaker's action and thought (without collaboration) → ←	Collaboration in action or non-abstract thought →	Collaboration in abstract thought
Collective Mono-logue:	↓ ↑ Stage IIB (first type) → Quarrel ←	↓ ↑ Stage IIB (second type) → Primitive argument	↓ ↑ Stage IIIB Genuine argument
	(Clash of contrary actions)	(Clash of un-motivated assertions)	(Clash of moti-vated assertions)

Stage I still partakes to a certain extent of the nature of ego-centric thought as it was described in the preceding chapter. At this first stage there is, strictly speaking, no conversation, since each child speaks only to himself, even when he seems to be addressing someone in particular. Besides, the children never speak about the same thing. And yet this collective monologue forms the starting point of childish conversation, because it is made up of separate groups, of bundles of consecutive remarks. When a child talks in this way, others will immediately answer by talking about themselves, and this gives rise to a sequence of four or five remarks, which form a conversational embryo, without, however, transcending the stage of the collective monologue.

Stages II and III, on the other hand, have some of the characteristics of conversation properly so-called and of socialized language. We have divided them into two series, A and B, which are parallel from the genetic point of view. (IIA corresponds to IIB, and IIIA to IIIB); the A series has as its origin an agreement in action and opinion (progressive collaboration), the B series has as its origin a disagreement, which begins with a simple quarrel and may evolve into more or less perfected arguments.

Stage IIA can be represented in either of two contemporaneous types. The first type (where the speaker associates his hearer with his own actions and thoughts) is represented by those conversations in which the child, although he only talks about what he is doing, associates with it the person to whom he is talking. There is association in the sense that every one listens to and understands the speaker, but there is no collaboration because each child speaks only of himself, of his own action, or of his own thoughts.

In the second type there is collaboration in action or in thought connected with action (non-abstract thought) in the sense that the conversation bears upon an activity which is shared by the talkers. The subject of conversation is thus some definite action, and not the explanation of a past or future action. It may also happen at this stage that some common memory is evoked, but there is never any question of explaining this memory (e.g. reconstructing some previously heard explanation) nor of discussing it (looking for what is, and what is not true in the memory or in the circumstances which complete it). The memory recalled in common at this IIA stage serves purely as a stimulus. One evokes it just as one tells a story, for the mere pleasure of doing so ("Do you remember how" . . . etc).

It is not until we come to stage IIIA, that we meet with abstract collaboration. By abstract we wish to designate those mental processes in the child which are no longer connected with the activity of the moment, but are concerned with finding an explanation, reconstructing a story or a memory, discussing the order of events or the truth of a tale.

The passage from one to the other of these two stages of the series A shows us a progressive socialization of thought. There was no *a priori* reason why these three types of conversation should represent successive stages. Type IIIA might quite conceivably have appeared before type IIA or the collective monologue, or simultaneously with them. As a matter of fact we shall see that this is not what happens; we shall see that there is progression according to age and in conformity with the table given above. But it goes without saying that the child, as he passes through stages IIA and IIIA, does not relinquish the conversation of the earlier stages. Thus a child who has reached stage IIIA will still indulge in occasional monologues, etc.

Parallel with this evolution is that by which children pass from stage IIB to IIIB, when instead of being in agreement with one another, as in the preceding stages, they are opposed either in opinion or in desire.

Stage IIB is also present in two different types. First of all we have the quarrel, a simple opposition of divergent activities. Just as we have seen that in the first type of stage IIA each child, although acting in isolation, can yet talk to the others about it and associate himself mentally with their activities, so here also, instead of associating himself with them, each child can criticize and abuse the others, can assert his own superiority, in a word, can quarrel. This type of quarrel is a clash of assertions, which are not only statements of fact, but are connected with desires, with subjective evaluations, with commands, and with threats. It may give rise to argument. Thus, after having said: "give me that—No—Yes—No—Yes, etc." the child may resort to statement of fact. "I need that.—No—Yes, etc." The first dialogue belongs to quarrelling, the second to argument. The reverse process is also possible; arguments can give rise to quarrels.

The second type of stage IIB is therefore primitive argument, i.e., argument without justification or proofs of the assertions made. Only in the third stage, IIIB, do we come to argument proper, with motivation of what is said.

Again, it is obvious that in the B series, once the child has reached the stages IIB and IIIB, he does not therefore cease to indulge in monologue or in arguments of a primitive nature. But a child old enough to quarrel is not necessarily capable of genuine argument.

There is between the stages II and III of the A series and the corresponding stages of the B series no *a priori* temporal connexion. But the evidence shows that genuine argument and abstract collaboration appear at the same age. Similarly, quarrelling and associating the hearer with one's action are contemporaneous. They are also contemporaneous with primitive argument and collaboration in action. This points to a certain parallelism.

Having established this schema, let us now examine each stage in turn.

§ 3 STAGE I: COLLECTIVE MONOLOGUE.—The last chapter has sufficiently familiarized us with what is meant by "collective monologue" to enable us to deal very briefly with it here. This stage does not belong to conversation proper, so the criterion which we used for classifying isolated remarks as collective monologue is entirely valid for marking out a whole group of such remarks. It may nevertheless be of interest to give some fresh examples of this category, in the first place for the sake of instancing a few cases under 5 and 6 years old, and secondly because this preparatory stage of conversation is numerically by far the most important, at any rate for children under 5.

We shall begin with examples of collective monologue of one term only, although the remarks are all addressed to someone.

> Den (4; 5) G[1] is talking volubly as she works. Béa (5; 10) G comes into the work-room. Den: *"You've got a sweater on, I haven't, Mummy said it wasn't cold."* Den goes on working. Béa does not answer.
>
> Den to Geo (6) in the building room: *"I know how to, you'll see how well I know. You don't know how.* (No answer. Den goes back to her place) *I know how."*
>
> Den to Béa: *"What do you want?* (No answer.) *I shall want some little holes."*
>
> Ari (4; 1) G to En (4; 11): *"What's your name, my name is Ari."* No answer. Ari, without any transition, to an adult: *"She's going to let her doll drop."*

These four-year-old monologues are thus entirely similar in function to the monologues quoted in the last chapter. They have, however, an element of paradox owing to the use made of questions and purely social forms of speech such as "You have put on, you'll see, you want" which the child uses without waiting for an answer, without even giving his companion time to get in a word. Den, for instance, is struck by Béa's jersey, but she immediately turns the subject on to herself. "I haven't," etc.

[1] (4; 5) G = Girl aged 4 years and 5 months.

Why does she speak to Béa? Not for the sake of telling her anything, still less for the sake of getting an answer, but simply as an excuse for talking. Similarly, Den's question to Béa is purely rhetorical, it is a pseudo-question which simply serves as an introduction to the remark which immediately follows. The social attitude is there only in form, not in substance. The same thing happens between Ari and En.

Collective monologues of two terms or more are of greater interest for our present purpose. Here are some examples:

> Pie (6; 5): "*Where could we make another tunnel? Ah, here Eun?*—Eun (4; 11): *Look at my pretty frock.*" (The End.)
>
> Cat (6; 2): "*Have you finished, Bur?*—Bur (4; 11): *Now it goes that way again,*" etc.

Talk of this kind clearly anticipates future conversation. The speaker expects an answer from his hearer. If the two remarks together constitute only a collective monologue, it is because the hearer is not listening. Thus there is as yet no conversation, because the successive terms are not adapted to one another. But conversation is there in embryo, because the several remarks are grouped into one bundle.

The age at which collective monologue marks a stage of development is between 3 and 4 to 5. The higher forms of conversation do not on the average appear before the age of 5, at any rate not between children of the same age and of different families.

§ 4. STAGE IIA. FIRST TYPE: ASSOCIATION WITH THE ACTION OF OTHERS.—This type has already been described as made up of those conversations in which each speaker talks only about himself and from his own point of view, but is heard and understood by each and all. But there is still no collaboration in a common activity. Here is an example. The children are busy with their drawings, and each one tells the story which his drawing illustrates. Yet at the same time they are talking about the same subject and pay attention to each other:

> Lev (5; 11): "*It begins with Goldylocks. I'm writing the story of the three bears. The daddy bear is dead. Only the daddy was too ill.*—Gen (5; 11): *I used to live at Salève. I lived in a little house and you had to take the funicular railway to go and buy things.*— Geo (6; 0): *I can't do the bear.*—Li (6; 10): *That's not Goldylocks.*—(Lev): *I haven't got curls.*"

This example is very clear. It is a conversation, since they are all speaking about the same thing, the class drawing, and yet each is talking for himself, without any attempt at co-operation. Here is another example:

> Pie (6; 5): "*It was ripping yesterday* (a flying demonstration).—Jacq (5; 6): *There was a blue one,* (an aeroplane) *there was lots of them, and then they all got into a line.*—Pie: *I went in a motor yesterday. And d'you know what I saw when I was in the motor? A lot of carts that were going past. Please teacher can I have the india-rubber?*—Jacq: *I want to draw that* (the aeroplanes). *It will be very pretty.*"

The subject of conversation is one and the same, and the dialogue has four terms. Just at first it might seem as though some common memory were being evoked, as in the cases of co-operation which the next grade will show us, but we shall see from what follows that each child is still speaking from his own point of view. Pie talks about his motor, Jacq plans to draw the aeroplane. They understand each other well enough, but they do not co-operate.

Here are two more typical examples which show very clearly that this association with the activity of each is intermediate between collective monologue and collaboration.

> Mad (7): "*On Sunday I went to see my Granny who lives in the 'Chemin de l'Escalade.'*—Geor (7; 2): *Do you know Pierre C.?—No.—I know him, he's my friend.*"
>
> Rom (5; 9): "*D'you know what I shall have for Christmas?—*Lev (5; 11) and To (4; 9): *No.—*Arm: *A bicycle with three wheels.—*Lev: *A tricycle. I've got one.*"

The reader will notice how Geor's thoughts are diverted by "Chemin de l'Escalade," etc. This looks like collective monologue. But the hearer has listened and understood, and this stage does therefore mark the beginnings of conversation proper, the beginnings of socialized language. But is this type of conversation only one among many others, or does it mark a genuine stage of development? We have seen that it does both these things.

Given the existence of such a stage of development, it goes without saying that no hard and fast rules can be laid down as to its precise limits. An enormous amount of material would be needed for any decisive statistics. The fact remains, however, that in the material at our disposal there are no examples of this type under 5 or even 5; 6, whereas there is a large number of collective monologues from 3 to 4 upwards.

Abstract collaboration hardly appears till about 7. The type of conversation under discussion therefore represents a definite stage of development in relation both to collective monologue and to abstract collaboration.

But in relation to active collaboration the present type cannot be said to occupy a position of before or after. Collaboration in play appears from the age of 4 and 4; 6. Collaboration may therefore sometimes be prior to "association with action," but the reverse is often the case, many children collaborating in work only after they have passed the present stage. In a word, this type of conversation and that which follows it are contemporaneous. They are the two possible modes of the same stage of development.

Again, it need hardly be pointed out that if at stage III the child learns the use of a new type of conversation, abstract collaboration, he does not for that reason discard the habits which he acquired at stage II. These different types coexist even in the adult, with the exception of collective monologue, which is a strictly childish form of conversation.

§ 5 STAGE IIA. SECOND TYPE: COLLABORATION IN ACTION OR IN NON-ABSTRACT THOUGHT.—In conversation of this type, the subject of the successive remarks, instead of being the activities of the respective speakers, is an activity in which they all share. The speakers collaborate, and talk about what they are doing. Instead of diffusion in relation to one and the same subject as in the preceding type, there is convergence.

Here is a typical example:

> Béa (5; 10) G wants to draw a flag. Lev (5; 11): "*Do you know the one my daddy has?—It isn't yours, it's mine. It's red and blue ... It's red, black and white, that's it—yes, first red, white and first black—I've got the right colour; I shall take a square.—No you must take two little long things—And now a square* (shows it to Lev)—*You must let me see if it's right when you've finished*" (which she did).

This is a very good example of collaboration in drawing. Lev advises Béa first as to colour then as to shape, and finally checks the result. Lev, it should be noted, knew the flag, and Béa did not. Hence the dialogue. Now, curiously enough, all the examples of collaboration in action under the age of 5; 6 or 6 are of this type, where a better informed or older child explains an action to a younger or less informed companion. It goes without saying that in reckoning the age at which this type of conversation first appears, no account need be taken of the age of the younger child, so long as his part in the dialogue is not an active one. Here are two examples. In the first the elder child only is active.

Rog (5; 6) to A (3; 9) who is drawing on the black-board: *"You want to draw something?—Something—But not so long as that. You must do them like this, and then like this, and then like this, and then some little windows, but not so long as that."* (The dialogue consists partly of gestures).

Rog (5; 6) asks Ez (6; 4) to explain a point in an educational game: *"Was there one of these ones with the yellow ones?—Jac (7; 2): You musn't show him.—Ez: There are yellow ones. He's doing it all wrong. That one's much easier. You can finish it now. Go along and finish it."*

Collaboration in these cases is help given by an older to a younger child With the very young children, i.e., those under 5½, collaboration between equals is first and foremost collaboration in play. Here are two examples.

Lev (5; 11): *"Den, I'll be the daddy and you're the mummy and Ari will be the nurse—Ari (4; 1): Yes, and the nurse'll take good care of the little children.—Den (4; 5) G: You're the daddy, Lev, you'll go out hunting, you'll go to Germany."*

Lev (5; 11): *"And then we'll play at balloons—Arn (5; 9): How, balloons?—You see, we could pretend we're in the sky. Who'll be the sand? Ari, you'll be the sand—No, No, not the sand—You'll be the balloon, me the basket,* who'll be the sand of the balloon?"

These conversations obviously presuppose collaboration, if not in action, at least in some common game or plan. As such, they no longer belong to the type of "association with the action of others."

Here, finally, is a case of collaboration in evoking a common memory. The example is unfortunately one of two terms only, because the conversation was interrupted by an adult.

Arn (5; 9): *"It's awfully funny at the circus when the wheels (of* the tricycle) *have come off.*—Lev (5; 11): *Do you remember when the gymnastic man but who couldn't do gymnastics, fell down . . .* "

Here, the collaboration is of thought only. In such cases there are two boundary problems to be solved. In the first place, there is between such dialogue as this and that represented by the preceding type (association with action) every degree of intermediate variety. But in the latter type each child talks about himself or about his personal recollections, here, on the contrary, the recollection is shared. This distinction is often of great practical value. When it cannot be applied, the two types of stage IIA can be grouped as one. On the other hand, it is always desirable to distinguish this collaboration in the evocation of a common memory from abstract collaboration. For the latter assumes in this case of a common memory that the speakers not only evoke it together, but that they discuss it, that they question or justify its foundation in fact, or that they explain the why and wherefore of events, etc. None of these characteristics is present in the last conversation we have reported. Lev and Arm are only trying to re-awaken in themselves one and the same pleasant experience, without any attempt to judge or explain the events.

In conclusion, collaboration in action or in non-abstract thought constitutes a type contemporaneous with the type preceding it, and these two together mark a stage of development which extends on the average between the ages of 5 and 7.

§ 6. STAGE IIIA. COLLABORATION IN ABSTRACT THOUGHT.— Conversations at this stage are the only ones in which there is any real interchange of thought. For even when they act in common, or evoke common memories, as in the conversations of the preceding type, children obviously have many more things in mind than they ever say. We shall see in chapter 5 that alongside of the practical categories of thought and of the interest he takes in his own activities, the child shows signs long before the age of 7 of being interested in the explanation of actions and phenomena. The numerous "whys" of children from 3 to 7 bear witness to this. The conversations which we shall class under the present type are those which bear 1° on the explanations of things and the motives of actions, 2° on the reality of events ("Is it true that . . . ?" "Why? . . . ," etc.)

Now it is a curious thing, and one that confirms the results of our investigations on Pie and Lev, that from the twenty children under observation we obtained only one conversation of this type, and not a very clear one at that. This shows once more how ego-centric are the intellectual processes of the child. It also enables us to place the beginnings of the socialization of thought somewhere between 7 and 8. It is at about this age, in our opinion, that conversations of this type first make their appearance. (Probably in both girls and boys.)

The only example obtained from our subjects is, as it happens, a dialogue between a girl of 7 and a boy of 6. These two children are searching together for the explanation, not of a mechanism, but of an action—the absence of their teacher. The corresponding question would therefore come under the "whys of intention and action" (see chapter 6) and would run: "Why has Mlle L. not yet arrived?"

> Mad (7; 6): *"Oh, the slow-coach!*—Lev (6; o): *She doesn't know it's late—Well, I know what she is.—And I know where she is.—She's ill.—She isn't ill since she isn't here."*

This mutual explanation is not, it must be admitted, of a very high intellectual order! The use of the word "since" in the argument should, however, be noted, though the proposition in which it occurs is of doubtful intelligibility.

For the sake of comparison let us give an example of this type of conversation overheard away from the *Maison des Petits* between two sisters of 7 and 8. This example contains, not only an explanation sought in common, as in the case of Mad and Lev, but also the mutual reconstruction of a memory. The memory is discussed and judged, not merely recalled as in the last stage.

> Cor (7): *"Once I wrote to the rabbit that I'd like to see him. He didn't come.—*Viv (8): *Daddy found the letter in the garden. I expect he* (the rabbit) *had come along with the letter, and he didn't find Cor and he went away again.—I went into the garden he wasn't there and then I forgot about it.—He saw Cor wasn't there. He thought 'she's forgotten' and then after that he went away."*

Cor and Viv both believe in fairies, at least they do so to one another in their conversations, prolonging in this way an illusion which has lasted several months. They have built a house for fairies in which they place little notes in the evening. The above conversation bears upon the outcome of one of these missives. They are explaining a failure to each other, and criticizing the course of events. This is enough to place this dialogue at the stage under discussion. It is extremely curious that we should have found no conversations of such a simple type among the children from 3 to 7 who work and play together at the *Maison des Petits*. Conversations of this type must surely occur between brothers and sisters under 7. But this circumstance in itself constitutes a special problem. As soon as there are elder and younger children, their conversation expresses, not so much an exchange or thoughts, as a special kind of relation, for the elder child is always regarded as omniscient, and the younger one treats this knowledge with some of the respect which he feels for the wisdom of his parents.

It need hardly be added that between conversations of stage IIIA and those of stage IIIB (genuine argument), there is every kind of intermediate variety.

§ 7. STAGE IIB. FIRST TYPE: QUARRELLING.—We now come to a set of developments parallel with the preceding ones. They consist of conversations which certainly express an interchange of thoughts between individuals, but an interchange occasioned not by progressive collaboration, but by divergence of opinions and actions. It may seem idle to distinguish two sets of developments on the basis of this difference only, but if this classification ever comes to be applied statistically on a large scale, the distinction may be seen to have its importance, particularly from the genetic point of view. It may well be through quarrelling that children first come to feel the need for making themselves understood. In any case, the study of arguing is, as the investigations of Rignano and P. Janet have shown, of great importance for the psychology of reflexion. It is therefore desirable to make a special study of the growth of arguing in children. We shall attempt it here, but only very schematically.

We may distinguish two stages of childish argument. The first consists in a simple clash of contrary tendencies and opinions. This gives us two more or less contemporaneous types—the primitive quarrel and the primitive argument. The second consists in arguments in which the speakers give the motives of their respective points of view. This stage corresponds to collaboration in abstract thought (IIIA). The first stage corresponds to IIA. Between the corresponding stages of series A and series B there is naturally a whole chain of intermediate links.

Here are a few examples of quarrels:

> Ez (6; 5): "*Ah! I've never had that.*—Pie (6; 5): *You've already had it to play with—That's for A.*—*Well I've never had it to play with.*"
>
> Lev (6; 0): "*I bagged this seat.*— . . . —*I shall sit here all the same.*—Béa (5; 0) G: *He came here first—No, I came here first.*"
>
> Ez (6; 3): "*You wait and see what a slap I'll give you*—Rog (5; 6): *Yes you just wait*—Lev (5; 10) (frightened): *No.*"

Lil (6; 10) G: "*She's nice.*—Ez (6; 5): *No.*—Mo (7; 2): *Yes, yes, yes.*—(They all rise and face each other). Ez to Mo: *You'll see what a slap I'll give you at break.*"

Quarrelling differs from primitive arguing simply in that it is accompanied by actions or promises of actions (gestures or threats). It is the functional equivalent of argument. In primitive argument the opposition is between assertions; here, it is between actions. Ez and Pie quarrel over a toy. Lev and a silent opponent defended by Béa quarrel over a seat, etc. Speech in these quarrels simply accompanies gesture, and is not always understood, as is shown by Lev (in the second quarrel) who repeats what Béa has just said in the fond belief that he is contradicting it.

In deciding upon the age of quarrelling a distinction should be drawn between quarrels with words and those without. The first alone are of interest to us. Now it is a remarkable fact that children between the ages of 4 and 5, although they are extremely quarrelsome, generally conduct their disputes without talking, and we have found no cases of spoken quarrels in three-termed dialogue prior to the age of 5½. There even seems to be a certain progression according to age from the wordless quarrel through the quarrel with words, but accompanied by actions, to the merely spoken quarrel devoid of actions, like that between Ez and Lev who did not slap each other in the end, but having had their say, were content to let the matter rest at that. But such a sequence is of course by no means universal. It simply indicates the progress of conversation in the particular little society which we were studying.

Quarrelling, in a word, is contemporaneous with the two types of stages IIA. Quarrelling and primitive argument merge into one another through a whole series of intermediate varieties of which we give two examples, both being classed as quarrels:

> Béa (5; 10) G: "*You said I was a ox!*—Jac (7; 2): *No, I said . . . silent*—*Oh, I thought you said I was a ox.*"
>
> Lev (5; 11): "*Gen, shew me your funicular railway. But that's not a funicular railway!*—Gen (6; 0) to Pie (6; 5): *He says it's not a funicular railway.* (Looking at Pie's drawing): *That's not pretty*—Pie: *Gen says that mine's not pretty. He shan't see it any more.* Lev to Pie: *Its very pretty.*"

In this last example Pie and Lev take sides against Gen. This is something more than simply arguing. The child is not trying to argue, but to tease or to defend himself. The first example is more subtle. Jac gives in at once to avoid an argument. Béa's tone at the outset, however, inclines us to class this dialogue as a quarrel.

§ 8. STAGE IIB. SECOND TYPE: PRIMITIVE ARGUMENT.— Argument begins from the moment when the speakers confine themselves to stating their opinions instead of teasing, criticizing, or threatening. The distinction is often a subtle one. We have just instanced intermediate examples which we placed among quarrels. Here is one which must be classed as an argument, because the speakers' tone is one of statement, although the subject-matter is one of blows.

> Ez (6; 4): "*You wait; at the Escalade, I'll be the strongest.*—Lev (5; 11): *At the Escalade, not at school.*—Ez; *Everywhere I'll be the strongest.*"

The argument is very primitive and not quite genuine, because there is no trace of a desire for logical justification in the assertions of Ez and Lev. The criterion of primitive argument is not an easy one to apply. We must therefore try to fix the point where the attempt is first made to justify and demonstrate the assertions made in the course of argument. We propose the following rule. There is demonstration (therefore genuine argument) when the child connects his statement with the reason which he gives for its validity by means of a conjunction (e.g. since, because, then, etc.), and thus makes his demonstration explicit. So long as the justification is only implicit, and the child expresses himself in a succession of disconnected statements, the argument is still only primitive. This rule is purely conventional, but it is useful because any subjective test as to whether demonstration is present or not tends to be still more arbitrary.

> Viv (7; 3) G.: "*My daddy is a tiger.*—Geo (7; 2): *No, he can't be. I've seen him.*—*My daddy is a godfather and my mummy is a godmother.*"

Geo implicitly justifies his assertion: "*He can't be*" with the proof; "*I've seen him.*" But there is no explicit connexion between the sentences. In order to find in the second a justification of the first, it would be necessary to follow a line of argument to which Geo nowhere gives expression. Geo, like Viv, confines himself to mere statement.

Similarly in the following example.

> Lev (5; 11): "*That's Aï.*—Mie (5; 5) G: *It's Mie* (Aï's sister).— Lev: *No, it's Aï.*—Ez (6; 4): *Its Mie, look.*" (He lifts Mie's cloak and shows her dress.)

The first three terms of the argument are definitely primitive, there is no demonstration. The fourth contains an element of justification, but by means of gesture, without any explicit reasoning. It serves the purpose in this particular case, but the instance is none the less primitive in character.

Justification of a statement may consist in an appeal to one's own authority or to that of others or of one's elders. But unless it is given in the form of reasoning, it does not constitute an argument. Here are two examples:

Lev (5; 10): "*It isn't naughty to bury a little bird*—Ari (4; 1): *Yes, it is naughty*—*No, no, no.* Lev to Je: *It isn't naughty is it?* Je (6; 0): *I don't know, I don't think so.*"

Aï (3; 9): "*I've got four little balls*—Lev (5; 10): *But there aren't four. You don't know how to count. You don't know how much four is. Let me see . . . etc.*"

In all these examples, it is easy enough to recognize primitive argument. The remarks are made as simple statements and not as explicit reasoning. If we compare these instances with the following example (of which the last remark comes very near to being genuine argument) and with the one example of genuine argument which we obtained, the difference will be seen at once:

Lev (5; 11): *We can only give some* [fish] *to those who speak English.*—Ez (6; 4): *We can't give her* [Béa] *any. I know English.*—Béa (5; 10): *No, I know English.*—Lev: *Then I'll give you the fish.*—Ez: *Me too.*—Mad (7; 6): *She doesn't know it.*— Lev: *Yes, she does.*—Mad: *It's because she wants some that she says that.*"

This conversation only becomes an argument towards the end. Mad and Lev begin by simply opposing their respective points of view to one another. But where a great advance is made on the previous examples is when Mad, in order to contradict Lev, gives an explanation of Béa's conduct. She therefore interprets the adverse point of view, and justifies her own by an explanation. Even if the other speakers are still arguing in a primitive manner, Mad, in her last remark, has reached the stage of genuine argument.

Primitive argument is thus, on the mental plane, the equivalent of quarrelling on the plane of action—a simple clash of contrary opinions and desires. There is therefore nothing surprising in the fact that these two types of conversation should be roughly contemporaneous. It is true that the quarrel without words, or at any rate without a three-termed dialogue is prior in appearance to argument, but according to our evidence the spoken quarrel, like the primitive argument, generally begins at about 5 or 5½. Genuine argument as represented by stage IIIA does not appear till about 7 or 7½. Before, therefore, it can be reckoned as one among other types of argument, primitive argument must be recognized as constituting a definite stage in the evolution of childish conversation, a stage, which though it has no very precise boundaries, yet corresponds to the objective results obtained from our statistics.

§ 9. STAGE IIIB: GENUINE ARGUMENT.—The statistical data are as follows. In the whole of our material we have found only one case of genuine argument in dialogue of more than three terms among the children under 7. This tallies exactly with the fact that collaboration in abstract thought does not appear, on an average, before the age of 7 or 7½. Indeed, these two different aspects, A and B, of stage III can be accounted for by one and the same circumstance. Up to a certain age the child keeps to himself, without socializing it, everything that is connected in his mind with causal explanation or logical justification. Now in order to argue, demonstrations and logical relations etc. have to be made explicit, all of which runs counter to the ego-centrism of the child under 7.

Here is the only case of genuine argument which we have obtained. The difference between it and the three preceding examples will be seen at once. Out of the five terms of the dialogue, three contain the word "because," which in one case at least points to a logical justification.

Pie (6; 5): "*Now, you shan't have it* (the pencil) *because you asked for it.*—Hei (6; 0): *Yes I will, because it's mine.*—Pie: *'Course it isn't yours. It belongs to everybody, to all the children.*—

> Lev (6; o): *Yes, it belongs to Mlle. L. and all the children, to Aï and to My too.*—Pie: *It belongs to Mlle. L. because she bought it, and it belongs to all the children as well.*"

It is surprising that a type of conversation apparently so simple should have occurred only once in the material we have collected. The truth is that the use of the word "because" is a very delicate matter. The logical "because" connects, not two phenomena of which one is cause and the other effect, but two ideas of which one is reason and the other consequence. Now this connexion is one which, as we shall see in chapter 1 of the second volume (examination of the sense of conjunctions, "because" etc.) it is still very difficult for the 7-year-old mind to make. There is therefore nothing surprising in the scarcity of genuine arguments with demonstrations in defence of the use of these conjunctions among children under 7.

After the age of 7 or 8, however, the logical "because" and "since" make frequent appearances in the children's conversation, thus enabling them to take part both in genuine argument and in collaboration in abstract thought.

Here are two examples taken at random from those conversations of children between 7 and 8, which are published from time to time[1] by Mlles. Audemars and Lafendel. These examples have been chosen at random from two pages in the collection:

> Ray: (She won't be an orphan). "*But she will go to a boarding school, since she has still got her daddy.*"
>
> Ray: (The chain of men is the most important of all), "*because they have worked a lot and invented a great many things.*"

A logical "since" and a logical "because" occur in this example. Such verbal forms abound in the conversation of these children,

[1] See *L'Educateur*, Lausanne, vol. 58, pp. 312–313.

whereas they are avoided or only used on very exceptional occasions by children under 7. It should be noted that with Ray the "because" is definitely logical, i.e., connecting two ideas or definitions, and not psychological, i.e., connecting an action with its psychological explanation.

The reasons, therefore, why genuine argument, like collaboration in abstract thought, appears only after the age of 7 or 7½ in the development of the child are of a very fundamental order. Does the absence of verbal forms expressing logical relations prevent genuine argument from manifesting itself, or does the absence of the desire to argue and collaborate explain the late appearance of these verbal forms? If we admit that thought in the child depends upon his interests and activities rather than *vice versa*, then the absence of the desire to argue and collaborate is obviously the initial factor. This is why we have begun our study of child logic with a study of the forms of conversation and of the functions of language. But there is, as a matter of fact, perpetual interaction between these two factors of evolution.

§ 10. CONCLUSION.—What conclusion are we to draw from these facts? Can we, in the first place, establish any numerical results from the material on which we have worked? This material consists of two books containing 500 remarks each. Among these there are several dialogues between children and adults, which have been omitted from the following calculations. This leaves us with about 400 remarks in each book, representing the talk of children between the ages of 3½ and 7. There are 31 conversations in one book and 32 in the other. These two groups may be distributed as follows.

					I	II	TOTAL	
Stage IIA 1st type	.	.	.	.	4	6	10	} 21
,, IIB 1st type	.	.	.	.	8	3	11	
Stage IIA 2nd type	.	.	.	.	9	16	25	} 40
,, IIB 2nd type	.	.	.	.	9	6	15	
Stage IIIA	.	.	.	.	.	1	0	1	} 2
,, IIIB	.	.	.	.	.	1	0	1	

The collective monologue is naturally excluded from statistics dealing with general conversations, and it can be judged of only by the number of remarks which are assigned to it. We have seen that the coefficient of ego-centrism (collective monologue, monologue and repetition) is 0.45 for the sum of the talk under investigation after subtraction of answers.

This result shows very clearly that genuine argument and collaboration in abstract thought constitute a stage of development which only intervenes after the age of 7. This is a very useful confirmation of the conclusions reached in the last chapter. The statistics of the remarks made by Lev and Pie seemed to justify the conclusion that intellectual processes (causal explanation, logical justification) in children of less than 7 or 7½ remain egocentric in character. It will be remembered that in all the talk classed as "information" we found very few cases of causal explanation or logical justification. Mental activity is either silent, or accompanied by monologues. Our present results, showing as they do the rareness of genuine argument and collaboration in abstract ideas before the age of 7, go to prove these same conclusions by a different method.

The fact that the stage of collaboration and genuine argument does not intervene till the age of 7 or 7½ is of the greatest importance. For it is between the ages of 7 and 8 that we can date the appearance of a logical stage in which the phenomenon of reflexion becomes general; if we agree with P. Janet in calling reflexion the tendency to unify one's beliefs and opinions, to systematize them with the object of avoiding contradiction.

Up till the age of 7 or 8 children make no effort to stick to one opinion on any given subject. They do not indeed believe what is self-contradictory, but they adopt successively opinions, which if they were compared would contradict one another. They are insensible to contradiction in this sense, that in passing from one point of view to another they always forget the point of view which they had first adopted. Thus in the course of interrogation, the same children aged from 5 to 7, will answer at one time that ants, flowers and the sun are living beings, and at another time that they are not. Others will affirm on one occasion that rivers have been dug out by the hand of man, and on another that they were made only by water. The two contrary opinions are juxtaposed in the children's minds. At one moment they adopt the one, then forgetful of the past, and in all sincerity, they come back to the other. This is a well-known fact in the examination of children up to the age of 7 or 8, even when the subjects are not deliberately inventing.

This absence of system and coherence will be examined elsewhere (Vol. II). It will suffice in the meantime to note that its disappearance coincides with the advent of genuine argument. This coincidence is not fortuitous. If, as we said a little while ago, a correlation be admitted to exist between a child's activity and his thought, then it is obviously the habit of arguing which will cause the need for inner unity and for the systematization of opinions to make itself felt. This it is, to which Janet and Rignano have drawn attention in connexion with the psychology of arguing in general. They have shown that all reflexion is the outcome of an internal debate in which a conclusion is reached, just as though the individual reproduced towards himself an attitude which he had previously adopted towards others. Our research confirms this view.

It should be stated in conclusion that these studies need to be completed by a general investigation of the conversations of children as they are carried on apart from work, as for instance at play in public gardens, etc. Enough has been said, however, for the schema which we have elaborated to serve in the studies ahead of us. The following chapter will complete our data by showing that if before the age of 7 or 8 children have no conversation bearing upon logical or causal relations, the reason is that at that age they hardly understand one another when they approach these questions.

3

UNDERSTANDING AND VERBAL EXPLANATION BETWEEN CHILDREN OF THE SAME AGE BETWEEN THE YEARS OF SIX AND EIGHT[1]

In the preceding chapters we have tried to determine to what extent children speak to each other and think socially. An essential problem has been left on one side: when children talk together, do they understand one another? This is the problem which we are now to discuss.

This question is not nearly so easy to answer as the preceding ones, and for a very simple reason. It is quite possible to determine immediately whether children are talking or even listening to one another, whereas it is impossible by direct observation to be sure whether they are understanding each other. The child has a hundred and one ways of pretending to understand, and

[1] With the collaboration of Mme Valentine Jean Piaget.

often complicates things still further by pretending not to understand, by inventing answers, for instance, to questions which he has understood perfectly well.

These conditions therefore oblige us to proceed with the utmost prudence; the different questions involved must be arranged in proper order, and only that one approached which concerns verbal understanding.

To show the soundness of the experiments we have instigated, let us start from observation of the child such as has been supplied by the preceding chapters. We have seen that in the highest types of conversation between children, i.e., collaboration and argument, two different cases are to be distinguished, which we have called stage II and stage III. The first case is connected with action (collaboration in action, or primitive argument still bound up with action and devoid of explicit reasoning); the second case makes use of abstraction. Let us call them, for the sake of brevity, the acted case and the verbal case. In the verbal case children collaborate or argue about a story to be reconstructed, a memory to be appreciated, or an explanation to be given (explanation of some phenomenon or other or of the words of an adult). Now discussions such as these take place on the verbal plane, without actions, without the aid of any material object with which the speakers might have been playing or working, without even the present spectacle of the phenomena or of the events about which they are talking. In the acted case, on the other hand, the collaboration or argument is accompanied by gestures, by demonstrations with the finger and not with words; it matters little, therefore, whether the talk is intelligible or not, since the talkers have the object under their eyes. Hence the quaint character of much childish talk. (That does that, and then that goes there, and it goes like that," etc.). Were it not entirely outside the scope of this study, the connexion should also be established between these "acted" conversations and the language by gesture and mime—language in movement, one might say—which is, after all, the real social language of the child.

Now in these two cases, "acted" conversation and "merely spoken" conversation, children naturally understand each other in a very different manner. (The second case, moreover, characterizes a stage which begins only at about seven years; it does not have its full effect, i.e., it does not lead children to understand each other till about the age of 8.) In "acted" conversation one gets the impression that the children understand each other well. Hence the success of the educational method (provided there is an adequate supply of educational games) which consists in letting one child explain to another, say, a certain way of doing sums, or a certain school regulation. Thus we owe to Mlle Descœudres the knowledge that in games of spelling (lotto, etc.), of arithmetic, and in exercises of manual skill (threading beads, etc.) even abnormal children collaborate very profitably, and understand each other better than master and pupil would do. This rule holds good even between children of the same age, from 5 or 6 upwards, although the understanding between elder and younger children is on the average higher. But all this concerns only "acted" conversation. As to merely spoken conversation it may be questioned whether children really understand each other when they use it; and this is the problem which we shall now attempt to solve. Let us begin by showing the importance of the subject.

An essential part of the intellectual life of the child takes place apart from contact either with any material that is really within his reach or with any concrete images. To say nothing of the ordinary schools where from the age of 7 the child no longer manipulates a single object, and where his thought sinks deeper and deeper into verbalism, cases of the following kind are of daily occurrence. A child sees a bicycle in the street, and mentally reconstructs its mechanism. (A Geneva boy can give this explanation on average from the age of 7 or 8½.) The same thing happens in the case of motors and trains. The child, from the age of 6 or 7, has images connected with the words "benzine," "electricity," "steam," etc. He has others connected with the concepts life, thought, feeling, etc., and he has ideas on the amount of life and feeling, so to speak, which may be accorded to animals, plants, stars, etc. . . . He hears people talk about countries, towns, animals, and instruments which are completely unknown to him, but about which he reasons nevertheless. Yet another kind of preoccupation is that concerning the amount of truth to be attributed to dreams, stories, the fantasies of play, etc. All these types of mental activity can take place only on the verbal plane, and in this sense they will always differ from those bearing upon toys and instruments, etc., which imply manual work or at least manipulation.

Now, as the last two chapters have shown, this verbal activity is not social; each child carries it on by himself. Each child has his own world of hypotheses and solutions which he has never communicated to anyone, either because of his ego-centrism, or for lack of the means of expression—which comes to the same thing, if (as we hope to show in this chapter) language is moulded on habits of thought. We shall even go so far as to say in a chapter in our second volume that a child is actually not conscious of concepts and definitions which he can nevertheless handle when thinking for himself. What then will happen when the chances of conversation lead children to exchange their ideas on the verbal plane? Will they understand each other or not? This is a cardinal question in the psychology of child thought, and will supply us with a necessary counter-proof. If we can prove that verbal thought is incommunicable between children we shall justify our hypotheses concerning childish ego-centrism, and at the same time explain some of the most characteristic phenomena of child logic, particularly that of verbal syncretism (cf. chapter 4.).

§ 1. THE METHOD OF EXPERIMENT.—In order to solve this

problem we have had to undertake an experiment which consists in making one child tell or explain something to another. This procedure will doubtless be criticized as being removed from everyday life, where the child speaks spontaneously, without being made to, and especially without having been told what to relate or explain to his listener. We can only reply that we found no other way of solving the problem. This method certainly has its drawbacks; still, once allowance has been made for the risks it incurs, it must be granted that in some of its aspects it recalls what happens in ordinary life; as when a child, immediately after hearing a story or receiving an explanation, goes off to tell the same story or give the same explanation to a younger brother or to a friend. The great thing is to turn the experiment into a game, to make it interesting. But this condition is not a very difficult one to fulfil if the children are taken during school hours, and consequently when they are under the spell of the unexpected. The matter can be introduced as an amusement or a competition: "Are you good at telling stories? Very well then, we'll send your little friend out of the room, and while he is standing outside the door, we'll tell you a story. You must listen very carefully. When you have listened to it all, we'll make your friend come back, and then you will tell him the same story. We shall see which of you is best at telling stories. You understand? You must listen well, and then tell the same thing . . . " etc. Repeat the instructions as often as necessary, and stress the need for a faithful rendering, etc.

Then one of the subjects is sent out of the room, and the set piece is read to the other. The more complicated passages are repeated, everything is done to make the subject listen, but the text is not altered. Then one or other of the following methods is adopted: (They have been used alternately, the one serving as a test of the other.) Either the child who has been waiting outside in the passage, and whom we shall call the *reproducer*, is sent for, and everything that the other child (whom we shall call the *explainer*) says to him is taken down in *extenso*; or else the explainer is asked to tell us a story in the first instance, and is then sent to tell the same story to the reproducer out in the lobby or in the garden, i.e., in our absence, and with the injunction to take as much time as he likes. In both cases the story, as told by the reproducer, is taken down verbatim. Both these methods have their drawbacks. In the first, the story told in our presence loses in spontaneity. In the second, we can no longer check matters so closely, and it may well be that the explainer, after having told us a story perfectly well, will take less trouble over it when he is talking to the reproducer. There is always a certain disadvantage in making the explainer repeat the same story twice. We therefore dispense with this initial test in the first method, as it is preferable to do for children between 7 and 8. Since the reproducer's degree of understanding is estimated in relation to that of the explainer, and not with reference to the original text, the fact that the explainer may occasionally blunder is of no importance. If, for instance, the explainer has understood 8 points out of 10 and the reproducer 4 points out of 8, the coefficient of understanding will be 0.8 $(= \frac{8}{10})$ for the explainer and 0.5 $(= \frac{4}{8})$ for the reproducer. It will not be 0.4 $(= \frac{4}{10})$ for the latter, because no account is taken of the two points omitted by the explainer. With children from 5 to 6, on the other hand, one is obliged to ask for a preliminary account of the story by the explainer, who very often has been thinking of everything rather than of paying attention.

The results obtained by these two methods have proved of equal value. By using them simultaneously we have therefore a means of testing our results, which will have to be borne in mind in our subsequent investigations.

When the experiment is over, the two children exchange parts; the explainer is sent out of the room and becomes the reproducer in this second test, a new story is told to the former reproducer who now becomes explainer, and everything is done as in the previous case.

After this exchange of stories, an exchange of explanations was organized, bearing upon mechanical objects. The explainer was shown a diagram of a tap or of a syringe (the drawing of a bicycle has also been used occasionally), and he was given in a fixed order the explanation of the workings of the several parts. This unusual choice of subject was not made at random, but in consideration of the interests of boys from 6 to 8. The latter are often too well-informed on these subjects for the experiment to be conclusive.

The method adopted for the explanations is as follows. The explainer, when he has had the diagram explained to him, takes possession of this diagram and explains it in his turn to the reproducer. The reproducer then gives his explanation, with the drawing still before him.

We have carried out with these methods some hundred experiments on 30 children from 7 to 8, taken in pairs (i.e., 15 couples with four experiments per couple, say two explanations and two stories), and on 20 children from 6 to 7 (ten couples with four experiments per couple).

Here are the stories which were used:

I. Epaminondas is a little nigger boy and he lives in a country where it is very hot. His mother once said to him: "Go and take this shortbread cake to your granny, but don't break it." Ep. put the shortbread under his arm, and when he got to his grandmother's the short-bread was in crumbs. His granny gave him a pat of butter to take back to his mother. This time Ep. thought to himself: "I shall be very careful." And he put the pat of butter on his head. The sun was shining hard, and when he got home the butter had all melted. "You are a silly," said his mother, "you should have put the butter in a leaf, then it would have arrived whole."

II. Once upon a time, there was a lady who was called Niobe, and who had 12 sons and 12 daughters. She met a fairy who had only one son and no daughter. Then the lady laughed at the fairy because the fairy only had one boy. Then the fairy was very angry and fastened the lady to a rock. The lady cried for ten years. In the end she turned into a rock, and her tears made a stream which still runs to-day.

III. Once upon a time, there was a castle, and in it were a king and queen who had three sons and one daughter. Near the castle was a wicked fairy who did not like children. She took the king and queen's children to the seashore, and changed them into four beautiful white swans. As their children had not come home, the king and queen went to look for them everywhere, and they came right down to the sea-shore. There they saw four beautiful swans, who told them that they were their children. The swans stayed on the sea for a very long time, and then they went away to a very cold country. After many years they came back to where their castle was. There was no castle there any longer, and their parents were dead. The swans went into a church and they were changed into three little old men and one little old woman.

In these three stories the events are related to one another in the greatest variety of ways, ranging from the most simple and natural to the most mythological. We now give the two mechanical explanations of which have made use most frequently. Between the causal relations which they imply, and the relations of events contained in the preceding stories, we shall have sufficient material for studying the way in which children understand and express the whole scale of possible relations.

(1) Look, these two pictures (I and II) are drawings of a tap (see p. 84).

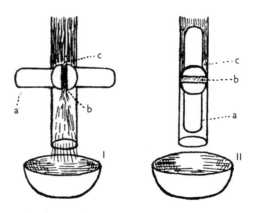

(2) This here (*a*) is the handle of the tap.

(3) To turn it on, look, you have to do this with your fingers (move the finger on diagram I and show the result on diagram II). Then it is like this (diagram II).

(4) You see (diagram I), when the handle is turned on like this (point to *a* and make horizontal movement), then the canal (point to *b*, call it also the little hole, door, or passage) is open.

(5) Then the water runs out (point to *b* in diagram I).

(6) It runs out because the canal is open.

(7) Look, here (diagram II), when the handle is turned off (point to *a* and make a vertical movement), then the canal (point to *b*; can also be called the hole or door or passage) is also shut.

(8) The water can't get through, you see? (point to *c*). It is stopped.

(9) It can't run out, because the canal (point to *b*) is closed.

The reader should note that each one of these points has to be made for the child. It often happens, for instance, that the subject understands, say, point (5) (the water runs out), and thinks that the water runs out simply because the handle of the tap has been

So far, then, the method is quite simple. You read one of the stories or explanations to the explainer, but you must not appear to be reading, and you must talk in the most natural manner possible. The explainer then tells the story to the reproducer, who finally serves it up to you again.

But this is not all. Once the reproducer's story has been obtained and taken down in its entirety, the explainer is taken aside for a few moments, and the reproducer is asked a certain number of questions on the points that have been omitted, so as to ascertain whether he has really failed to understand them. He may either have forgotten them or he may not know how to express them. In order to judge of the child's degree of understanding these factors must at all costs be eliminated, so as to clear the ground for a more searching investigation. If in the story of Niobe, for example, the end is forgotten, the child is asked whether there is nothing about a stream. Thus by means of questions, vague at first and then more and more precise, and with the help of that division into points which we have just given for explanations and which we shall give in the next paragraph for stories, the reproducer's degree of understanding can be properly put to the test. When this has been done, the explainer is questioned in the same manner, to see whether he has really understood the points which appear doubtful.

§ 2. PARCELLING OUT THE MATERIAL.—Such experiments as these will be seen to resemble on many points the experiments made by Claparède and Borst, by Stern, etc., on evidence. For in the manner in which the explainer, and even more so the reproducer, distort the story they have heard, we can see various factors at work, such as memory of facts, logical memory, etc., all of which we shall call by the same name—the factors of evidence. Now it is important to eliminate these factors in order to study understanding or the lack of it independently of distortions of fact due to other causes. How then are we to avoid the factors of evidence, which are of no interest to us here? By the device of parcelling out the material.

We have divided each of our set pieces into a certain number of points, as is done in the sifting of evidence, so as to see which of these points have been reproduced or omitted by the subjects, and instead of choosing a large number all bearing on questions of detail, we have restricted ourselves to a small number of rubrics connected solely with the understanding of the story. In estimating the correctness of each point, moreover, we have taken no notice in parcelling out the material of the factors that were not essential to the understanding of the story: Thus in the tale of Niobe the name of Niobe plays no part whatsoever; it is sufficient if mention is made of "a lady" or even "a fairy." Similarly, "12 boys and 12 girls" can be changed into "many children" or "three children," etc., provided a difference is made between the number of children belonging to "the lady" and that of those belonging to the fairy.

Here, in detail, are the points taken into consideration:

I Niobe. (1) Once there was a lady (or a fairy, etc.). (2) She had children (provided they outnumber these of the other fairy). (3) She met a fairy (or a girl, etc.). (4) This fairy had few children (or none at all, provided their number is inferior to the first lot). (5) The lady laughed at the fairy. (6) Because the fairy had so few children. (7) The fairy was angry. (8) The fairy fastened the lady (to a rock, a tree, to the shore, etc.). (9) The lady cried. (10) She turned into a rock. (11) Her tears made a stream. (12) Which flows to this day.

It is obvious that each of these points except point (7), which can easily be taken for granted, and points (9) and (12) which are supplementary to the body of the story, are necessary to the comprehension of the story. It will be seen, moreover, that we are very generous in our estimates, since any alteration of detail is tolerated.

The stories of Epaminondas and of the four swans were parcelled out according to exactly the same principles.[1] As for the points which we made use of in the mechanical explanations, they have already been given in the preceding paragraph.

Having disposed of this part of the subject, we then proceeded to estimate the understanding of the children as follows. In the first place, we tried to reduce our results to numbers and coefficients of understanding. We are not ignorant of the objections of all sorts which are raised against the use of measurement in psychology. We are aware of the inaccurate and arbitrary character of such methods of evaluation, and above all of that element of dangerous fascination which makes statisticians lose sight of the concrete facts which their figures represent. But we must not, on the other hand, judge the psychologists to be more naïve than they really are. It is too often the reader who takes the figures literally, whilst the psychologist moves more slowly to his conclusions. Our figures will yield much less than they seem to contain. We shall look to them in this work, not so much for an exact measurement—that seems to us premature—as for an

[1] We give in detail the points which were used, in case anyone ever repeats our experiments with the same set pieces.

I. Epaminondas: (1) A little nigger boy. (2) A hot country. (3) His mother sends him to take a shortbread cake. (4) Which arrives broken (in crumbs, etc.). (5) Because he had held it under his arm. (6) His granny gives him some butter. (7) Which arrives melted. (8) Because he put it on his head. (9) And because it was very hot.

II. The four swans: (1) A castle. (2) A king and queen. (3) Who had children. (4) There was a fairy. (5) She did not like children (or was wicked, etc.). (6) She changed them into swans. (7) The parents find their children, or the swans. (8) These go away. (9) To a cold country. (10) They come back again. (11) The castle and the parents are no longer there. (12) They are changed into (13) old people. (14) In a church.

We have distinguished between points (12) and (13) because it sometimes happens that the children think the old people have appeared in the story without realizing that they are the swans transformed.

aid to research and to the practical solution of the problems. In giving the solution of these problems we shall rely far more on the methods of pure observation and clinical examination than upon rough numerical data. These will serve at best to sharpen our criticism, and in this capacity their legitimacy cannot be questioned. Let the reader then be not too hastily shocked, but quietly wait for our conclusions. In the meantime, let us confine ourselves to the quest for schemas of objective evaluation, i.e., schemas, which, though founded on pure conventions, admit of being put into practice by every one with the same result.

We shall distinguish, in the first place, *general understanding, i.e.,* the manner in which the reproducer has understood the whole of the story told by the explainer, and *verbal understanding bearing upon causal or logical relations.* The latter bears upon certain points in the stories, and will concern us later on.

Within general understanding we shall distinguish on the one hand, between implicit understanding (i.e., what the child has understood without necessarily being able to express it) and explicit understanding (i.e., what the child reproduces spontaneously), and on the other, between the understanding of the explainer in relation to the adult and the understanding of the reproducer in relation to that of the explainer.

α = What the reproducer has understood in relation to what the explainer has understood.

β = What the reproducer has understood in relation to what the explainer has expressed.

γ = What the explainer has understood in relation to what the adult has expressed.

δ = What the explainer has expressed in relation to what he has understood.

When something is explained to the explainer, one of three things may happen. Either he does not understand, and therefore cannot repeat anything; or else he understands, but either cannot or will not repeat it (for lack of the means of expression or because he thinks the thing goes without saying and is known to his hearer, etc.); or, finally, he understands and repeats correctly. It is important to consider these three cases separately. One of the chief causes of misunderstanding among children may be due to some personal trait in the explainer. When such a factor is present it is expedient to make allowance for it. Here is an example of the parcelling out of which we spoke:

> Schla (6; 6) to Riv (6; 6). Explanation of the drawing of the tap: *"You see, this way* (diagram I) *it is open. The little pipe* (c) *finds the little pipe* (b) *and then the water runs out. There* (diagram II) *it is shut and it can't find the little pipe that runs through. The water comes this way* (diagram I, c) *it comes in the little pipe. It is open, and there* (II) *it is shut. Look, you can't see the little pipe any more* (II) *it is lying down, then the water comes this way* (c) *and wouldn't find the little pipe any more."*

If the reader refers to the points given in the preceding paragraph, he will find what follows. Point (I) is understood by Schla; he had told us just before speaking to Riv that it was about a tap. But he forgets to mention it to Riv, probably because for himself it goes without saying. Point (2), the part played by the handle is also understood. Schla had said to us: *"There are two little bars there* (a). *When you turn them, it runs out because they turn the pipe round."* This explanation is good. In this exposition to Riv, on the other hand, no mention is made of the handle of the tap. Schla contents himself with saying: "It is open" or "it is shut," which seems to him sufficient to recall the movement with which one turns the handle of the tap. Is this carelessness or forgetfulness, or does Schla think that Riv has understood things sufficiently clearly? We shall not discuss these points for the moment. It will be sufficient for us to note their importance in the mechanism of childish language. Point (3) is also understood (*"When you turn"*). Schla knows and tells us that it is with the fingers that the handle of the tap is made to revolve. He does not say so to Riv either, because it goes without saying or for some other reason. As to the four other points, it is obvious that they are all correctly understood and expressed by Riv. The connexion between the fact that "it is *open*" and that the water runs through the canal b is very well indicated, as is also the movement of the water. The opposite connexion (between the closing of the canal, the movement of the handle and the stoppage of the water) is also indicated.

The nine points of the explanation have been understood by Schla. Even though in talking to Riv he may not have expressed himself clearly and explicitly throughout, still, so far as he himself is concerned, the child has understood everything and can give us spontaneous proof of having done so (otherwise we would have tested him with the questions of which we spoke in a previous paragraph). If then we calculate the coefficient of γ we get

$$\gamma = \frac{\text{Number of points understood by the explainer}}{\text{Number of points to be understood}} = \frac{9}{9} = 1.00.$$

The points not expressed to the reproducer (to Riv) do not enter into this coefficient. They do so, on the other hand, in the calculation of the coefficient of δ

$$\delta = \frac{\text{Number of points expressed to the reproducer}}{\text{Number of points understood by the explainer}} = \frac{6}{9} = 0.66.$$

The significant of the coefficients γ and δ will now be clear. The first gives a measure of the explainer's understanding in relation to the experimenting adult. The second gives a measure of the value of the explanation given by the explainer to the reproducer.

Let us now see how much Riv has understood of the explanation given by Schla. Here are Riv's words verbatim:

> Riv (6; 6) "Here (I, c) *there's the pipe, and then it is opened, and then the water runs into the basin, and then there (II, c) it is shut, so the water doesn't run any more, then there's the little pipe (II, b) lying down, and then the basin's full of water. The water can't run out 'cos the little pipe is there, lying down, and that stops it.*"

Point (1) (the word tap) is omitted. But has Riv understood it? We ask him "What is this all about?—*A pipe*—Is it a tap?—*No.*" He has therefore not understood, which is hardly surprising as Schla has not told him. Point (2) is also omitted. We show Riv the handle (*a*) and ask him what it is. He does not know a thing about it. Nor has he understood what must be done to make the little pipe turn round (*b*), although he might have guessed this through hearing Schla say, "*It is open*," etc., even without understanding that the two *a*'s represent the handle. Thus points (3), (4) and (7) have been missed. We now test this interpretation by means of several questions. "What must you do to make the little pipe lie down?" etc. All the rest, however, has been understood.

Concerning Riv's understanding, two things have to be established. In the first place, there is its relation to Schla's understanding, i.e., not only to what Schla has expressed, but also to what he has understood without expressing it (α). Secondly, there is the relation of Riv's understanding to what Schla has made quite explicit (β). In this connexion, points (4) and (7), which are expressed by Schla ("*There it is shut, and can't find the little pipe that runs through,*" etc.), are not understood by Riv. Now Riv might have discovered, even without knowing that the *a*'s represent the handle of a tap, that in order to close the canal *b* or make it lie down, something would have to be turned, or "shut off." But this relation has completely escaped his notice, though pointed out by Schla, and emphasized with gesture. It may be objected that Schla has not expressed this relation very clearly, but the point is that he has expressed it in the childish manner of juxtaposition (cf. § 6). Instead of saying: "It can't find the little pipe *because* it is shut," Schla says: "It is shut, and it can't find the little pipe." This is the style in which Riv thinks. Why should not Schla understand him, since he too must surely think in the same manner?

Riv has therefore understood four points out of the six that have been expressed and out of the nine that have been understood by Schla. This yields the two coefficients α and β.

$$\alpha = \frac{\text{Everything understood by the reproducer}}{\text{Everything understood by the explainer}} = \tfrac{4}{9} = 0.44.$$

$$\beta = \frac{\text{Everything understood by the reproducer}}{\text{Everything expressed by the explainer}} = \tfrac{4}{6} = 0.66.$$

Since points (4) and (7) are expressed by Schla in the style of juxtaposition, they might be considered as not expressed, so that coefficient β would be changed to $\tfrac{4}{4} = 1.00$. We shall agree, however, to look upon juxtaposition as a means of expression until we make a special study of it later on (§ 6).

The meaning of the coefficients α and β is therefore clear. Coefficient α indicates how much the explainer has been able to convey to the reproducer. Its variations are therefore due to two factors distinct from one another though combined in this case into a single measure: 1° The fact that the explainer cannot or will not always express himself clearly; 2° the fact that the reproducer does not always understand what the explainer says, even when the latter expresses himself quite clearly. These two factors, the explainer's capacity for understanding, and the reproducer's capacity for expressing himself are indicated by coefficients δ and β respectively. Coefficient α therefore, which virtually contains them both, represents—in so far as the experiments are not artificial, nor the method of parcelling out arbitrary—a measurement of verbal understanding between one child and another, since it measures both the manner in which one of the speakers makes himself understood and the manner in which the other understands. This coefficient α, moreover, is a true measure of the understanding between child *and child*, since it is calculated in relation to what the explainer has actually remembered and understood of the set piece, and not in relation to what he ought to have understood. If Schla had understood only 4 points instead of 9, α would be ¼ and γ would be 0.44. Understanding between child and child would be perfect, however deficient might be that between child and adult.

The coefficient β is a measure of the understanding between child and child in the restricted sense, i.e., of the understanding of the reproducer in relation to what the explainer has been able to express. The respective values α and β must therefore not be confused, since each has its own particular interest.

In order to show straight away what can be deduced from such coefficients, we can say that in the case of Schla and Riv, which we have just examined, one child has understood the other definitely less than this other understood us. Riv understood Schla in a proportion of 0.44 (α = ⁴⁄₉), and Schla understood us in a proportion of 1.00 (γ = ⁹⁄₉). What is the cause of this lack of understanding between Schla and Riv? Is it Riv's deficient understanding, or Schla's faulty exposition? Riv's understanding in comparison to what Schla has expressed is 0.66 (β = ⁴⁄₆). The value of Schla's exposition in comparison to what he has himself understood is also 0.66 (δ = ⁶⁄₉). We may conclude from this, that the non-understanding between

Schla and Riv is due as much to the deficient exposition of the one as to the deficient understanding of the other.

The dissection of the stories follows exactly the same method. Special kinds of understanding (causality, etc.) will be examined later on.

§ 3. NUMERICAL RESULTS.—By parcelling out in this way the 60 experiments made on our 30 children from 7 to 8 (all boys), we reached the following results.

Once again, however, we lay stress on the fact that we do not consider that our problem can be solved by figures. We have far too little confidence in the value of our method of parcelling out, and especially in the general value of our experiments, to come to such hasty conclusions. Our experiments are carried out "just to see," and are meant only as a guide to any future research.

The figures which we shall give are therefore meant only as a help to observation of facts and to clinical examination. They contain, it is true, a statistical solution of the problem. But we shall adopt this solution only as a working hypothesis, in order to see in the later paragraphs whether it really tallies with the clinical evidence, and whether this tallies with the facts revealed by everyday observation.

Having disposed of these preliminary considerations, let us pass on to the actual figures. With regard to the stories, understanding between children as indicated by the coefficient α was found to be only 0.58. Now the explainer understood us on the average quite well, since the coefficient γ reaches 0.82. The explainer's power of exposition also proved quite good, the coefficient δ being 0.95. It is therefore the understanding of the reproducer which is at fault; β is only 0.64.

It should be noted that if we subtract the deficit due to the explainer ($1.00-0.95 = 0.05$) from the deficit due to the reproducer ($0.64-0.05 = 0.59$), we get the total deficit (0.54). This will be of use to us later on.

With regard to explanations, understanding between children is also greatly inferior to understanding between explainer and adult. Here the coefficient α is 0.68 and γ 0.93. Explanations are therefore generally better understood than stories, both between children and between children and adults. This may be an accident, due to the method of parcelling out (the nine points of the explanations are perhaps easier to remember, because they are more comprehensive). Whether this is so or not is of no consequence. What matters is not this value 0.68, taken by itself, but the interrelations which it implies. The deficit on the part of reproducer and explainer is quite different in this case from what it was in the stories. The explainer does not express himself nearly so well; δ is only 0.76 instead of 0.95 as in the case of the stories. But the proportion of what the explainer has expressed which is understood by the reproducer (β) is 0.79 instead of 0.64, as in the case of the stories. Explanations, therefore, seem to resemble the procedure of ordinary life much more closely than do stories. This impression receives further confirmation from the fact that if the share of the explainer indicated by coefficient (δ) be added to the share of the reproducer (β), the result is not equal but inferior to the total deficit. 1.00−0.76 = 0.24 and 0.79−0.24 = 0.55 < 0.68.

This circumstance is easy to explain. In the case of the stories, when the explainer expresses himself badly, the reproducer cannot supplement obscure or forgotten passages. He has a tendency to distort even correctly given material, and especially a tendency not to listen to his interlocutor. This was abundantly shown in the spontaneous conversations of children which we gave when dealing with the collective monologue (e.g. when Pie says to Béa: "I am doing a staircase, look," and Béa answers: "I can't come this afternoon, I've got a Eurhythmic lesson.") In the case of mechanical explanations, on the other hand, the reproducer has already been interested on his own account in the handling of taps and syringes. He has the diagrams before him, and can think about their meaning while the explainer is talking. Thus even if the explainer has not been listened to, or if he is obscure and elliptical, the reproducer can reconstruct the required explanation. This is why the complete understanding α is better than one would expect from the sum of the deficits indicated by the coefficients δ and β. The relations, moreover, seem to us to exist independently of the particular mode of parcelling out which we have adopted.

The value of coefficient α, therefore, does not necessarily imply that the absolute understanding is good. It does not mean that the explainer is capable of making the reproducer understand something new and hitherto unknown to him. On the contrary, the added deficits yield 0.56, whereas in the case of the stories they amount only to 0.59. Roughly speaking, then, the understanding of explanations is less good than that of stories. If, therefore, α is better in the case of explanations, it is because the reproducer has identified himself more fully with what he is reproducing; and this he was enabled to do thanks to the diagrams and to his own previous interests. Apparent comprehension has been in this case a mutual stimulus to individual reflexion. And this is the initial stage of all understanding, even with adults.

The fact that the explainer's capacity for exposition (δ) is better in the case of stories than in that of explanations has nothing that need surprise us. Explanation presupposes a certain number of verbal expressions difficult to handle, because connected with causal relations. Stories are told in a much simpler style.

These conclusions receive complete confirmation from the results obtained between the ages of 6 and 7. We experimented on 20 children of this age, of whom eight were girls.[1] With these,

[1] It is certainly regrettable to mingle the sexes in an enquiry of this kind, but we found no appreciable differences between the boys and those eight girls probably because of the latter's small number. Our 40 experiments between 7 and 8 may therefore be regarded as fairly homogeneous.

too, understanding between children was weaker than understanding of the adult by the child, and in more marked proportions than between the years of 7 and 8. Thus in the case of explanations, children's understanding of each other was $\alpha = 0.56$, and of us, $\gamma = 0.80$. With regard to stories, their understanding of each other was $\alpha = 0.48$, and of us, $\gamma = 0.70$. It should be noted that these coefficients $\gamma = 0.80$ and $\gamma = 0.70$ prove that the use of the same explanations and stories is justified in spite of the difference of age in the subjects, since the explainer has been able to understand us in the above proportions.

What is the cause of this relative lack of understanding amongst themselves in children from 6 to 7? Does the fault lie with the explainer's means of expression, or with the reproducer's capacity for understanding? The explainer expresses himself as well from 6 to 7 as from 7 to 8 ($\delta = 0.76$), and almost as well in the case of stories ($\delta = 0.87$ as compared to 0.95). The amount understood by the reproducer of what the explainer has duly expressed is once again low (0.70 and 0.61), and, curiously enough, in exactly the same proportions as in the cases observed between 7 and 8. In the stories, the coefficient α is equal to the sum of the deficits indicated by β and δ:

$$1.00 - 0.87 = 0.13 \text{ and } 0.61 - 0.13 = 0.48 = \alpha.$$

In the case of explanations, on the other hand, the coefficient α is greater than the sum of the deficits:—

$$1.00 - 0.76 = 0.24 \text{ and } 0.70 - 0.24 = 0.46 < 0.56.$$

In conclusion we obtain the following table:

	Explanations.					Stories.			
	α	γ	β	δ		α	γ	β	δ
6–7 years	0.56	0.80	0.70	0.76		0.48	0.70	0.61	0.87
7–8 years	0.68	0.93	0.79	0.76		0.54	0.82	0.64	0.95

What conclusions can we draw from these figures? We have undertaken to be cautious. Shall we assert straight away that children understand each other less than they understand us, at any rate in so far as verbal understanding is concerned? This is what the experiments would seem to show. But in these we took special care to make ourselves intelligible, which is not always done by those who talk to children. It is true that in everyday life there is often what Stern has called "convergence" of the language used by parents towards a childish style of speech. Parents instinctively use easy expressions, of a concrete and even animistic or anthropomorphic nature, so as to come down to the mental level of the child. But side by side with this there are all the manifestations of verbalism, there is everything that the child picks up and distorts, and there is everything that passes him by. We need only remind our readers of the very definite results obtained by Mlle Descœudres and M. Belot on the lack of understanding between children and adults.[1]

We shall therefore confine ourselves to the following conclusions. In verbal intercourse it would seem that children do not understand each other any better than they understand us. The same phenomenon occurs between them as between them and us: the words spoken are not thought of from the point of view of the person spoken to, and the latter, instead of taking them at their face value, selects them according to his own interest, and distorts them in favour of previously formed conceptions. Conversation between children is therefore not sufficient at first to take the speakers out of their ego-centrism, because each child, whether he is trying to explain his own thoughts or to understand those of others, is shut up in his own point of view. This phenomenon occurs, it is true, among adults. But these have had

---

[1] A. Belot, "Les écoliers nous comprennent ils?" Bull. Soc. Alf. Binet. A. Descœudres, "Guerre au verbalisme," Interm. des Educ., 1913, "Encore du verbalisme," ibid., 1917.

at least some practice in argument or conversation, and they know their faults. They make an effort to understand and be understood, unless indeed distrust or anger reduces them to a childish state, because experience has shown them the appalling density of the human mind. Children have no suspicion of all this. They think that they both understand and are understood.

Such, then, is our working hypothesis. Analysis of our material will show us what it is worth. Let the reader not ascribe to us more than we are actually saying. We are merely postulating that the language of children and between children is more ego-centric than ours. If this can be verified by analysis, it will explain a number of logical phenomena such as verbal syncretism, lack of interest in the detail of logical correspondences or in the "how" of causal relations, and above all, incapacity for handling logical relations, a task which always implies that one is thinking about several points of view at the same time (chapters 4 and 5, and early chapters of Vol. II).

§ 4. EGO-CENTRISM IN THE EXPLANATIONS GIVEN BY ONE CHILD TO ANOTHER.—There emerges from our statistics the paradoxical fact, common in children from 7 to 8 and 6 to 7, that stories are less well understood by the reproducer than are mechanical explanations, even though they receive a better exposition on the part of the explainer. In the case of stories the numerical value of the exposition is 0.95 and 0.87 respectively, and the coefficient β 0.64 and 0.61; for mechanical explanations the exposition amounts to 0.80 and 0.70, and the coefficient β to 0.80 and 0.70. This enables us to conclude that the reproducer's understanding is partly independent of the exposition given by the explainer. This exposition is one, therefore, that is very inadequate. When we say, e.g., that its value is 0.95, all we mean is that the points expressed by the explainer are in a proportion of 0.95 to those which he has understood. But the manner in which these expressed points are connected and presented to the hearer may be very bad. In other words, the explainer's style may be said to present a certain number of features which prevent it from being intelligible, or at any rate from being very "socialized." These are the features which we must now try to elaborate.

The most striking aspect of explanations between one child and another which we have had occasion to study in the course of these experiments is constituted by what may be called the *ego-centric character* of childish style. This feature is in full agreement with those of the spontaneous language of children, which we described in an earlier chapter. We must take our stand on this agreement between the products of pure observation and the products of experiment, for it alone will enable us to find the significance of the latter. Now we have seen that the child of 6 to 7 still talks to a great extent for himself alone, without trying to gain the attention of his hearer. Thus a portion of the child's language is still ego-centric. When, moreover, the language becomes socialized, the process at first only touches the factual products of thought, i.e., in talking to each other children avoid the use of causal and logical relations (because, etc.), such as are used in all "genuine argument" or in "collaboration in abstract thought." Before the age of 7 or 8 these two kinds of relations are therefore still unexpressed, or rather, still strictly individual. Observation shows that up till the age of about 7 or 8, the child, even when he can think of them himself, does not spontaneously give explanations or demonstrations to his equals, because his language is still saturated with ego-centrism.

Now this is the very phenomenon which we met with in our experiments. The explainer always gave us the impression of talking to himself, without bothering about the other child. Very rarely did he succeed in placing himself at the latter's point of view. It might be thought that this was because he was addressing himself to the experimenter as though he were reciting a lesson, and forgot that he had to make his playmate understand. But spontaneous language between children exhibits exactly the same features. Moreover, the explainer sprinkles his exposition with such expressions as: "You understand, you see, etc," which shows that he has not lost sight of the fact that he is talking to a friend. The cause of his ego-centrism lies much deeper. It is extremely important, and really explains all the ego-centrism of childish thought. If children fail to understand one another, it is because they think that they do understand one another. The explainer believes from the start that the reproducer will grasp everything, will almost know beforehand all that should be known, and will interpret every subtlety. Children are perpetually surrounded by adults who not only know much more than they do, but who also do everything in their power to understand them, who even anticipate their thoughts and their desires. Children, therefore, whether they work or not, whether they express wishes or feel guilty, are perpetually under the impression that people can read their thoughts, and in extreme cases, can steal their thoughts away. The same phenomenon is undoubtedly to be found in Dementia Precox and other pathological cases. It is obviously owing to this mentality that children do not take the trouble to express themselves clearly, do not even take the trouble to talk, convinced as they are that the other person knows as much or more than they do, and that he will immediately understand what is the matter. This mentality does not contradict ego-centric mentality. Both arise from the same belief of the child, the belief that he is the centre of the universe.

These habits of thought account, in the first place, for the remarkable lack of precision in childish style. Pronouns, personal and demonstrative adjectives, etc., "he, she" or "that, the, him," etc., are used right and left, without any indication of what they refer to. The other person is supposed to understand. Here is an example:

> Gio (8 years old) tells the story of Niobe in the role of explainer: "*Once upon a time there was a lady who had twelve boys and twelve girls, and then a fairy a boy and a girl. And then*

> *Niobe wanted to have some more sons* [than the fairy. Gio means by this that Niobe competed with the fairy, as was told in the text. But it will be seen how elliptical is his way of expressing it]. *Then she* [who?] *was angry. She* [who?] *fastened her* [whom?] *to a stone. He* [who?] *turned into a rock, and then his tears* [whose?] *made a stream which is still running to-day.*"

Fom this account it looks as though Gio had understood nothing. As a matter of fact he had grasped nearly everything, and his understanding in relation to us was $\gamma = 0.91$ $(\delta = 0.80)$. He knew for instance that the fairy was angry *"because she* (N.) *wanted to have more children than the fairy."* The pronouns distributed at random are therefore a characteristic of the style, and not a proof of lack of understanding. Gio knows perfectly well that it was the fairy who fastened N. to the rock and not *vice versa.*

It is easy to foresee the results of such a style. The reproducer, Ri (8 years old), begins by taking N. for the fairy, and by thinking that it is N. who fastens the lady. After being put right on this point, he reproduces the story as follows:

> *There was a lady once, she had twelve boys and twelve girls. She goes for a walk and she meets a fairy who had a boy and a girl and who didn't want to have 12 children. 12 and 12 make 24. She didn't want to have 24 children. She fastened N. to a stone, she became a rock, etc.* $(\beta = 0.72)$.

Another example:

> Kel (8 years old) also tells the story of Niobe and says of the fairy: *"She fastened the lady to a rock. She* [who?] *cried for ten years. They are still running to-day."* The word "tears" is taken for granted. As it cannot be heard that the verb is in the plural[1] this

---

[1] The French for tear, "larme", is feminine and referred to by the personal pronoun "elle" in the singular, and "elles" in the plural. Phonetically the two are indistinguishable. [Translator's Note.]

style is incomprehensible. It sounds as if it were the lady or the rock that was running. We ourselves did not understand in the first instance.

In the case of mechanical explanations, the explainer assumes from the beginning that the "doors," "pipes," and "bars" are known to the reproducer, so that instead of beginning by show- ing them and explaining their uses, he speaks of them as familiar objects. Here is an example:

> Pour (7; 6) explains the tap to Pel (7; 0): "*The water can go through there* [points to the large pipe in fig. 1, without designat- ing the exact spot, the opening] *because the door* [which door?] *is above and below* [the movable canal *b* which he does not show] *and then to turn it* [turn what?] *you must do so* [makes the movement of turning fingers but without pointing to the handles *a*]. *There, it* [what?] *can't turn round* [= the water can't get through,] *because, the door is on the right and on the left. There, because the water stays there, the pipes can't get there* [the pipe is lying down. Note the inversion of the relation indicated by the word 'because.' What ought to have been said was: 'The water stays there because the pipes can't . . . etc.'] *and then the water can't run through*."

The words used by Pour, the "door," the "pipes," are supposed to be known by Pel; so much so, that Pour forgets to show these objects in the diagram. And yet Pour, as our interrogatory proves has a fair understanding of the detail of the diagram ($\gamma = 0.88$). Only his style is faulty. In his reproduction, con- sequently, Pel talks about doors which he takes literally without seeing where they are. "*The water can't run because it is stopped, and there are doors that stop it, they are shut, and then the water can't run through.*" What is most remarkable is that Pel manages to under- stand pretty well everything, but by his own effort ($\alpha = 0.75$).

As to what Pour has said to Pel, this remains for the latter a purely verbal affair.

It will perhaps be objected that such phenomena are due to the scholastic atmosphere which gives rise to verbalism. On this hypothesis the explainer speaks, not to make himself understood, but for the sake of speaking, as one recites a lesson. But we have already answered this objection by pointing out how, in their spontaneous conversations, children express themselves in the same vague manner, because they talk much more for themselves than for their hearer. Take, for example, the slip-shod use of words even in "association with the action of each" (chapter 2, § 4) where children talk to one another spontaneously.

> "*The daddy bear* [which one] *is dead. Only* [?] *the daddy* [the same or another?] *was too ill*"—"*There was a blue one*" [talking of aeroplanes without mentioning them.] "*I want to draw that*," meaning by "that" probably a flying race or anything else connected with it.

We find the same inaccuracy in the qualifying words, the same method of alluding to objects supposedly known. Here is one more example of explanation, which was observed in the course of our experiments, and of which the style exactly resembles that of explanations given spontaneously by children.

> Toc (8 years old). Fragment of the explanation of the tap: "*That and that* [the two extremities of canal *b*] *is that and that* [*id.* on diagram II] *because there* [diagram I] *it is for the water to run through, and that* [diagram II] *you see them inside because the water can't run out. The water is there and cannot run.*" Toc therefore points to the two extremities of a canal without saying anything about a canal or alluding to the handle (*a*), in short,

without naming any of the objects which he is discussing. Still, having got so far, he believes, as he tells us, that his hearer (Kel, 8 years old) has understood everything. Kel is able, indeed, to repeat more or less the same words, but without attaching any concrete meaning to them. We ask him before Toc: "What was done so that the water should stop running?—*It was turned round*—What was?—*The pipe* (b) [correct].—How was the pipe turned round (b)?— . . . What is this for (the handle, a)?— . . . (He doesn't know)." Toc is then astonished to see that Kel has understood nothing, and he begins his explanation all over again. But, and this is the point we wish to emphasize, for it proved to be very usual, his second exposition is no clearer than the first: "*This is a thing* [the handle (a) which he had forgotten to mention] *like this* [diagram I] *this way it's that the water can't run. When this thing is like that* [diagram II] *it means that the water can't run.*" Thus, even when he wants to make things clearer to Kel, Toc forgets to tell him that it is the handle which turns the canal or which is moved with the fingers, etc. In a word, unless Kel guesses—and this is just what he fails to do in this particular case—the language used is unintelligible. But the main reason for Toc talking in this way is his belief that things go without saying, and that Kel understands immediately.

These features of ego-centric style are still more pronounced between 6 and 7, which goes to prove that they are not scholastic habits. Between 6 and 7 the children are still in the so-called Kindergarten classes, which are far less coloured with verbalism than those above them. These children, moreover, play amongst themselves far more than in the elementary classes. Now the ego-centrism of their explanations is far more pronounced; which proves that this ego-centrism is due to the general factors of language and thought which we laid stress on in the preceding chapters dealing with spontaneous language.

Riv (6 years old), for example, begins his explanation of the syringe by pointing to diagram III and saying: "*You see, there* (b) *is the piston* [what piston? the piston of what?] *then you pull it and it makes a squirt* [concluded too quickly]. *Then it leaves room for the water* [why does it make this room?] *When you push the little piston* [he no longer points to it] *it makes the water come out, it makes a squirt, you see? That is the bowl there* (a) *and then the water.*"

Now Riv has completely understood ($\gamma = 1$). Moreover, he is very definitely addressing himself to his hearer Schla, as is shown by the expressions "*you see, you understand,*" and by the interest which both the children have evinced in the matter. It goes without saying that Schla has not understood a thing:

Schla (6 years old) reproduces Riv's explanation: "*He told me that it was . . . something. There was something, and then there was something where there was water, and then the water came out. That is where the water was. That* (a) *is the place where the water was, and the water squirted the two bowls and poured into them*" ($\alpha = 0.33$).

As will be seen by comparing these two texts, it is only Riv's inaccuracy that has confused Schla. Otherwise the explanation would have been adequate. From Riv's last sentences the whole mechanism might have been reconstructed. But Riv, thanks to Schla, has taken the syringe for a tap, and consequently has understood nothing of the movement of the piston.

Another example:

Met (6; 4) G, talking of Niobe: "*The lady laughed at this fairy because she* [who?] *only had one boy. The lady had twelve sons and twelve daughters. One day she* [who?] *laughed at her* [at whom?] *She* [who?] *was angry and she* [who?] *fastened her beside a stream.*

She [?] *cried for fifty months, and it made a great big stream.*"
Impossible to tell who fastened, and who was fastened. Met
knows perfectly well ($\gamma = 0.83$), but Her (6; 3) G, who is listening, naturally understands things the wrong way round. She
thinks it is the fairy "*who laughed at the lady who had six boys
and then six girls,*" and that it was the fairy who was fastened,
etc. ($\alpha = 0.40$).

Finally, one of the facts which point most definitely to the
ego-centric character of the explanations of children is the large
proportion of cases in which the explainer completely forgets to
name the objects which he is explaining, as in the cases of taps
and syringes. This holds good for half of the explainers from 6 to
7, and for one-sixth of those between 7 and 8. They assume
that their hearer will understand from the outset what they are
talking about. Naturally, in such cases, the reproducer gives up
trying to understand, and repeats the explanation he has
received, without attempting to assign a name to the object in
question.

§ 5. THE IDEAS OF ORDER AND CAUSE IN THE EXPOSITIONS
GIVEN BY THE EXPLAINERS.—Other factors are at work which
help to render the explainer's exposition rather unintelligible to
the reproducer. These are an absence of order in the account
given, and the fact that causal relations are rarely expressed, but
are generally indicated by a simple juxtaposition of the related
terms. The explainer, therefore, seems not to concern himself
with the "how" of the events which he presents; at any rate, he
gives only insufficient reasons for those events. In a word, the
child lays stress on the events themselves rather than on the
relations of time (order) or cause which unite them. These factors, moreover, are probably all connected in various degrees
with the central fact of ego-centrism.

The absence of order in the account given by the explainer
manifests itself as follows. The child knows quite well, so far as

he himself is concerned, in what order the events of a story or the different actions of a mechanism succeed one another; but he attaches no importance to this order in his exposition. This phenomenon is due once more to the fact that the explainer speaks more to himself than to the explainer, or rather to the fact that the explainer is not in the habit of expressing his thoughts to his companions, is not in the habit of speaking socially. When an adult narrates, he is accustomed to respect two kinds of order: the natural order given by the facts themselves, and the logical or pedagogic order. Now it is to a great extent because of our concern with clarity and our desire to avoid misunderstanding in others that we adults present our material in a given logical order, which may or may not correspond with the natural order of things. The child, therefore, who, when he explains his thoughts, believes himself to be immediately understood by his hearer, will take no trouble to arrange his propositions in one order rather than another. The natural order is assumed to be known by the hearer, the logical order is assumed to be useless. Here is an example:

> Ler (7; 6) explains the tap: "*It's a fountain. It either runs, or it doesn't run, or it runs. When it is like that* [diagram I] *it runs. And then there's the pipe* [c] *that the water goes through. And then, when it is lying down* [b] *when you turn the tap, it doesn't run. When it is standing upright, and then you want to turn it off, it's lying down.* [Note the curious treatment of the temporal subclauses]. *And then that is* . . . [the basin]. *And then when it is standing upright* [again the canal b] *it is open and when it is lying down it is shut.*"
>
> Del (7 years old): "*That is a tap, and then you turn it on and then the water runs into the basin, and then to find its way, it goes through the little pipe.* [Note the inversion of these two propositions] *and then there is the handle that you turn round* . . . etc."

This mode of exposition, which consists in connecting propositions by "and then" is typical. The conjunction "and then" indicates neither a temporal, a causal nor a logical relation, i.e., it indicates no relation which the explainer could use in order to link his propositions together for the purpose of a clear deduction or demonstration. The term "and then" marks a purely personal connexion between ideas, as they arise in the mind of the explainer. Now these ideas, as the reader may see, are incoherent from the point of view of the logical or of the natural order of things, although each one taken separately is correct.

Order may be absent even from the account of the stories, but this is rarer. Here is an example:

> Duc (7 years old): "*Once upon a time, there were four swans, and there was a king and a queen who lived in a castle and had a boy and a girl. Near by, there was a witch who did not like the children and wanted to do them harm. They turned into swans, and then they were on the sea . . . etc.*" The swans are made to appear before the meeting of the witch and the children, although the sequel shows that Del is perfectly familiar with their origin.

But there is considerable difference between the exposition of explainers between 7 and 8 and that of those between 6 and 7. This is one of the most important points brought out by the parcelling out of our material, and one which only goes to show how independent of scholastic habits this material is. The absence of order which we have described is more or less exceptional between 7 and 8. Between 6 and 7, it is the rule. It seems pretty certain, therefore, that the capacity for arranging a story or an explanation in a definite order is acquired some time between the ages of 7 and 8. The question, of course, will have to be approached by other methods, for it would be highly desirable to prove what is at present only a hypothesis, viz., that the capacity for order makes its appearance at the same time as genuine argument, as collaboration in abstract thought, (see conclusion of chapter 2) and at the same time as incipient understanding among children (a stage between 7 and 8 during which β goes beyond 75 per cent for explanations and reaches 0.79). But there are indices which point to such a chronology. We know, for example, that it is at 7 that Binet and Simon fixed the three messages test (to carry out three messages in a given order). Now, before the age of 7, children succeed in carrying out the messages, but not in the given order. Terman, it is true, has brought the test age down to 5, but this seems to us excessive. It is at the lowest a test for 6-year-old children. Now it is easier to follow a certain order in actions than in a spoken account. This leads us back to the view that between 7 and 7½ is the age when the desire for order in the expositions given by children first makes its appearance.

Here, for instance, are two terms of comparison, the story of the four swans told by a child of 7½ who is typical of that age, and the same story told by a typical child of 6; 4:

> Cor (7; 6): "Once upon a time, in a great big castle, there was a king and a queen who had three sons and one daughter. Then there was a fairy who didn't like the children, then she brought them to the seashore, then the children changed into swans, and then the king and queen they looked for the children till they could find them. They went down as far as the seashore, and then they found the four children changed into swans. When the swans had gone away on the sea, they went towards the castle, they found the castle all destroyed then they went to the church, then the three children were changed into little old men and one little old woman." Thus the order of events has been respected.
>
> Met (6; 4) G: Once there was a fairy, there was a king and then a queen. Then there was a castle, there was a wicked fairy [the same] who took the children [which children?] and changed them

into swans. She led them to the seashore [Inversion]. *The king and queen came in, and couldn't find them. They went to the seashore and found them. They went into a castle* [the same one. Met knows this] *and changed them into little old people. After that* [!] *they found them.* [This had already been said. Met knows quite well that it was prior to the transformation into old people]. It may be claimed that this lack of order is simply due to a lack of memory. This is certainly one of the factors at work, but not the only one. The proof of this is that when we read the story over again to Met, she proceeded to tell it as follows: *"Once there was a king and a queen. There were three children, one little girl and three boys. There was a wicked fairy who had changed the children into white swans. Their parents looked for them and found them by the seashore. And then* [!] *they had been changed into swans* [reversion to what has already been said]. *They said it was their children. They had a castle* [wrongly placed]. *Their parents died. They went away to a very cold country* [inversion]. *They went into a little church and they were changed into little old men and a little old woman."*

Or again, this opening to the story of Niobe: Cé (6 years old): *"There's a lady who was called Morel, and then she turned into a stream . . . then* [!] *she had ten daughters and ten sons . . . and then after that* [!] *the fairy fastened her to the bank of a stream and then she cried twenty months, and then after that* [!] *she cried for twenty months and then her tears went into the stream, and then . . . etc."*

The question may of course be raised, whether the explainer has understood. This we have always verified by appropriate questions. With regard to mechanical explanations, the objection cannot be maintained. Logical order is far more independent of understanding, and in the majority of cases the child understands clearly (the subsequent interrogatory also confirms this), but presents his material incoherently. Here is a good example of this incoherence on the part of an explainer who has understood everything:

> Ber (6; 3). "*You see this tap, when the handle is straight like this* [*a* diagram I] *lying down, you see the little pipe has a door and the water can't get through* [there is no connexion between these facts. There seems to be a mistake. As a matter of fact, Ber has passed from diagram I to diagram II] *then the water doesn't run, the door is shut. Then, you see here* ['then' has no meaning here. He points to diagram I] *you find the little door* [b] *and then the water comes into the basin and then the two sides of the handle* [a] *are like that* [this has already been said] *then the water can run, and then the pipe is like that* [b in diagram II] *then there is no little door then the water can't find the little door. Then the water stays here* [c, diagram II]. *When the tap is on* [accompanying movement] *there is a little pipe, then the water can get through and the handle, oh, well! it is lying down* [a, diagram I] *whereas here, the little pipe is straight* [diagram II, he calls straight what he had called lying down in the preceding proposition] *the handle is straight* [a, diagram II, this time straight means vertical] and the little pipe [b, of which he has just spoken as being straight] *is lying down.*"

This type of explanation is paradoxical. Ber's understanding is excellent ($\gamma = 1.00$, there is a wealth of detail and of vocabulary (e.g. the word "whereas" which generally appears somewhere about the age of 7),[1] but the order is muddled to the point of unintelligibility. Even the words (straight and lying down) are taken in a sense which varies from one moment to another. The result was that the listener Ter (6 years old) hardly understood a thing, and was obliged to reconstruct the whole explanation

[1] As was shown in the reports of the *Maison des Petits*. Cf. Descœudres, *Le Développement de l'enfant de deux à sept ans*, p. 190.

himself, in which task he did not particularly distinguish himself
($\alpha = 0.66$).

There is no need to multiply the examples which are all pretty
much alike. We must rather seek to establish the nature of a
certain peculiarity which is connected with this lack of order in
the explanations, we mean the fact that when a child is relating
an event or describing a phenomenon he is in no way concerned
with the "how" of these happenings. For, given that a child has
simply to note facts without occupying himself with their connexions, he is not likely to worry himself about how these facts
are produced in detail. He is content to feel this detail, but ego-
centrically, i.e., without trying to express it. If such-and-such a
condition exists, then such-and-such effect will result, no matter
how. The reason given is always incomplete. We shall begin by
giving a few examples, and shall afterwards try to explain this
absence of interest in the "how" of mechanisms. Here are first of
all a few cases observed in connexion with stories:

> Duc (7 years old), already quoted on p. 110, relates the trans-
> formation of the children into swans without pointing out that
> it was the fairy who caused this transformation. "*They turned
> into swans*," and that was the end of it.
> Maz (8 years old) also says: "*There was a fairy, a wicked fairy.
> They turned themselves into swans.*" There is here mere juxta-
> position of the two affirmations, with no explicit indication
> concerning the "how." Blat (8 years old) says: "*They turned
> themselves into swans*," etc.

In such cases as these the explainer knows perfectly well
"how" the transformation took place; it was the work of the fairy.
Sometimes the reproducer understands, sometimes not. In the
following cases the omission of the "how" is more serious
because the explainer himself is not always interested in the
mechanism which he neglects to explain.

Schi (8 years old) explains the syringe: "*You put the water in there and then you pull. The water goes in there* [c]*, you push and then it squirts.*" Schi has more or less understood ($\gamma = 0.77$) but he mentions neither the hole nor the empty space left by the piston as it is drawn up, etc. The result is that the listener understands inadequately ($\alpha = 0.55$).

Gui (7; 6) says among other things: "*The tap goes this way, and that prevents you making* [!] *the water run.*" He defines neither the function of the canal nor the effect of the handle on the rotation of the canal.

Ma (8 years old) says that the water cannot run out of the tap "*because it is shut, so that the water shan't get out, because it is shut, they have turned off the tap.*"

In a word, all these explanations take the essential thing (the position of the canal, *b*) for granted, instead of referring to it explicitly: the explainer has understood the "how," but in his opinion it goes without saying and is of no interest.

Such vague expressions as these abound among very young children and also among older ones. We need not record them all. But it is interesting to note how frequent they are, and to find out why the child troubles himself so little with the "how" of things, both for his listener and for himself. This indifference concerning the "how" of phenomena constitutes a well-known trait in the spontaneous explanations of children. Why should Schi find it quite natural that by "pulling the piston" the water should go into the syringe, just as though the piston made the water go up; that by turning the tap we stop "making" the water run, just as though the water acted in obedience to the dictates of the handle of the tap? This is an instance of defective adaptation of childish thought to the details of the mechanism. But is not this lack of adaptation perhaps more or less directly connected with the ego-centrism of thought? For the child, as for us, the criterion of the value of an explanation is the *satisfaction* felt by the subject when he pictures himself *creating* the effect which has to be explained with means which he now considers as causes. Now when we think for ourselves, everything seems quite simple; imagination works more easily, autism is stronger, thought, in other words, takes on new powers. Between two phenomena, A and B, known to be connected by a causal chain which alone will explain the "how" in question, we feel it unnecessary to define this relation any further. This is because we know that we have only to look for it to find it—no matter how—and because we are not very exacting when it is a question of proving things to ourselves. In the end—or rather, from the outset—ego-centric thought ignores this question of "how." When, on the other hand, we want to explain our ideas to other people, then the difficulties begin to appear, the need is felt for clearly defined relations, and the connecting links are no longer skipped, as when individual fantasy held its sway.

We do not claim that these considerations explain the lack of interest shown by the explainers and by children in general in the "how" of phenomena. We only believe that we have given one of the elements in this lack of adaptation. There are other and deeper elements, which we shall meet with again in chapter 5. In the meantime, this one must suffice: since explainers, as we have seen, generally speak from their own point of view, without being able to enter into that of their listeners, their interests remain ego-centric, and tend to omit information about the "how" of mechanisms. The reasons given for phenomena, are therefore generally incomplete.

This peculiar phenomenon of "incomplete reason or cause" is all the more interesting to observe in our present results, because it can quite easily be produced experimentally, and because we shall meet with it again in a chapter of our second volume, when we shall deal with the question of causal conjunctions. Our subjects, moreover, present a special case of this indifference to the "how" of mechanisms, and one which we shall meet with again

(Vol. II.); we mean the apparent inversion of the expression "because." The conjunction "because" seems in these cases to introduce the consequence instead of the cause, as it does when correctly used. This confusion is due simply to the fact that the child does not bother about the "how" which connects the various events of which he is speaking.

> Here is an example: Pour (7; 6) in the text of his which we quoted in the last section, instead of saying "the water stays there because the pipe is lying down" or in Pour's own style, "the water stays there because the pipes can't get there," says exactly the opposite: *"Because the water stays there the pipes can't get there."*
>
> Here is another example in which the inversion is not of a "because" but of a "why" (we shall meet with such inversions in the spontaneous language of children in Chapter 5, § 2): instead of saying, "Why does the water run here and not run there? Because here the tap is turned on and there it is turned off." Mart (8 years old) says: *"Why is the tap turned on here and turned off there?* [It is because] *here the water is running and there the water is not running."* This "why" has all the appearance of being a "why of motivation" (= "why was the drawing made of the tap turned off?") But in reality this is simply an inversion, due once more to lack of interest in the detail of the mechanism.

These apparent inversions of cause and effect are due, as we shall show at greater length in our second volume, to the circumstance that "because" does not yet denote an unambiguous relation of cause and effect, but something much vaguer and more undifferentiated, which may be called the "relation of juxtaposition," and which can best be rendered by the word "and." Instead of saying "the water stays there because the pipe is lying down," it is of no consequence to the child whether he says "the pipe is lying down *and* the water stays there" or "the water stays there *and* the pipe is lying down." When the child replaces "and" by "because," he means to denote, sometimes the relation of cause and effect, sometimes the relation of effect and cause.

This fact is due to the important phenomenon of *juxtaposition.* Juxtaposition, which really covers all the facts enumerated in this section, is the characteristic corresponding to that which, in connexion with drawing, M. Luquet has called "synthetic incapacity." This it is which renders the child incapable of making a coherent whole out of a story or an explanation, but makes him, on the contrary, tend to break up the whole into a series of fragmentary and incoherent statements. These statements are juxtaposed to the extent that there exists between them neither temporal, causal, nor logical relations. The result is, that a collection of propositions juxtaposed in this way lacks something more than sequence, it lacks any sort of verbal expression denoting a relation. These successive statements are, at the best, connected by the term "and." In the child's mind this term undoubtedly answers to a certain dynamic relation, which might be expressed by "this goes with," and which might take on several meanings, including that of causality. But the question is whether the child is conscious of these different meanings, whether he would be able to express them, and, finally, whether he succeeds by means of this juxtaposition in making his listener understand what he is talking about. It may well be, on the contrary, that the feeling of relations remains ego-centric, and therefore incommunicable and practically unconscious. We shall see later on that as a matter of fact the use of juxtaposition is little understood by the reproducer. Here is an example:

> Mart (8 years old): "*The handle is turned on and then the water runs, the little pipe is open and the water runs. There, there is no water running, there the handle is turned off, and then there is no water running, and here the water is running. There, there is no water running, and here there is water running.*"

It is obvious that there is no whole here, no synthesis, but only a series of statements in juxtaposition. Indeed, there is not a single "because" in the whole explanation, nor a single explicit causal relation. Everything is expressed factually; the connexion between the handle and the canal *b*, between the position of the canal *b* and the passage of the water, all this is denoted simply by "and" or "and then." It may be objected that we often express ourselves in the same way. But then we arrange our propositions in a certain order, and above all we succeed in making ourselves understood. Whereas, although Mart has understood everything ($\gamma = 1.00$), his listener has only understood part of the relations ($\beta = 0.77$). We must be careful also not to confuse the "and" which marks a succession in time as when "the fairy fastened N. *and* N. cried," and the "and" which replaces a "why" and which alone is an "and" of juxtaposition. The mere absence, moreover, of the word "because" is not sufficient to characterize the phenomenon of juxtaposition. This absence must be accompanied by a real incoherence in the sequence of propositions. Here is one more example:

> Ber (*cf.* p. 111): "*When the handle is straight* [I] . . . *the little pipe has a door and then* [II] *the water can't get through*" and "*you'll find the little door and then the water goes into the basin and the handle is like this.*" We have in this example absence of order, absence of causal relations between the propositions, and absence of explicit connexions such as "because" or "then." It is therefore a definite case of juxtaposition.

In a word, these remarks all lead us to the conclusion that the child prefers factual description to causal explanation. He confines himself to describing the parts of the mechanism, to enumerating, if necessary, the principal movements that take place, but factually, and without bothering about the "how" of things. It sometimes happens, moreover, that this description consists of a series of propositions devoid of logical or temporal order, without these propositions being connected by explicit relations such as "because" and "afterwards," etc. In such cases as these we have "juxtaposition."[1]

It is interesting to note in our material the presence and constancy of those features on which we have already laid stress in connexion with the function of child language and with the spontaneous explanations between one child and another, studied under the heading of "adapted information" (chapter 1, § 6). This shows very clearly that the relative lack of understanding between children which we are emphasizing here is not merely an artificial product of our experiments, but is deeply rooted in the very nature of childish language such as we are able to observe it in natural conditions. We set aside the question of language by gesture, which expresses causality in its own way, but without special words or explicit designations.

One of the consequences of this factual way of talking, i.e., this way that is unadapted to causality, is that the child expresses himself better when he tells stories than when he gives mechanical explanations. As we have seen, the coefficient δ is always higher in the stories than in the explanations.

§ 6. THE FACTORS OF UNDERSTANDING.—Given all the characteristics of explanation between one child and another, two alternatives as results are possible. Either owing to the fact that their characteristics are due to a structure of thought which is common to all children, i.e., owing to the fact that all children are ego-centric, they will understand each other better (being used to the same way of thinking) than they understand us; or, on the contrary, by reason of this very ego-centrism, they will fail to understand each other properly, since each one is really thinking only for himself. The experiments have shown that

---

[1] We shall return to the phenomenon of juxtaposition in greater detail in the course of Vol II, especially in connexion with the conjunction "because."

from the point of view of verbal understanding, the second hypothesis is the more in accordance with the facts.

The time has now come for us to examine whether this lack of understanding is to be altogether laid to the charge of the explainer, or whether the reproducer does not in his manner of understanding show signs of peculiarities, which it may be worth our while to notice.

In the first place, we have seen that the main factor in rendering the explainer obscure and elliptical is his conviction that his listener understands from the outset, and even knows beforehand everything that is said to him. In this connexion it should be noted that the listener adopts exactly the complementary attitude: he always thinks he has understood everything. However obscure the explanation, he is always satisfied. Only two or three times in the whole course of our experiments has the reproducer complained of the obscurity of the explanation that has been given him. It may be objected that scholastic habits have helped to render him so easily satisfied. But here again the objection misses the mark, because this feature is more pronounced among very young children. It is the reproducers of 7 or 8 who have asked of the explainer the few questions we have had occasion to note. The little ones, for their part, were always and immediately satisfied. The earlier chapters showed us, moreover, that one of the characteristics of children's conversations is that each imagines he is understanding and listening to the others, even when he is doing nothing of the kind.

How then are we to characterize the stage of understanding between children before the age of 7 or 8? It is no paradox to say that at this level, understanding between children occurs only in so far as there is contact between two identical mental schemas already existing in each child. In other words, when the explainer and his listener have had at the time of the experiment common preoccupations and ideas, then each word of the explainer is understood, because it fits into a schema already existing and well defined within the listener's mind. In all other cases the explainer talks to the empty air. He has not, like the adult, the art of seeking and finding in the other's mind some basis on which to build anew. Conversely, the reproducer has not the art of grasping what is standing between him and the explainer, and adapting his own previously formed ideas to the ideas which are being presented to him. If there are, previous to the experiment, no schemas common to the two children, then the words spoken by the explainer excite in the mind of the reproducer any schema which may have been suggested by some accidental analogy or even some simple consonance; the reproducer then thinks he has understood, and simply goes on thinking without ever emerging from his ego-centric groove.[1] This is the reason why mechanical explanations are better understood than stories, even though they are more difficult to reproduce. The exposition, even if it is faulty, excites analogous schemas already existing in the listener's mind; so that what takes place is not genuine understanding, but a convergence of acquired schemas of thought. In the case of stories, this convergence is not possible, and the schemas brought into play are usually divergent.

We need not recall examples of these divergent schemas, which were sufficiently illustrated by the accounts of reproducers given in sections 2 and 4. We shall simply quote one or two examples of schemas of purely verbal origin.

After hearing one of Gio's versions, Ri (8 years old), tells the story of Niobe as follows: "*Once upon a time, there was a lady*

[1] It may be of interest in this connexion to recall that M. N. Roubakine (see Ad. Ferrière, "La psychologie bibliologique d'après les documents et les travaux de Nicolas Roubakine," *Arch. de Psych.*, Vol. XVI, pp. 101–102) came to an analogous conclusion in his studies on adult understanding in reading. He showed that when they read each other's writings, adults of differing mental types do not understand each other.

who was called Vaïka. She had twelve sons. A fairy only had one. Once, one day, her son made a stain on the stone. His mother cried for five years. It [the stain, as Ri afterwards informed us] *made a rock, and her tears made a stream which is still running to-day."*

The idea of the stain (in French: "tache") arose in Ri's mind when Gio pronounced the words: "The son of the fairy fastened (French: "attaché") her to the stone." The alliteration "tache–attaché" is thus sufficient to build up a new structure in Ri's mind, viz., that the mother cried because of the stain which made the rock. Now we think in sentences, not in words; it is therefore not only the single word "fastened" that has been misunderstood, but the latter part of the story which has been completely altered.

Herb (6 years old) tells the story of the four swans, after having heard it told by Met (see § 5): *"There was once a queen and a king and then four children, one girl and three boys; and then there was all the children dressed in white. Their father and mother looked for them and they found them by the sea shore. He said to the wicked queen* [= the fairy]: *"Are those children yours?" The wicked queen said: "No, they are not yours." "*

Here again, it looks as though it were only the words "turned into swans" that had been altered (= dressed in white). But there is more in it than this. The idea of a disguise has appreciably altered the end of the story. Instead of thinking of a metamorphosis of children into animals who go away to a distant country, Herb has turned the story into one of simple kidnapping. The fairy has disguised the children in order to keep them, and the parents have failed to find them or recognize them because of the disguise.

The process of alteration is clear. Owing to one syllable or one word being imperfectly understood a whole schema arises in the mind of the reproducer, which alters and obscures the rest of the story. This schema is due to the fact that ego-centric thought is, as we saw in chapter 1, essentially unanalytical. The result is that it ignores isolated words and deals with whole sentences, understanding them or altering them as they stand without analysing them. This phenomenon is, moreover, a very general one in the verbal intelligence of the child, and will be studied in the next chapter under the name of *Verbal Syncretism*.

Finally, to what extent, we may ask, does the reproducer understand the explainer's manner of expressing causality? We have seen that a causal connexion is generally replaced by a simple relation of juxtaposition. Is this juxtaposition understood by the reproducer as a relation of causality? This is the question we have to answer. Here are a few results obtained from children between 7 and 8 in connexion with the question of the tap. Points 4, 6, 7 and 9 were taken down separately, as being exclusively concerned with causality (4 = when the handle is horizontal the canal is open; 6 = the water runs because the canal is open; 7 and 9, the contrary). The four coefficients were calculated with reference only to these four points. In this way a measure of the understanding of causality is obtained, whether the explainer has expressed the causal relations by juxtaposition or not.

$$\alpha = 0.48 \qquad \gamma = 0.97 \qquad \beta = 0.68 \qquad \delta = 0.52$$

The results are practically the same for children between 6 and 7 ($\alpha = 0.49$, $\beta = 0.68$).

The significance of these figures is clear. For one thing, causality is well understood by the explainer—$\gamma = 0.97$ is an excellent coefficient, above the average of the explainer's mechanical explanations, which is between 0.93 and 0.80; but it is badly expressed ($\delta = 0.52$). This last circumstance emphasizes the prevalence of the phenomenon of juxtaposition. The result of this faulty verbal expression is just what might be expected: the reproducer is very unsuccessful in understanding the explainer ($\alpha = 0.48$, as compared to 0.68 for mechanical explanations between 7 and 8, and 0.56 between 6 and 7). Causal relations are therefore imperfectly understood by children, whether they are expressed by juxtaposition or not.

What part exactly does the phenomenon of juxtaposition play in this imperfect understanding? In order to solve this problem, we took down separately all definite cases of juxtaposition in the explanation of the tap and the syringe or in the stories, i.e., all the cases where a causal relation is expressed simply by juxtaposition (with or without "and") of the connected propositions. We then sought to establish in what proportion of cases this relation of juxtaposition was understood as a causal relation. Take, for instance, this phrase of an explainer: "The handle is like that, and the little pipe is closed." In how many cases will the reproducer understand (whether he expresses it or not is of no consequence; the child's degree of understanding is always tested by supplementary questions) that the little pipe is closed *because* the handle has been turned? Out of some forty clear cases of relation by juxtaposition, only a quarter were understood, i.e., in only a quarter of the cases did the listener grasp the causal relation. This is a crucial point. Relation by juxtaposition is therefore an ego-centric mode of conceiving causality; it can never be used by the child as a means of adapted expression.

Are these results peculiar to our particular method of experiment, or do they correspond to something that can be observed in the spontaneous life of the child? It will be sufficient to recall the results of the last two chapters to realize that this imperfect understanding of causality among children is a perfectly spontaneous thing; children do not talk about causality among themselves before the age of 7 or 8. Such explanations as they give each other are rare and factual. The questions they ask one another contain very few "whys," and hardly any requests for causal explanation. Before the age of 7 or 8, causality is the object of ego-centric reflexion only. This reflexion gives rise to the well-known questions of child to adult, but the schemas implied by these questions or produced by the answers of adults remain incommunicable, and therefore invested with all the characteristics of ego-centric thought.

§ 7. CONCLUSION. THE QUESTION OF STAGES AND THE EFFORT TOWARDS OBJECTIVITY IN THE ACCOUNTS GIVEN BY CHILDREN TO ONE ANOTHER.—One last question which can be asked in connexion with our experiments is this. To what extent do children try to be objective when they talk to one another? It should be noted in the first place that the objectivity of thought is closely bound up with its communicability. It is in ego-centric thought that we give rein to our imagination. When we think socially, we are far more obedient to the "imperative of truth." When, therefore, does this effort towards objectivity in explanation or story between one child and another first make its appearance? If we can fix this moment, we shall at the same stroke be able to determine that critical period when understanding between children first comes to be *desired* and therefore possible.

In this connexion, our material supplies a fairly definite answer. On the one hand, it is only from the age of 7 or 8 that there can be any talk of genuine understanding between children. Till then, the ego-centric factors of verbal expression (elliptical style, indeterminate pronouns; etc.) and of understanding itself, as well as the derivative factors (such as lack of order, in the accounts given, juxtaposition, etc.) are all too important to allow of any genuine understanding between children. Between the ages of 7 and 8 these factors become less active, and some of them (lack of order) even disappear. On the other hand, there exists between children of 6 and 7 and those of 7 and 8 a fundamental difference as regards their efforts to be objective. This convergence of two independent phenomena is certainly not fortuitous, and it has enabled us to place the beginnings of verbal understanding between children, approximately between the ages of 7 and 8.

We have often wondered during our experiments to what extent the explainers, when they made their expositions, and the reproducers, when they repeated what they had heard, really tried to give a true account, and to what extent they simply believed themselves to be doing so. It often happens, for instance, that the explainer, not having the end of his story or his explanation in mind, seems to invent the end, or at least to alter it, as though he were making it up. It also happens that the reproducer seems to give up the attempt faithfully to reproduce what he has heard, and rather than repeat what he has not understood, embarks upon some story of his own. In this respect there is a great difference between the two groups of children.

In the case of boys from 7 to 8 it is quite safe to say that both explainer and reproducer try to give a faithful account of what they have heard. They have a sense of what is meant by the faithful rendering of a story or the truth of an explanation. When they invent, which happens rarely, they know it, and willingly own to it. This shows up all the more clearly because of the marked difference which exists in this respect between stories and mechanical explanations. Mechanical explanation arouses a more lively interest; both explainer and reproducer try to understand it; the results therefore are better. Stories arouse less interest; the explainer tells them with less enthusiasm; even when he is faithful, which is usually the case, the effort to be objective is greater.

The younger children, on the other hand, find it far more difficult to distinguish between romancing and a faithful rendering. When the child has forgotten something or understood it imperfectly, he fills in the gap by inventing in all good faith. If he is questioned on what he has heard, he stops inventing, but left to himself he will believe what he has made up. Romancing, or conscious and deliberate invention, is thus connected with an

4

SOME PECULIARITIES OF VERBAL UNDERSTANDING IN THE CHILD BETWEEN THE AGES OF NINE AND ELEVEN[1]

We laid stress in the first chapters on the ego-centric nature of child thought, and we tried to point out the importance which this phenomenon might assume in the use of reasoning in general. We tried in particular to bring out the three following points in which ego-centric differs from socialized thought. 1° It is non-discursive, and goes straight from premises to conclusion in a single intuitive act, without any of the intervening steps of deduction. This happens even when thought is expressed verbally; whereas in the adult only invention has this intuitive character, exposition being deductive in differing degrees. 2° It makes use of schemas of imagery, and 3° of schemas of analogy, both of which are extremely active in the conduct of thought

[1] With the collaboration of Mlle Alice Deslex.

and yet extremely elusive because incommunicable and arbitrary. These three features characterize the very common phenomenon called the syncretism of thought. This syncretism is generally marked by a fourth characteristic to which we have already drawn attention, viz., a certain measure of belief and conviction, enabling the subject to dispense very easily with any attempt at demonstration.

Now childish ego-centrism seems to us considerable only up till about 7 or 8, the age at which the habits of social thought are beginning to be formed. Up till about 7½, therefore, all the child's thought, whether it be purely verbal (verbal intelligence) or whether it bear on direct observation (perceptive intelligence), will be tainted with the consequences of ego-centrism, and of syncretism in particular. After the age of 7 to 8, these consequences of ego-centrism do not disappear immediately, but remain crystallized in the most abstract and inaccessible part of the mind, we mean the realm of purely verbal thought. In this way, a child may cease between the ages of 7 and 11 to 12 to show any signs of syncretism in his perceptive intelligence, i.e., in those of his thoughts that are connected with immediate observation (whether these are accompanied by language or not), and yet retain very obvious traces of syncretism in his verbal intelligence, i.e., in those of his thoughts that are separate from immediate observation. This syncretism, which appears only after the age of 7–8 will be called *Verbal Syncretism*, and will alone concern us in this chapter.

It is not our intention to embark upon a comprehensive study of verbal syncretism, nor to make a catalogue of the various forms which this phenomenon assumes in children. We shall only analyse one fact of experience which is connected with syncretism, and which we came upon quite by chance while we were making investigations with the object of standardizing a test of understanding.

We occasionally make use at the *Institut Rousseau* of a test of understanding which is very well suited to the examination of schoolboys or of children from 11 to 15. The subject is given a certain number of proverbs such as: "Drunken once will get drunk again." "Little streams make mighty rivers," etc. (10 proverbs at a time). Then 12 sentences in no particular order, 10 of which express severally and in a new form the same ideas as were expressed in the proverbs. As, for example, the sentence "It is difficult to break old habits" corresponds to the proverb "Drunken once will get drunk again." The child is asked to read the proverbs and to find the sentences which fit them.

Now we applied this test to children of 9, 10, and 11, and this is what happened.

In the majority of cases the children did not understand the proverbs in the least; but they thought they had understood them, and asked for no supplementary explanation of their literal or hidden meaning. This is a very common characteristic of verbalism, and as such very interesting. It may be objected that it can be accounted for by such scholastic habits as fear or discipline, by false shame, by the suggestion of the experiment. This may sometimes happen, but not in the great majority of cases, where the child really believes that he has understood. In these cases the experiment only reproduces a phenomenon which is well known in daily life. The child hears the remarks of adults (whether they have been addressed to him or not), and instead of interrupting to ask for explanations, he instantly imagines that he has understood. Or else, he tries to find out for himself, he incorporates what he has heard to his own schemas, and straightway gives to all the words a meaning which may be more or less constant and precise, but is always categorical. This, however, concerns us only indirectly, and it is not on the imperfect understanding of proverbs that we wish to lay stress in this chapter.

The second thing we noticed was this. The children often found, sometimes without hesitation, sometimes after feeling their way about a little, sentences which corresponded with the proverbs they had failed to understand, and which in the eyes of the subject really fulfilled the condition of "meaning the same thing" as the respective proverbs. The children therefore understood the instructions and applied them in their own manner. Naturally this correspondence between the proverb and the sentence "meaning the same thing" contained elements so surprising and so absolutely incomprehensible that we were at first inclined to think that the children were inventing. But this again does not concern us directly. It is obvious that if the children imagine they have understood the proverbs, they will have no difficulty in finding a corresponding sentence. The fact that this correspondence is absurd to the logical adult need not astonish us, and is not what we wish to talk about. But how does this correspondence come about? This is where we touch upon verbal syncretism.

A third point must be added to the other two. We believe that we have shown this correspondence to be due neither to chance nor merely to what is called verbalism, i.e., the automatic use of words devoid of sense. On the contrary—and it is only on the peculiar nature of this correspondence that we shall lay stress in this chapter—we can discern in this activity of understanding and invention on the part of the child several of those schemas of analogy, of those leaps to conclusions which are the outstanding characteristics of verbal syncretism. It is from this point of view that we deem it useful to analyse this handful of experimental facts, however insignificant they may seem to the reader at first sight.

Our material has thus been collected by the most deplorable method. But in science every opportunity must be utilized, and it is well known that the residue of experiments planned for a definite object is often more interesting than the experiments themselves.

Even with these reservations we would never have ventured to

make the children look for the correspondence between proverbs they did not understand and sentences having the same
meaning as these proverbs, had it not been that each one of our
subjects was able to find the correct correspondence for at least
two or three proverbs out of the total number (10, 20 or 30
according to the experiments), and thus proved that he was able
to carry out the instructions, and to understand what a proverb
is. Once we had entered upon these investigations, moreover, the
conviction grew upon us that in daily life the child often hears
phrases, thinks he understands them, and assimilates in his own
way, distorting them as much as the proverbs of which we made
use. In this connexion the phenomena of verbal syncretism
have a general bearing upon the whole verbal understanding of
the child, and are therefore well worth studying. We only hope
that in the circumstances we shall not be blamed for the method
we have adopted. It is not a method at all. We have simply
made experiments "just to see." Our results contain only suggestions, which are meant to be taken up and tested by other
methods.

§ 1. VERBAL SYNCRETISM.—We must first say a few words by
way of introduction to the subject of syncretism, independently of the circumstances in which we happen to have
observed it.

Recent research on the nature of perception, particularly in
connexion with tachistocopic reading, and with the perception
of forms, has led to the view that objects are recognized and
perceived by us, not because we have analysed them and seen
them in detail, but because of "general forms" which are as
much constructed by ourselves as given by the elements of the
perceived object, and which may be called the schema or the
gestaltqualität of these objects. For example, a word passes through
the tachistocope far too rapidly for the letters to be distinguished separately. But one or two of these letters and the
general dimensions of the word are perceived, and that is

sufficient to ensure a correct reading. Each word, therefore, has its own "schema."[1]

M. Claparède, in a note on the perceptions of children, has shown that these schemas are far more important for the child than for us, since they develop long before the perception of detail. For example, a child of 4 who did not know his letters and could not read music managed to recognize the different songs in a book from one day or one month to another, simply by their titles and from the look of the pages. For him, the general effect of each page constituted a special schema, whereas to us, who perceive each word or even each letter analytically, all the pages of a book are exactly alike. Children therefore not only perceive by means of general schemas, but these actually supplant the perception of detail. Thus they correspond to a sort of confused perception, different from and prior to that which in us is the perception of complexity or of forms. To this childish form of perception M. Claparède has given the name of *syncretistic perceptions*,[2] using the name chosen by Renan to denote that first "wide and comprehensive but obscure and inaccurate" activity of the spirit where "no distinction is made and things are heaped one upon the other" (Renan). Syncretistic perception therefore excludes analysis, but differs from our general schemas in that it is richer and more confused than they are. It was the existence of this syncretism of perception which enabled Decroly to teach children to read by letting them recognize words before letters, thus following the natural course of development from syncretism to the combination of analysis and synthesis, and not from analysis to syncretism.

This movement of thought from the whole to the part is a very general one. It will be remembered how this point was

[1] See Mach, *The Analysis of Sensations*. See Bühler, *Die Gestaltwahrnehmungen*, Vol. 1, 1913, p. 6.

[2] *Arch. de Psych.*, Vol. VII (1907), p. 195.

emphasized by M. Bergson in his criticism of associationism. "*Association*," he said, "is not the fundamental fact; it is by *dissociation* that we begin, and the tendency of every memory to gather others around it can be explained by a natural return of the mind to the undivided unity of perception."[1]

Students of linguistics in particular are constantly detecting this process in language, as when they show how the sentence is always earlier than the word, or when, like M. Bally, they analyse the phenomenon of "lexicalization." They also point out the affiliation which we shall have occasion to deal with later (Vol. II.) between the phenomenon of syncretism and that of juxtaposition. M. Hugo Schuchardt has recently pointed out that not only is the word-sentence earlier than the word, but also that the word is derived from the juxtaposition of two sentences, which juxtaposition then brings about the need for co-ordination and finally for lexicalization.

From the point of view of the psychology of language M. Lalande has shown what is the bearing of these linguistic considerations upon the study of thought. He recalls the observations of M. O. F. Cook, according to which the Golahs of Liberia do not know that their language is made up of words. Their unit of consciousness is the sentence. Now these sentences, like ours, contain a certain number of words, and Europeans who learn the language can ascribe to these words a constant meaning. But the Golahs have never consciously realized their existence nor the constancy of their meaning; just like those children who can make a correct use of certain difficult terms in their speech, and are yet incapable of understanding these terms taken by themselves. M. Lalande completed these data by an examination of the spelling of illiterate adults. These show a tendency to run together words that should be separate (le courier va pasé ma cherami), or to divide single words (je fini en ten beras en bien

---

[1] H. Bergson, *Matière et Mémoire*, Paris, 11th ed. (1914), p. 180.

for)[1] in complete disregard of the meaning of the units created in this way. This, however, does not prevent these same persons from talking perfectly good French.

In a word, the line of development of language, as of perception, is from the whole to the part, from syncretism to analysis, and not vice versa. If this is so, then we must expect to find the same phenomenon of syncretism in the understanding of language itself. The phenomena emphasized by M. Cook and M. Lalande are relevant to the conscious realization of words taken as linguistic units and of words already understood in their relation to the rest of the sentence. What happens then, when, for example, the child is confronted with sentences which he does not understand, either because of the difficulty of the thought which is expressed, or because of the difficulty of the words which are employed? Will he begin with analysis, and try to understand words or groups of words, taken separately, or will the child's understanding move by general schemas which themselves will give a meaning to the particular terms in question? In other words, is there a syncretism of understanding just as there is a syncretism of perception and of linguistic consciousness? This chapter will be devoted to establishing the existence of such a syncretism and to describing some of the principal phenomena connected with it.

This syncretism of understanding must not be confused with the phenomenon which we shall meet with again presently (chapter 5, § 3), and which we have called elsewhere *syncretism of reason* or of explanation.[2] This is the name given to that process by which one proposition calls forth another, or one cause an effect, not because of any implication which has been logically

---

[1] The correct French spelling would be, "le courier va passer ma chère amie" (the post is just coming, my dear) and, "je finis en t'embrassant bien fort" (I end with a loving kiss). [Translator's Note].

[2] Jean Piaget, "Essai sur la multiplication logique," etc., *Journ. de Psych.*, 1922, pp. 244, 258 *et seq.*

analysed nor because of any causal relation which has been made explicit in all its detail (analysis of the "how"), but once again because of some general schema, which connects the two propositions or the two representations of phenomena. This schema is given immediately, in an indistinct and general manner, so that the two propositions or the two phenomena are taken in a lump and regarded as an indissoluble whole. Example: Béa (5 years old) *"the moon doesn't fall down, because it is very high up, because there isn't any sun, because it is very high up."* The fact of the moon not falling down, the fact of its being very high up, and the fact of its shining when the sun is not there constitute one solid whole, since these features are always perceived together. The result is that the child explains one of these features simply by an enumeration of the others.

The syncretism of understanding and that of reasoning are of course dependent on one another. We shall see how these two forms combine in connexion with the phenomena which will be described in this chapter.

Finally, we wish to recall, in connexion with syncretism, the fine work done by M. Cousinet on the ideas of children.[1]

Under the name of "immediate analogy" M. Cousinet has described one of the phenomena closely connected with the syncretism of perception. According to him, children who confuse two perceptions under a single name have not previously compared them (a child does not explicitly compare an owl and a cat before referring to the former as "miaou"), but they see the compared objects as alike before making any inference. The analogy is therefore not mediate but immediate, because the subject "does not compare perceptions but perceives comparisons." If, therefore, says M. Cousinet, children perceive different things as identical, it is because each childish representation forms an

---

[1] Roger Cousinet, "Le rôle de l'analogie dans les représentations du monde extérieur chez les enfants," *Rev. Philos.*, Vol. LXIV. p. 159.

"indissoluble lump," in other words because their perception is syncretistic.

M. Cousinet's argument seems to us perfectly sound; but we believe that there is more than "immediate analogy" in the syncretism of understanding and reasoning which we shall presently describe. Most of M. Cousinet's examples are factual, and show evidence of syncretism of perception or of conceptual representation only. They are perceptions added to perceptions. This of course is the form in which syncretism first presents itself, and we have no quarrel whatsoever with M. Cousinet's highly suggestive exposition; what we do think however, is that the idea of syncretism is richer than that of "immediate analogy." As we have just been seeing, even in "mediate" operations like understanding or reasoning we can have syncretism, i.e., the formation of general schemas, which bind the propositions together and create implications, without ever resorting to analysis. We therefore suggest our notion of the syncretism of thought as being more comprehensive than the notions of syncretism of perception and immediate analogy, and as containing them both in the nature of special cases.

§ 2. SYNCRETISM OF REASONING.—In Geneva our experiments were carried out on about twenty boys of 9 and fifteen girls of the same age, and at Lavey (in Vaud) on a similar number of subjects between 8 and 11. We wish to remind our readers that the tests employed[1] were originally intended to measure the degree of understanding in children between 11 and 16. The children on whom we worked were below the level required for most of the proverbs. In order, however, that the experiment should not be absurd, we analysed only the answers given by children who had been able to discover and defend the correct correspondence for at least one or two proverbs, and had thus

---

[1] For the list of proverbs used and for the ready-reckoner see M. Claparède's new book, *Comment diagnostiquer les aptitudes chez les écoliers*, Paris, Flammarion.

proved their capacity for carrying out the instructions necessary for the experiment. The number of correct answers for the 9-year-olds fluctuated between one (two cases) and 23 (one case).

Let us now submit to analysis some cases of the syncretism of reasoning. They will prepare our mind imperceptibly for the mechanism of the syncretism of understanding. Syncretism of reasoning may be said to occur in the materials which we have collected whenever a proverb is compared to a corresponding sentence, not because of any logical implication contained in the text, but because of an implication built up in the child's imagination by means of a general schema in which the two propositions are united. For this syncretistic implication to be seen in its purest form, the proverb and the sentence chosen by the child should both be understood by him. We are then faced with the spectacle of two propositions, which taken separately might have been quite well understood, being actually distorted by syncretism, which then unites them by means of a fictitious implication. In the cases where the separate propositions are also misunderstood, we have the additional phenomenon of "syncretism of understanding" which will be studied later on. The two cases are always more or less mixed.

Here is a case of almost pure syncretistic reasoning:

Kauf (8; 8) G. (3/10)[1] connects the proverb: "When the cat's away the mice can play," with the following phrase: "Some people get very excited but never do anything." Kauf, who would understand the meaning of each of these sentences if they were separate, yet declares that they mean "*the same thing*."—"Why do these sentences mean the same thing?— *Because the words are about the same*—What is meant by 'some people' . . . etc?—*It means that some people get very excited, but afterwards they do nothing, they are too tired. There are some*

[1] This fraction signifies: 3 correct correspondences out of 10.

> *people who get excited. It's like when cats run after hens or chicks.*
> *They come and rest in the shade and go to sleep. There are lots of*
> *people who run about a great deal, who get too excited. Then*
> *afterwards they are worn out, and go to bed."*

The mechanism of syncretistic implication shows here very clearly. The proverb has been understood verbally by Kauf. According to her it means: *"The cat runs after the mice."*

The symbolic or ethical meaning of the proverb is not specified by Kauf until she has found a corresponding sentence. How does this correspondence or implication arise? By a simple fusion of the two propositions in one common schema. The words: "When the cat's away" are fused with the words: "Some people never do anything," and take on the meaning of: "the cat has a rest and goes to sleep." The words "the cat runs" are brought into connexion with "some people get very excited." The result is that the two propositions imply one another. This implication does not come about analytically, through reflexion upon the given text, but syncretistically, i.e., through simple projection of the proverb into the sentence by a process of immediate fusion. Thus there is no analysis of detail, but the formation of a general schema. Such is implication by syncretism, which will be found in all syncretistic reasoning, and which consists in a general fusion of two propositions.

With Kauf of course this syncretism of reasoning is connected with syncretism of understanding. This is how the sentence comes to be verbally distorted in favour of a general schema which actually contradicts the proverb. Kauf has confined herself to adding a corollary to the proverb, which was not given in the text; she imagines that the cat is away, "to take a rest." The meaning of the words, however, has not been altered, whereas the actual words of the corresponding sentence have been garbled: the word "but" has been taken in the sense of "and then." Thus the understanding of this sentence is itself syncretistic, i.e., it is a function of the general schema, whereas the understanding of the proverb existed before this schema.

Here is another example:

> Mat (10; 0) G. (2/10) connects the proverb "So often goes the jug to water, that in the end it breaks" with the sentence "As we grow older we grow better." Now the proverb has been understood verbally. For Mat it means: "*You go to the water so often that the jug cracks; you go back once again and it breaks.*" The corresponding sentence is explained as follows: "*The older you get the better you get and the more obedient you become—* Why do these two sentences mean the same thing?—*Because the jug is not so hard because it is getting old, because the bigger you grow, the better you are and you grow old.*"

The syncretism here is of reasoning only, since neither of the propositions has been altered in favour of a common schema. Mat's reasoning, moreover, seems rational enough except that it seems curious to compare a jug that gets broken to a man who grows old. It may be claimed that this absurdity is due to the fact that a child of 10 cannot realize that the symbolism of a proverb is exclusively ethical. This is undoubtedly one of the factors at work, although at this age children realize perfectly well that all proverbs are symbolic. But this factor alone does not explain the child's power to connect everything with everything else by means of general schemas, and to compare a jug to a child simply because both grow older.

It is obvious, moreover, that this last example is far less syncretistic than the first, and that it approximates to the simple judgment of analogy of the adult. This gives us two extreme cases, between which there is a whole series of fluctuating intermediate cases. We give one of these by the same little girl, Mat:

> "White dust will ne'er come out of sack of coal" is compared

to "Those who waste their time neglect their business." The proverb is understood verbally: *"I thought it meant that white dust could never come out of a sack of coal, because coal is black"*— Why do these two sentences mean the same thing?—*People who waste their time don't look after their children properly. They don't wash them, and they become as black as coal, and no white dust comes out.*—Tell me a story which means the same thing as: "White dust will ne'er . . . etc."—*"Once upon a time there was a coal merchant who was white. He got black and his wife said to him: "How disgusting to have a man like that." And so he washed, and he couldn't get white, his wife washed him and he couldn't get white. Coal can never get white, and so he washed his skin, and he only got blacker because the glove* [washrag] *was black."*

It is quite clear in a case like this that the mechanism of the subject's reasoning cannot be explained by judgments of analogy affecting the details of the propositions. Having once read the proverb, the child is ready to attach to it any symbolic significance which chance may reveal in the perusal of the corresponding sentences. All that the proverb has left in his mind is a schema, a general image, if one prefers—that of the coal which cannot become white. This is the schema which has been projected, whole and unanalysed, into the first of the corresponding sentences which was fitted to receive it (those who waste their time . . . etc). Not that this sentence really has anything in common with the proverb; it can simply be imagined to do so. Now—and this is where syncretism comes in—the child who fuses two heterogeneous sentences in this way does not realize that he is doing anything artificial; he thinks that the two propositions united in this way involve one another objectively, that they imply one another. The corresponding sentence into which the proverb has been projected actually reacts upon the latter, and when the child is asked to tell a story illustrating the proverb, the story will bear witness to this interpenetration. To reason syncretistically is therefore to create between these two propositions relations which are not objective. This subjectivity of reasoning explains the use of general schemas. If the schemas are general, it is because they are added on to the propositions and are not derived from them analytically. Syncretism is a "subjective synthesis," whereas objective synthesis presupposes analysis.[1]

Here are some more examples which bring out very clearly this super-added element, which has not been deduced by logical analysis, but imagined by subjective comparison.

Nove (12; 11) (3/12) compares "Filing can turn a stake into a needle" to "Those who waste their time neglect their business,"—"*because by filing, that means the more you file it* (a stake) *the smaller it gets. People who don't know what to do with their time file, and those who neglect their business turn a stake into a needle; it gets smaller and smaller, and you don't know what has become of the stake* [therefore it has been neglected]."

Péril (10; 6) (7/10) identifies "The cowl does not make the monk" with "Some people get very excited but never do anything." Because: "*Even if you make a cowl, the monk isn't in it, the cowl cannot talk.*" This comment seems more like a simple illustration which Péril does not yet take literally. But he goes on: "*Because people who get very excited may get excited but they do nothing, because the cowl does not make the monk, people who get very excited do not make anything either.*"[2] Here the identification is more serious: the empty cowl is compared to a man who is excited! The words "do not make" take on a more and more concrete significance in the child's mind. "Tell us a story

---

[1] The reader will now realize why the ego-centrism of child thought brings syncretisms in its wake. Ego-centrism is the denial of the objective attitude, and consequently of logical analysis. It therefore gives rise to subjective synthesis.

[2] In the French the verbs "do" and "make" are throughout represented by the single verb "faire" [Translator's note].

which means the same thing as "The cowl does not make the monk."—*There was once a dressmaker who was making a dress for a person, and while she was making the dress this lady suddenly died. The dressmaker thought she could make everything and that the dress would take the place of everything, but she soon saw that the dress would not do instead of the dead lady.*" In this way the corresponding sentence and the proverb gradually melt into one another. They do so because the words "make the monk" gradually call up the image of "getting excited so as to represent a monk," and because the words "never do anything" take on the meaning of "do not succeed in replacing the monk." Thus are the two propositions completely identified, thanks to a purely subjective schema.

Xy (12 years old): "Whoever trusts in the help of others risks being left without support." = "He who sows thorns must not go unshod," because *"Whoever trusts in the support of others must have a support, and whoever walks on thorns must have shoes."*

There is no need to multiply examples; we shall meet with plenty more. Let us rather consider how to interpret this syncretism of childish reasoning. Two hypotheses are possible. The first would explain the observed facts by invoking the process of reasoning from analogy, by what M. Cousinet has called "mediate analogy." In reasoning of this kind the subject argues from the resemblance of two elements, taken respectively from two different objects, to the inclusive similarity of the two objects compared. In the case of the proverb and the corresponding sentence the child would take his stand upon an observed resemblance between two substantives or two negations, etc., and would then conclude that the two phrases were identical, after he had assimilated the remaining elements one to another term by term. The second hypothesis would explain the facts with the aid of general schemas, of an immediate syncretistic fusion of the two propositions. As he reads the proverb, the child makes for himself a schema in which such things as the symbolic meaning of the proverb, the mental imagery released by the words, the rhythm of the sentence, the position of the words in relation to conjunctions, negations, and punctuation, all enter as elements. All these factors would thus give rise to a unique schema, in which would be condensed the various concrete images called up by reading the proverb. Then comes the search for the corresponding phrase. By now the schema is ready to be projected whole into the words and ideas which present themselves. Some of these may actually resist it, but in so far as they can tolerate the schema, its very existence will tend to warp the subject's understanding of the corresponding phrase even before he has finished reading it. The corresponding phrase is assimilated, one might almost say digested, by the schema of the proverb. Once the digestion has taken place, moreover, a return shock takes place, and the proverb is digested in its turn by the schema of the corresponding phrase. This is where we have evidence that the syncretism of reasoning is a wider and more dynamic process than the syncretism of perception which M. Cousinet has described under the name of "immediate analogy."

The difference between these two hypotheses is often imperceptible, for the apparition of a whole general schema may in many cases be released by a partial analogy. But this much can be vouched for in our children's answers: the presence of such schemas can always be detected. As for partial analogies, they are sometimes the outcome of general schemas, and they sometimes precede them. The manner in which the child assimilates the two phrases is therefore in no way analytical or deductive. When Kauf compares "When the cat's away, the mice can play" to the corresponding phrase which we mentioned, she justifies her comparison by saying: *"because the words are more or less the same."* Now the two phrases have not a word, not even a synonym in common. "Away" is assimilated to "get very excited," but this is an assimilation of schemas, not an analysis of detail, because the child imagines that the cat has gone away to rest after having been very excited. Is it then the phrase "[the mice can] play" which has been brought into connexion with "get very excited?" But this comparison is only possible on the basis of a general schema. Similarly, when Mat wishes to justify her assimilation of "So often goes the jug to water . . . etc." to the phrase which we quoted, she tells us that the two propositions have two similar words, "*big* and *old*." But it is she who has put the word "old" into the interpretation of the proverb "*because it* [the jug] *gets old.*" Here again, the analogy of detail appears after that of the general schema, or at least as its function. Even if we admit that this analogy of detail appeared first, and was the occasion for the formation of a general schema, this would not be sufficient to explain the nature of the schema: "The jug becomes less hard as it grows older, just as the man becomes wiser (or better) as he grows older." It is obvious that the analogy of detail and the general schema are given together, and that there has been not inference from the part to the whole, but immediate fusion or assimilation. Besides, we have seen that very often no analogy of detail can account for the syncretism in question. In Mat's other example ("From sack of coal . . . ") there is not a single verbal analogy between the two propositions that have been brought together. This is equally clear in the case of Péril. The words "do not make the monk" take on a more and more concrete and vivid meaning as the two phrases are fused together. It is therefore no analogy between the words "make the monk" and the words "never do anything" which has allowed the child to make this assimilation, but it is the progressive assimilation which has fortified the analogy.

In conclusion it must be said that there is a mutual dependence between the formation of general schemas and that of analogies of detail. Analogies of detail make the formation of general schemas possible, but are not sufficient for their formation. Conversely, general schemas give rise to analogies of detail, but are likewise not sufficient for their formation.

Syncretism of reasoning is, therefore, in the first instance the assimilation of two propositions in virtue of the fact that they have a general schema in common, that they both, willy nilly, form part of the same whole. A enters into the same schema as B, therefore A implies B. This "implication" may appear in the form of an identification, as in the present experiments, where the child is asked to find two phrases that mean "the same thing." It can also take the form of implication properly so called, or of a "because," as in the cases which one of us previously published as examples of the syncretism of reasoning.[1] In the example which we recalled a little way back, "the moon doesn't fall down because there is no sun, because it is very high up," the features "doesn't fall down," "the sun goes out when the moon appears," and "the moon is very high up" form one single schema, because they characterize the moon. Now it is quite enough for this schema to be present in the child's mind for him to say: the moon doesn't fall down *because* ... etc. Here the schema brings about a definite implication.

§ 3. THE NEED FOR JUSTIFICATION AT ANY PRICE.—From the frequent occurrence of this pseudo-logical or pseudo-causal "because," we can draw the conclusion that childish thought and ego-centric thought in general are perpetually determined by a need for *justification at all costs.* This logical or pre-logical law has a deep significance, for it is probably owing to its existence that the idea of chance is absent from the mentality of the child. "Every event can be accounted for by its surroundings," or again, "Everything is connected with everything else, nothing happens by chance"—such might be the tenets of this creed. The, for us, fortuitous concurrence of two natural phenomena or of two remarks in conversation is not due to chance; it can be

---

[1] Article mentioned in § 1.

accounted for in some way which the child will invent as best he can. With regard to reflexion on natural phenomena, we shall see many examples of this law in connexion with the "whys" of children (chapter 5, § 2). A large number of these questions are put as though the child completely excluded chance from the course of events. A few examples of the same phenomenon in connexion with verbal intelligence have been cited by one of us under the somewhat equivocal heading of the "principle of reason." When a child is asked the reason for something, and does not know, he will always and at any cost invent an answer, thus testifying to this particular desire to establish connexions between the most heterogeneous objects. For instance, a child is told as a test of his powers of reasoning, to put a slip of blue paper into a box if he finds one penny in it, a slip of white paper if he finds two pennies, etc. The subject puts in the white slip at random. "Why must you put in the white slip?—*Because white is the same colour as a penny*" or "*Because its colour shines* (like nickel)" etc.[1] This example shows that arbitrary instructions do not satisfy a child. The result is that he will always find a justification for everything, which to us is simply "given" without any reason, which is simply "assumed."

Now these facts, which we have pointed out without explaining them, are constantly to be met with in connexion with the proverbs; the child always justifies the most unexpected combinations. Here are a few examples in which syncretism brings about these justifications at any price:

> Witt (10 years old): "Qui s'excuse s'accuse" = "Those who are too kind-hearted have everything taken away from them in the end"—"*because the other person took something away, and so he excused himself.*"
>
> And (9; 6): Same proverb = "Whoever goes to sleep late will

wake up late"—*because he excuses himself because he got up late* [for having got up late].

Dut (8; 10): "Drunken once will get drunk again" = "By pleasing some we displease others"—"*because when someone is drinking, you go and disturb him.*"

Hane (9; 3): "White dust will ne'er come out of sack of coal" = "We must work to live"—"*because money is needed to buy coal.*"

Ec (9; 1): "By wielding his hammer a blacksmith learns his trade" = "Men should be rewarded or punished according to what they have done"—"*because if we learn our trade properly, we are rewarded, and if we don't, we are punished*" and "The sheep will always be shorn" = "By practising a thing very often we learn to do it well" because "*by much practice of shearing sheep we learn to shear well enough to do others, when we have others.*"

Again Ec: "The flies buzzing round the horses do not help on the coach" = "It is difficult to correct a fault that has become a habit"—"*because the flies are always settling on the horses, and they gradually get into the habit and then afterwards it is difficult for them to cure themselves.*" And "To each man according to his works" = "Whoever goes to sleep late will wake up late"— "*because if you have something to learn you go to bed late. His works, that means ours, and so we wake up late. Our works are the things we have to do, you have things to do and you have to go to bed late so as to know them.*" This last example brings in a more definite general schema than the preceding ones.

Xy (12; 11): "To every bird his own nest is beautiful" = "Insignificant causes may have terrible consequences" because "*a bird builds his nest very carefully, whereas if you do things carelessly, it may have terrible consequences*" and "While you are idling, the joint is burning" = "People who are too busy correcting the faults of others, are not always the most blameless themselves" because "*when one is too busy correcting other people's faults, one leaves the joint to burn.*"

The mechanism of these justifications is plain. They are cases of syncretism, in which the general schema is reduced to the minimum, and amounts to what M. Cousinet has called "immediate analogy."

The faculty for justification at any price which we see in children is thus a consequence of syncretism. Syncretism, which is the negation of analysis, calls forth this effort by which every new perception is connected somehow or other with what immediately precedes it. The connexion is sometimes complex and presents itself in the form of a general schema, in which the old fits term by term into the new, sometimes it is simpler and more immediate, and will supply us with cases, like those which we are considering, of justification at any price. It may still be objected that these justifications can be sufficiently accounted for by the notion of immediate analogy, without bringing in that of syncretism. We believe, on the contrary, that if it were not for his syncretistic habits of thought, if it were not for the fact that he can perceive nothing but general schemas which engender this perpetual conviction that everything is connected with everything else, the child would never produce these arbitrary justifications in such abundance. It is obvious, moreover, from the examples we have given that between syncretism properly so-called and the other cases there is every kind of intermediate variety. Here again, it is thanks to the general schema under formation that the analogy of detail is brought into being.

There is therefore in the childish imagination an astonishing capacity for answering any question and disposing of any difficulty with some unexpected reason or hypothesis. For the child, there is no "why" that does not admit of an answer. A child can always say: "I don't know" in order to get rid of you; it is only very late (between 11 and 12) that he will say: "One cannot know." It may be suggested that these justifications are given out of *amour-propre*, so as not to remain *a quia*, etc. But this does not explain the wealth and unexpectedness of the hypotheses brought forward; these recall the exuberance of symbolist mystics or of interpretational maniacs far rather than the tendency shown by adults (e.g., examination candidates) to hedge, when they are taken off their guard. If anyone disputes the existence of the desire to justify at any price, he will have to explain the affiliation between the justifications of children and those of interpretational maniacs in the first stages of the disease. The peculiarities which we have mentioned are very similar to those which Dr Dromard attributes to interpretational maniacs[1]— *imaginary reasoning*, in which every possibility becomes a probability or a certainty; *diffusion of interpretation*; i.e., that process of "linking up, in virtue of which one interpretation is called forth by an earlier one, and rests in its turn upon one subsequent to it." ("I graft one thing on to another, and in this way I gradually build up a scaffolding of the whole," Patient G); *radiation*, i.e., "the fortuitous and unexpected production of innumerable interpretations gravitating at a certain distance around the main idea, which represents the centre and rallying point of every part of the system"; *symbolism*, or the tendency to find in every event and every sentence a hidden meaning of greater depth than that which is apparent, etc. M. Dromard is therefore right in concluding that "in their manner of thinking, of perceiving and of reasoning interpretational maniacs recall some of the essential traits of primitive and of child thought."[2]

The hypothesis which attributes the exuberance of these childish interpretations to mere invention is one which occurs very readily to the mind in connexion with the various facts recorded in this chapter; we shall show by and by what it amounts to. The objection should also be put aside according to which the interpretative character of children's justifications is

---

[1] G. Dromard. "Le délire d' interpretation," *Journ. de Psych.*, Vol. VIII (1911), pp. 290 and 406.

[2] *Ibid.*, p. 416.

due to the fact that we experimented with proverbs. All the phenomena with which we are dealing in this chapter are embodied in the reflexions of children as observed in ordinary life. Many people, for instance, have studied the spontaneous etymology which children practise, or their astonishing propensity for verbalism, i.e., the imaginative interpretation of imperfectly understood words; and both these phenomena show the child's facility in satisfying his mind by means of arbitrary justifications. Moreover, as we have repeatedly pointed out, the child does not know at the beginning of the experiment that the proverb has a hidden meaning. All we do is to remind him that a proverb is "a sentence that means something," and to ask him to find a sentence which "means the same thing." If there were not in the child a spontaneous tendency towards justification at any price, and towards interpretative symbolism, he would never, within the limitations of our experiments, have manifested the phenomena which we have been examining.

We can therefore conclude that the desire for justification at any price is a universal law of verbal intelligence in the child, and that this law itself is derived from the syncretistic nature of childish reasoning. The fact that for the syncretistic point of view everything is related, everything is connected to everything else, everything is perceived through a network of general schemas built up of imagery, of analogies of detail and of contingent circumstances, makes it quite natural that the idea of the accidental or the arbitrary should not exist for the syncretistic mentality, and that consequently a reason should be found for everything. On the other hand, syncretism is the outcome of childish ego-centrism, since it is ego-centric habits of thought that induce the child to fly from analysis and to be satisfied with general schemas of an individual and arbitrary character. We can now understand why it is that the justifications of children, rooted as they are in syncretism, have the character of subjective and even of pathological interpretations due to a regression to a primitive mode of thinking.

§ 4. SYNCRETISM OF UNDERSTANDING.—Up till now we have had to do only with those children who more or less understood both of the two sentences to be compared. So far as the corresponding sentences are concerned, there can be no doubt about this. With regard to the proverbs, we may say that they have been verbally understood, i.e., that in reading them the child has had a concrete idea of their meaning, missing only their moral significance. Yet they all had the feeling that each proverb had a symbolic sense, although we never laid any stress on this point. Given these conditions of adequate understanding, we believe that the phenomena which we described a little way back belong quite definitely to syncretistic reasoning.

How does this phenomenon of syncretism originate? So far, we have looked upon the faculty for forming general schemas as given, and as the outcome of nonanalytical habits of thought derived from ego-centrism. We must now examine the mechanism more closely, and pass to the study of syncretistic understanding. In view of the phenomena studied in the first chapters of this book, we can take it that when a child listens to someone else talking, his ego-centrism induces him to believe that he understands everything, and prevents him from understanding word for word the terms and propositions that he hears. Thus, instead of analysing what he hears in detail, he reasons about it as a whole. He makes no attempt to adapt himself to the other person, and it is this lack of adaptation which causes him to think in general schemas. In this sense, egocentrism may be said to be contrary to analysis. Now, a very easy way of studying the mechanism of the formation of these syncretistic schemas is to note in our experiments when one of the words in the proverb or in the corresponding phrase is unknown to the child. Will he be interested in this word, as would be a mind free from ego-centrism, which tended to adapt itself to the interlocutor's point of view, and will he try to analyse this word before advancing another step in his reasoning? Or will he assume that the word is known to him, and then go on with his thinking as though no difficulty were present at all? We shall see that ego-centric habits of thought are the strongest, and that the child reasons as though he had not listened to the interlocutor, and as though he understood everything. The result is that the unknown word is assimilated as a function of the general schema of the phrase or of the two phrases. Syncretistic understanding consists precisely in this, that the whole is understood before the parts are analysed, and that understanding of the details takes place—rightly or wrongly—only as a function of the general schema. It is therefore in syncretistic understanding that we shall find the connecting link between the ego-centric habits of thought already known to us through the last three chapters and the syncretism to which they give rise.

If we wish to get some idea of this syncretism of understanding in the child, we need only think of the way in which persons gifted with intuition translate a language with which they are unfamiliar, or understand difficult propositions in their own language. They will often understand the general trend of a page written in a foreign tongue, or of a page of philosophy, for example, without understanding all the words or all the details of the exposition. A schema of understanding has been constructed, relatively correct (as appears from the more complete understanding subsequently obtained), but resting only on a few points which have been spontaneously related. In these cases such a schema precedes analytical understanding.

Now, this is the method used by the child. He lets all the difficult words in a given phrase slip by, then he connects the familiar words into a general schema, which subsequently enables him to interpret the words not originally understood. This syncretistic method may of course give rise to considerable mistakes, some of which we shall presently examine; but we believe it to be the most economical in the long run, and one which eventually leads the child to an accurate understanding of things by a gradual process of approximation and selection.

Here is an example of this method in connexion with our proverbs:

> Vau (10; 0) identifies "To each according to his works" with "Some people get very excited, and then never do anything." Now he does not know the word "according." But from the first he thinks that he understands it, and in the following manner. He connects these two propositions "*because they are just about the same thing*"; one sentence means: "*every one does his works, each has his works,*" and the other: "*Each wants to do something but they never do anything.*" Except for the antithesis, therefore, the schema is similar for both phrases. What then is meant by "according to"? It means "*Let them come. Let each one come to his work.*" Half an hour later we ask Vau to repeat the two sentences by heart. He reproduces the first as follows: "*Each according to work.*" The expression "according to" has definitely taken on the meaning of "coming"; Vau reproduces the corresponding sentence as follows: "*Some people come for nothing*"— Why do the two phrases mean the same thing?—*Because some people went, but never did anything. There* [in the proverb] *they went but they did something.*"

This case shows us very clearly a child ignorant of a word, but unaware of his own ignorance. The result is, that the unknown word is interpreted in function of the general schema of the two phrases compared. Vau made no attempt to analyse the details of the phrases in so far as they were incomprehensible. He decided that they meant the same thing, and then proceeded to interpret the various terms in function of the general schema which had been formed independently of the unknown word. If, therefore, we bring this mechanism of word understanding into relation with syncretism, it is because in this type of understanding the mind goes from the whole to the part exactly in the same way as it does in primitive perception.

Here are some more examples:

> Kauf (8; 8) G. assimilates "The sheep will always be shorn" to the following phrase: "Small people may be of great worth," without knowing the word "worth," and comes to the conclusion that the latter phrase means: "*It means that they may get bigger later on.*" Once again the unknown word is used as a function of the general schema. The sheep, says Kauf, will always be shorn, because as he grows older he grows bigger. The two sentences therefore mean the same thing "*because sheep can get bigger as they grow older, sheep are small when they are young, when people are young they are small, and as they grow older they get bigger.*" [= They are of great worth in the sense that has just been expounded.]

The same corresponding sentence is assimilated by Don (9 years old) to the proverb "The flies buzzing round the horses do not help on the coach," from which Don concludes that "worth" means "*something which is large,*" or "*a large number of flies.*" Here, once more, it is the schema that gives the meaning to the unknown word.

We need not dwell any longer on these facts which are those of current observation. It is they that explain the phenomenon of verbalism. If children have so much facility in using an unknown word, without noticing that they do not understand it, it is not because they think they can define it, for out of its context the word means nothing to them. But the first time they met with it, the whole context gave to the word a meaning that sufficed, owing to the syncretistic connexion between all the terms of the context, and owing to the pseudo-logical justifications always ready to emerge.

We can see at the same time how the syncretism of understanding explains that of reasoning, and bridges the gulf between ego-centric thought and the phenomena described in the last few sections. This is more or less how things happen. When the child hears people talk, he makes an effort, not so much to adapt himself and share the point of view of the other person as to assimilate everything he hears to his own point of view and to his own stock of information. An unknown word therefore seems to him less unknown than it would if he really tried to adapt himself to the other person. On the contrary, the word melts into the immediate context which the child feels he has quite sufficiently understood. Words which are too unfamiliar never call forth any analysis. Perception and understanding are thus syncretized, because they are unanalysed, and they are unanalysed because they are unadapted. From this syncretistic "reception," so to speak (perception or comprehension) to syncretistic reasoning there is only a step, the step of conscious realization. Instead of passively nothing that such-and-such a phrase "goes with" (feeling of agreement) such-and-such another, or that the fact of the moon not falling down "goes with" the fact of its being very high up, the child can ask himself, or be asked by someone "why" this is so. He will then create implications, or discover various justifications, which will simply render more explicit this sense of "agreement" which he felt in all things. The illogical character of childish "whys," or the absence of the notion of chance revealed in primitive "whys" are therefore due to syncretism of understanding and of perception itself, and this in its turn is due to the lack of adaptation which accompanies ego-centrism.

We can now sum up in a few words the problem discussed in § 2: Do syncretistic relations between propositions arise out of analogies of detail, or vice versa? This question, which we have already answered by saying that the two are mutually dependent, can also be stated in connexion with syncretistic understanding and perception. Does the child understand the sentence as a function of the words, the whole as function of the parts, or vice versa? These questions are idle in connexion with easy sentences or familiar objects, but they become interesting as soon as there is adaptation to new objects of thought.

With regard to perception, the subject will have to be pursued later, but this much it seems possible to establish. In the case quoted by M. Claparède, for instance, the question may be raised whether the child who recognized one page of music amongst many others was guided (as the hypothesis of syncretism would suggest) by the general effect of the page, or by some particular detail (such as the ending of a line or the portion of the page blackened with an agglomeration of notes). Now there is solidarity between the general effect of the page and the separate effect of the isolated details. If there is a general effect, it is because over and above the vague mass which serves as a background, certain details are picked out at random and are specially noticed. It is because of these distinctive details that there is a whole, and vice versa. The proof that this is neither a sophism nor a truism is that we adults, who are accustomed to analyse each group of notes and each word, no longer see either the general effect nor the outstanding details. If the distinguishing details are no longer present, it must be because there is no longer any general effect, and vice versa. As soon as we half close our eyes, however, certain groups of notes and certain words stand out, and it is by means of them that the page takes on, now a certain general physiognomy, now its opposite, in a continuous rhythm of alternation. There is the same solidarity between the distinctive details and the general effect in children's drawings. This is why a child, if he wishes to express the figure of a man, is content to put down together a few details, insignificant or essential (a head, a button, legs, a navel, etc. at random) which we would have chosen in quite another manner, our perception not being syncretistic to the same degree.

It is therefore no truism to say that the general schema and the analysis of details are mutually dependent. The two elements are quite distinct, and the one calls forth the other according to a rhythm which it is quite easy to observe.

Exactly the same thing happens in syncretistic understanding. In some cases it seems as though only the schema mattered, and that the words were only subsequently understood. Here is an example:

> Péril (10; 6) identifies "Drunken once will get drunk again" with "Whoever goes to sleep late will wake up late" "*because there are the same words in the sentence before the comma, and the words that are repeated in the two sentences are put in the same places; in both sentences there is a word that is repeated.*" It would therefore seem that Péril had been guided purely by the schematized general form. But he argues from this to an indentification of the meaning of the words: "*Because whoever has drunk wants to go on drinking, and whoever goes to sleep late will also wake up late.*"

In other cases the child seems to be on the look-out only for words resembling each other in sense or in sound ("petit" and "petites," "habit" and "habitude"); in fact he seems to start from the understanding of particular words. But here again the general schema is built up just as definitely. In syncretism of understanding, as in that of perception, there is solidarity between the details and the general schema. One may appear before the other, and is therefore independent of it; but it will call forth the other and be called forth by it by a process of alternation which prolongs itself into an indefinitely protracted oscillation. As this rhythm is repeated, the details are more and more analysed, and the whole is more and more synthesized. The result is, that to begin with, only the largest and most distinctive details are noticed, and only the coarsest of general schemas are constructed. At first, therefore, the distinctive details and the general effect are more or less mixed up together; then analysis and synthesis develop concurrently and at the expense of this initial syncretism.

It will now be understood why in syncretistic reasoning the use of explicit analogy is so inextricably intertwined with that of general schemas which mutually imply one another. It is because, through a succession of conscious realizations on the part of the subject, syncretism of reasoning grows out of that of understanding and perception.

§ 5. CONCLUSION.—Our readers will perhaps be inclined to take the view that ego-centric thought, which gives rise to all these phenomena of syncretism, is closer to autistic or dream thought than to logical thought. The facts which we have been describing are in several of their aspects related to dreaming or day-dreaming. We mean such things as the picking out of verbal and even punning resemblances, and, above all, the way in which the mind is allowed to float about at the mercy of free associations, until two propositions are brought together which originally had nothing in common.

This is not the place to carry out an exhaustive comparison between syncretism and autistic imagination. Besides, we have already pointed out the relation which exists between patho-logical interpretation and children's justification at any price. Nevertheless, it may be useful at this point to note that every-thing leads us to consider the mechanism of syncretistic thought as intermediate between logical thought and that process which the psycho-analysts have rather boldly described as the "symbol-ism" of dreams. How, after all, does autistic imagination function in dreams? Freud has shown that two main factors contribute to the formation of the images or pseudo-concepts of dreaming and day-dreaming—*condensation* by which several disparate images melt into one (as different people into one person), and *transference* by which the qualities belonging to one object are transferred to another (as when someone who may bear a certain resemblance to the dreamer's mother is conceived of as his actual mother). As we have suggested elsewhere[1] there must be every kind of intermediate type between these two functions and the processes of generalization (which is a sort of condensation) and abstraction (which is a sort of transference). Now syncretism is precisely the most important of these intermediate links. Like the dream, it "condenses" objectively disparate elements into a whole. Like the dream, it "transfers," in obedience to the association of ideas, to purely external resemblance or to punning assonance, qualities which seem rightly to apply only to one definite object. But this condensation and transference are not so absurd nor so deeply affective in character as in dreams or autistic imagination. It may therefore be assumed that they form a transition between the pre-logical and the logical mechanisms of thought.[2]

We ought certainly to be careful not to underestimate thought carried on by means of syncretistic schemas, for in spite of all the deviations which we have described, it does lead the child on to a progressive adaptation. There is nothing unintelligent about these schemas; they are simply too ingenuous and too facile for purposes of accuracy. Sooner or later they will be submitted to a rigorous selection and to a mutual reduction, which will sharpen them into first-rate instruments of invention in spheres

[1] J. Piaget. "La psychanalyse dans ses rapports avec la psychologie de l'enfant," *Bullet. Soc. Alf. Binet*, No. 131–133, pp. 56–7.

[2] One more proof of the analogy between syncretism and imagination has been supplied by M. Larsson's fine work (H. Larsson, *La Logique de la poésie*, transl. Philipot, Paris, Leroux, 1919). M. Larsson has shown that artistic imagination (which is one of the forms of autism) consists first and foremost in seeing objects not analytically as does intelligence, but syncretistically, i.e., by means of general perceptions. Art brings out the *Gestaltqualitäten* of things, and the intropathic effort made by the artist consists in reviving this primitive total perception.

of thought where hypotheses are of use. It is only at the age of the children we have studied that this exuberance hinders adaptation, because it is still too closely connected with autistic imagination.

These analogies between syncretism and autistic imagination also explain why the answers which we obtained from the children so often seemed to have been invented. The impression must often have been created that the children we questioned were making fun either of us or of the test, and that the many solutions which they discovered at will could have been exchanged for any others that might have suggested themselves, without the child being in any way put out. This would considerably diminish the value of the facts we have studied. This objection is one that it is always very difficult to meet, because in questioning a child we have no criterion for ascertaining whether he is inventing or whether he really believes what he says. On the other hand, there are three criteria which we wish to suggest for this kind of research, and which, if simultaneously applied, would enable us to distinguish between invention and truth. Now, in the case of the phenomena described above, we believe there has been no invention, and that the resemblance to invention which marks the answers obtained was due precisely to the analogy between syncretism and imagination, invention being one of the forms of childish imagination. Here are the three criteria which enable us to draw this conclusion instead of denying all value to our results.

First criterion: *Uniformity or Numerical Constancy of the Answers*. When the same experiment is carried out on a great many different subjects, the answers obtained either all resemble each other, or are diverse and unclassifiable. In the first of the two cases there is far less chance of there having been invention than in the second. It may well be that answers which the child gives according to his fancy or simply as a game follow a law as regards both form and content. What is less probable is that the same question put to 40 or 50 different children should *always* call forth invention, instead of provoking sometimes an adapted, sometimes fabricated answer. Now in the case of our proverbs, all the answers were alike in content as well as in form.

Second criterion: The *Difference of Age* in the children. Certain questions provoke romancing in children of a given age (e.g., from 5 to 6) who do not understand them, and therefore treat them as a game. Between 7 and 8 the same questions will be understood, and therefore taken seriously. When all the children of the same age answer in the same way, the question may still be raised whether there has not been invention owing to general incomprehension. But if for several years in succession the answers are practically the same, then the chances of invention have been decreased. Now this is what our proverbs reveal. Between 9 and 11 we get the same results, and the subjects examined outside of these limits gave answers of a similar nature. As the years increased, there was simply a more or less sensible diminution of syncretism.

Third criterion: *Finding the right Answer*. It is easy to see, once the child finds the right answer, whether his method changes, and whether he suddenly denies what till then he apparently believed. If so, then there is a chance that invention has taken place. If, on the other hand, there is continuity between the methods which lead to error and those which lead to the right solution, if there are imperceptible stages of development, then the chances are against invention. Now in the case of our proverbs, right answers and wrong lay side by side in the child's mind, and the right answers did not exclude the presence of syncretism from the method by which the correspondence between proverb and sentence was found.

We can therefore conclude that our children's answers are not due to invention. One can never be sure, however, that in some cases the answers have not been invented. We have even become certain of the contrary in connexion with one or two examples which stood out from among the others by reason of their being more arbitrary in character. For the rest, if our material does show any signs of invention, this is due to the fact that syncretism, like all manifestations of the egocentric mentality, occupies, as will be shown later on, a position half-way between autistic and logical thought.[1]

[1] For a more detailed treatment of this parallel between autistic and child thought, see our article, "La pensée symbolique et la pensée de l'enfant," *Arch. de Psych.*, Vol. XVIII, p. 273 (1923).

how are those interests to be classified? In order to solve this problem it is sufficient to make a list extending over a certain stretch of time, if not of all the questions asked by a child, at least of those asked of the same person, and to classify these questions according to the sort of answer which the child expects to receive. But this classification is a nicer matter than one would think, and we shall therefore be more concerned with the creation of an instrument of research than with its practical application.

The material on which we shall work consists of 1,125 spontaneous questions asked of Mlle Veihl over a period of ten months by Del, a boy between 6 and 7 (6; 3 to 7; 1). These questions were taken down in the course of daily talks lasting two hours; each talk was a sort of lesson by conversation, but of a very free character during which the child was allowed to say anything he liked. These talks had begun long before lists were made of the questions, so that the child found himself in a perfectly natural atmosphere from the start. Also, what is more important, he never suspected that his questions were being noted in any way. Mlle Veihl possessed the child's full confidence, and was among those with whom he best liked to satisfy his curiosity. No doubt the subject-matter of the lessons (reading, spelling, general knowledge) had a certain influence on the questions that were asked, but that was inevitable. The chance occurrences of walks or games—which, incidentally, played their own small part in these interviews—had just as much influence in directing the subject's interests. The only way to draw a line between what is occasional and what is permanent in the curiosity of a child, is to multiply the records in conditions as similar as possible. And this is what we did. Finally, it need hardly be said that we abstained as carefully from provoking questions as from picking and choosing among those that were asked.

Nevertheless, as this investigation was originally destined to help only in the study of "whys," these alone have been taken down in their entirety during the first interviews in which the experimenter was at work. For a few weeks, all other questions were only taken down intermittently. On some days, it goes without saying, all questions were taken down without any exception, but on others, only the "whys" were taken into account. Questions 201 to 450, 481 to 730, and 744 to 993, however, represent a complete account of all the questions asked during the corresponding periods of time. The statistical part will therefore deal only with these three groups of 250 questions each, or else with the "whys."

I. "WHYS"

Before broaching the difficult problem presented by the types of question asked by Del, let us try, by way of introduction, to solve a special and more limited problem—that of the different types of "whys."

The question of children's "whys" is more complex than it at first appears to be. It is well known that the whys which appear somewhere about the age of 3 (Stern mentions them at 2; 10, 3; 1 etc., Scupin at 2; 9, Rasmussen between 2 and 3 etc.), are extremely numerous between this age and that of 7, and characterize what has been called the second age of questions in the child. The first age is characterized by questions of place and name, the second by those of cause and time. But its very abundance leads us to look upon the "why" as the maid-of-all-work among questions, as an undifferentiated question, which in reality has several heterogeneous meanings. Stern was right in pointing out that the earliest "whys" seem more affective than intellectual in character, i.e., that instead of being the sign of verbal curiosity, they rather bear witness to a disappointment produced by the absence of a desired object or the non-arrival of an unexpected event. But we have yet to ascertain how the child passes from this affective curiosity, so to speak, to curiosity in general, and finally to the most subtle forms of intellectual interest such as the search for causes. Between these two extremes there must be every shade of intervening variety, which it should be our business to classify.

There is a certain category of childish "whys" which do seem, from a superficial point of view, to demand a causal explanation for their answer. Such an one is this, one of the earliest questions of a boy of 3: *"Why do the trees have leaves?"* Now, if such a question were asked by an adult, educated or otherwise, it would imply at least two groups of answers. One group of answers, the finalistic, would begin with the word "to" ("to keep them warm," "to breath with," etc.), the other, the causal or logical, would begin with the word "because" ("because they are descended from vegetables which have leaves" or "because all vegetables have leaves." It is, therefore, not possible to see at first which of these two shades of meaning is uppermost in the child's question. There may even be a quantity of other meanings which elude our understanding. The question may be merely verbal, and indicate pure astonishment without calling for any answer. This is often the case with the questions of children; they are asked of no one, and supply in effect a roundabout way of stating something without incurring contradiction. Very often, if one does not answer a child immediately, he will not wait, but answer himself. We have already (chapter 1) come across several of these ego-centric questions, which are strictly speaking pseudo-questions. But this will not be taken into account in the classification which follows. However ego-centric a question may be, it is always interesting that it should have been expressed in the form of a question, and the type of logical relation (causality, finalism etc.) which it presupposes is always the same as that which would characterize the question if it were asked of anyone. In this connexion, the question which we quoted admits of many more meanings for the child than for the adult. The child may have wanted to know, from anthropomorphism and apart from any interest in the tree itself, "who put the leaves on the trees." (Why have the trees got leaves? Because God put them there). He may have purposive or utilitarian ideas in relation to humanity. (Why . . . etc.—So that it should look pretty. So that people might sit in its shade, etc.), or in relation to the tree itself, which the child would endow with more or less explicit aims (because it likes to, etc.). In a word, a large number of interpretations are always possible when a child's "why" is isolated from its context.

The lists of "whys" belonging to the same child, such as we are going to discuss, will therefore by the mere fact that they make comparisons possible, help to solve the two following problems, which without this method are insoluble: 1° What are the possible types of "whys," classified according to the logical type of answer which the child expects or which he supplies himself? 2° What is the genealogy of these types?

§ 1. PRINCIPAL TYPES OF "WHYS."—There are three big groups of children's "whys"—the "whys" of *causal explanation* (including *finalistic* explanation), those of *motivation*, and those of *justification*. Inside each group further shades of difference may be distinguished. After a certain age (from 7 to 8 onwards) there are also the whys of *logical justification*, but they hardly concern us at the age of Del, and they can be included in the "whys of justification" in general.

The term *explanation* is to be taken in the restricted sense of causal or finalistic explanation. For the word "explain" carries with it two different meanings. Sometimes it signifies giving a "logical" explanation, i.e., connecting the unknown with the known, or giving a systematic exposition (explaining a lesson or a theorem). "Whys" referring to logical explanation ("Why is half 9, 4.5?") are to be classified as "logical justification." Sometimes, on the contrary, the word "explain" means carrying back our thought to the causes of a phenomenon, these causes being efficient or final according as we are dealing with natural phenomena or with machines. It is in the second sense only that we shall use the word explanation. "Whys" of causal explanation will therefore be recognizable by the fact that the expected answer implies the idea of the cause or of final cause. Here are some examples taken from Del: "*Why do they* (bodies) *always fall?*"—"*Lightning . . . Daddy says that it makes itself all by itself in the sky. Why?* [does it make itself in this way]"—"*Why haven't they* [little goats] *got any milk?*"—"*Why is it so heavy* [a two-franc piece]?"

Let us designate as *motivation* that sort of explanation which accounts, not for a material phenomenon, as in the last category, but for an action or a psychological state. What the child looks for here is not, strictly speaking, a material cause, but the purpose or the motive which guided the action, sometimes also the psychological cause. "Whys" of motivation are innumerable, and easy to classify: "*Are you going away? Why?*"—"*Why do we always begin with reading?*"—"*Why doesn't daddy know the date? He is quite grown up.*"

Finally, let us designate as "whys" of justification those which refer to some particular order, to the aim, not of some action, but of a rule. "Why do we have to . . . etc." These "whys" are sufficiently frequent in the case of Del to justify the formation of a separate category. The child's curiosity does not only attach itself to physical objects and the actions of human beings, it goes out systematically to all the rules that have to be respected— rules of language, of spelling, sometimes of politeness, which puzzle the child and of which he would like to know the why and the wherefore. Sometimes he seeks for their origin, i.e., his idea of it, the object of the "grown-ups" who have decided that it should be so, sometimes he looks for their aim. These two meanings are confused in the same question—"why . . . etc.?" We have here a collection of interests which can be united under the word "justification" and which differ from the simple interest in psychological motivation. Here are examples of it, some less obvious than others: "*Why not 'an'* [in the spelling of a word]? *You can't tell when it is 'an' or 'en.'"*—*"Why not 'in'* [in 'Alain']? *Who said it shouldn't be, the grown-ups in Paris?"*—*"Why do people say 'strayed,' does it mean lost?"*—*"Black coffee, why black? All coffee is black . . ."*

These, then, are the three great classes of "whys" which it is possible to establish straight away. But it need hardly be said that these are "statistical" types, i.e., that between them there exists every kind of intermediate variety. If all the existing transitional types could be arranged in order, and their shades of difference expressed in numbers, then the three main types would simply represent the three crests of a graph of frequency. Between these summits there would be the intermediate zones. In psychology, as in zoology, we must needs adopt a classification into species and varieties; even though its application is purely statistical, and though an individual sample taken at random cannot be placed for certain in one class rather than another until its true nature and derivation have been established by experiment and analysis.

It is obvious, for instance, that between the "causal explanation" of physical objects called forth by the questions of the first group, and psychological "motivation," there are two intermediate types. Alongside of the explanations which the child himself considers as physical (the cloud moves because the wind drives it along) there are those which he looks upon as mixed up with motivation (the river is swift because man or God wanted it to be), and there are those which we ourselves consider mixed (the two-franc piece is heavy because it is in silver, or because it was made to weigh more than a one-franc piece, etc.). Causal explanation therefore often inclines to motivation. But the converse also happens. In addition to the "whys of motivations" which refer to a momentary intention (Why are you going away?) there are those which involve explanations of a more psychological nature, and appeal no longer to an intention, but to cause properly so-called (Why does Daddy not know the date?), which brings us back to the first type of question. The result is, that we can give no fixed form to the criterion used to distinguish causal explanation from motivation. The decision in each case as to whether the child wanted to be answered with a causal explanation or with a motivation would be too arbitrary. The criterion can only be practical, and will have to adapt itself to the contents of the question. When the question refers to physical objects (natural phenomena, machines, manufactured objects, etc.), we shall class it among the "whys" of causal explanation; when the question refers to human activities, we shall class it among the "whys" of motivation. This classification is a little arbitrary, but the convention is easy to follow. In our opinion the attempt to define the child's motive too closely would be still more arbitrary, for that would be to put the purely subjective judgment of each psychologist in the place of conventions, which may be rigid, but which are known to be only conventions.

The distinction, between motivation and justification, on the other hand, is even more difficult to establish with any precision. In the main, "whys" of justification imply the idea of rules. But this idea is far less definite in the child than in us, so that here again we are obliged to use a criterion bearing on the matter rather than on the form of the question. The justification of a rule is very closely allied to motivation, to the search for the intention of him who knows or who established the rule. We shall therefore say that "whys" of justification are those which do not bear directly on a human activity, but on language, spelling and, in certain cases to be more closely defined, on social conventions (bad manners, prohibitions, etc.).

If we insist upon this third class of "whys," it is because of the following circumstance. We have shown throughout the last three chapters that before 7 or 8 the child is not interested in logical justification. He asserts without proving. Children's arguments in particular consist of a simple clash of statements, without any justification of the respective points of view. The result is, that the word "because" corresponding to a logical demonstration ("because" connecting two ideas of which one is the reason for the other) is rarely used by the child, and, as we shall see in the next volume, is even imperfectly understood by him; in a word, it is alien to the habits of thought of the child under 7 or 8. Now, corresponding to this group of logical relations, to the "because" which unites two ideas, there is obviously a group of "whys of justification" whose function is to find the logical reason for a statement, in other words, to give a proof or to justify a definition. For example "why is 4.5 half of 9?" This is not a case of causal or psychological motivation, but quite definitely one of logical reasoning. Now, if the observations made in the course of the last chapters are correct, we shall expect—and our expectation will prove to be justified—this type of "why" to be very rare under the age of 7 or 8, and not to constitute a separate class. But—and this is why we wish to keep the "whys of justification" in a separate category—there is for the child only a step from a rule of spelling or grammar to the definition of a word, etc., and from the definition of a word to a genuine "logical reason." Everyone knows that childish grammar is more logical than ours, and that the etymologies spontaneously evolved by children are perfect masterpieces of logic. Justification in our sense is therefore an intermediate stage between simple motivation and logical justification. Thus, in the examples quoted, *"Why do people say "strayed"?" [instead of saying lost] inclines to the "whys" of motivation; "Why black coffee, all coffee is black"* seems to appeal to a logical reason (which would be a link between a reason and conclusion); and the other two seem to be intermediate "whys" which appeal to a certain form of spelling, etc.

To sum up. "Whys of justification" are an undifferentiated class before the age of 7 or 8. After the age of 7 or 8 this class is replaced—such at least is our hypothesis—by two other classes. One of these, "logical justification or reason," is to be contrasted with causal explanation and motivation. The other, "justification of rules, customs, etc." can be considered as intermediate between logical justification and motivation. Before the age of 7 to 8, these two classes can therefore be united into one.

This gives us the following table:

	Form of the question		Matter of the question
Explanation (causal)	{ Cause	}	Physical objects
	{ End		
Motivation	Motive		Psychological actions
Justification	{ Justification proper		Customs and rules
	{ Logical reason . . .		Classification and connexion of ideas

In addition to this, it should be pointed out that there are certain classes of questions beginning with such words as "how," "what is," "where . . . from," etc., which correspond word for word with the classes of "whys" of which we have just spoken. This will supply us with a very useful counter-proof.

§ 2. "WHYS OF CAUSAL EXPLANATION." INTRODUCTION AND CLASSIFICATION BY MATERIAL.—We have no intention of attacking the vast subject of causality in childish thought. On the contrary, we have concentrated on the problem of the formal structure of reasoning in the child. As it is very difficult to isolate the study of causality from that of children's ideas in general, the subject should by rights be excluded from our investigation. Nevertheless, two reasons compel us to broach the matter here and now. In the first place, one of the objects of this chapter was to show that in Del's case there are very few "whys of justification"; we must therefore analyse the sum of the answers obtained, in order to become aware of this absence. In the second place, it is quite possible to study causality from the point of view of the structure of reasoning, and in particular of the influences of ego-centrism, without encroaching too far on the actual domain of ideas. We shall, in spite of this, however, say a few words about these ideas, and then draw our conclusions in the next paragraph on the structure of the questions which have been asked.

"Whys of causal explanation" raise a number of problems which are of paramount importance in the study of the child intelligence. It is indeed a matter for conjecture whether a child feels in the same degree as we do the need for a causal explanation properly so-called (efficient cause as opposed to finalism). We ought therefore to examine the possible types of causality which could take the place of causality properly so-called. Stanley Hall has shown that out of some hundreds of questions about the origin of life (birth) 75% are causal. But he never stated his criteria. He simply pointed out that among these causal questions a large number are artificialistic, animistic, etc.[1] The difficulty therefore still remains of classifying these types of explanation and of finding their mutual relations to each other.

Now we had occasion in two earlier chapters (1 and 3) to show that the child between 6 and 8 takes very little interest in the "how" of phenomena. His curiosity reaches only the general cause, so to speak, in contrast to the detail of contacts and of causal sequences. This is a serious factor in favour of the *sui generis* character of "whys of explanation" in the child. Let us try to classify those of Del, starting from the point of view of their contents, and not bothering about their form.

Classifying these "whys" by their contents consists in grouping them according to the objects referred to in the question.

In this connexion,[2] out of the 103 "whys of causal explanation" 88 refer to nature and 22 to machines or manufactured articles. The 81 "whys" concerning nature can be subdivided into 26 questions about inanimate objects (inanimate for the adult), 10 about plants, 29 about animals and 16 about the human body.

[1] Stanley Hall, "Curiosity and Interest," *Pedag. Sem.*, Vol. X. (1903). See numerous articles which have since appeared in the *Pedag. Sem.*
[2] Out of 360 "whys" taken down in ten months, 103, *viz.* 28% were found to be "whys of causal explanation."

What is most remarkable about this result is the feeble interest shown in inanimate physical objects. This circumstance should put us on our guard from the first against the hypothesis according to which Del's "whys" would refer to causality in the same sense as ours. A certain number of the peculiarities exhibited by the "whys" concerning the physical world will enable us to state the problem more precisely.

In the first place, some of Del's questions bear witness to the well-known anthropomorphism of children. It may be better described as *artificialism*, but nothing is known as yet about its origin or its duration. For example: "*Why [does the lightning make itself by itself in the sky]? Is it true? But isn't there everything that is needed to light a fire with up in the sky?*" These artificialistic questions, which are rarely quite clear, obviously do not presuppose an efficient mechanistic causation analogous to ours.

Other and more interesting "whys" raise the problem of *chance* in the thought of the child. These for example: Del had thought that Bern was on the lake. "The lake does not reach as far as Bern"—"*Why?*" or *Why does it not make a spring in our garden?*" etc. Mlle V. finds a stick and picks it up. "*Why is that stick bigger than you*"—"*Is there a Little Cervin and a Great Cervin?*"—No—*Why is there a Little Salève and a Great Salève?*" Questions of this kind abound with this child; we shall come across many more, and they will always surprise us. We are in the habit of alotting a large part to chance and continency in our explanations of phenomena. All "statistical causality," which for us is simply a variety of mechanical causality, rests on this idea of chance, i.e., of the intersection of two independent causal sequences. If there are no springs in the garden, it is because the series of motives which lead to the choice of the garden's locality is independent of the series of causes which produced a spring a little distance away. If the two lines of sequences had crossed, it would only be by chance, as there is very little likelihood of their crossing. But it is clear that this idea of chance is derivative: it is a conclusion forced upon us by our powerlessness to explain. The result is, that the child is slow in reaching the sort of agnosticism of ordinary adult life. For lack of a definite idea of chance, he will always look for the why and wherefore of all the fortuitous juxtapositions which he meets with in experience. Hence this group of questions. Do these questions then point to a desire for causal explanation? In a sense they do, since they demand an explanation where none is forthcoming. In another sense they do not, since obviously a world in which chance does not exist is a far less mechanical and far more anthropomorphic a world than ours. Besides, we shall meet with this problem of causality again, in connexion with other varieties of "why."

The following questions, however, seem to really belong to the order of physical causality:

(1) "*Why do they* [bodies] *always fall?*" (2) "*It* [water] *can run away, then why* [is there still some water in the rivers]?" (3) "The water goes to the sea—*Why?*" (4) "*There are waves only at the edge* [of the lake]. *Why?*" (5) "*Why does it always do that* [stains of moisture] *when there is something there* [fallen leaves]?" (6) "*Will it always stay there* [water in a hole worn away in the sandstone]?—No, the stone absorbs a lot.—*Why? Will it make a hole?*—No—*Does it melt?*" (7) "*Why does it get colder and colder as you go up* [as you go north]?" and (8) "*Why can you see lightning better at night.*"

It is worth noting how difficult it is to determine what part is played by finalism in these questions and what by mechanical causality. Thus "whys" 3, 7, and 8 could easily be interpreted as finalistic questions: you see the lightning better in order to . . . etc. It is only in questions 1, 4, 5, and 6 that we can be at all sure of any desire for a causal explanation, because the objects are uncircumscribed, and clearly independent of human or divine intervention. Lightning, on the other hand, is, as we have just seen, spontaneously conceived of as "manufactured" in the sky; rivers, as we shall show later on, are thought of as put into action by man, etc.

In a word, these questions asked about the physical world are far from being unambiguously causal. Questions about plants do not throw much light on the matter. Some point to a certain interest in the circumstances of the flower's habitat: *"Why are there not any* [bluebells] *in our garden?"* Others, more interesting, refer to the life and death of plants: *"Has it rained in the night?— No.—Then why have they* [weeds] *grown?" Why do we not see those flowers about now* [the end of summer]?"—*"They* [roses on a rose-tree] *are all withered, why? They shouldn't die, because they are still on the tree"—"Why does it* [a rotten mushroom] *drop off so easily?"* We shall come across this preoccupation with "death" in connexion with other questions, which will show that this interest is of great importance from the point of view of the idea of chance. The first group of questions raises the same problems as before: the child is still very far from allowing its share to chance in the nexus of events, and tries to find a reason for everything. But is the reason sought for causal, or does it point to a latent finalism?

Questions on animals are naturally very definite in this connexion. About half of them refer to the intentions which the child attributes to animals. *"Does the butterfly make honey?—No.—But why does it go on the flowers?"—"Why do they* [flies] *not go into our ears?"* etc. These "whys" ought to be classified as "whys of motivation," but we are confining this group to the actions of human beings. If it were extended to include animals, there would be no reason for not extending it to include the objects which at 6 or 7 the child still openly regards as animated, such as (according to the research work done at the *Institut Rousseau* on the ideas of children) stars, fire, rivers, wind, etc. Among the other questions, only four are causal, and curiously enough, are again concerned with death:

"*They* [butterflies] *die very soon, why?*"—"*Will there still be any bees when I grow up?*"—Yes, those that you see will be dead, but there will be others.—"*Why?*"—"*Why do they* [animals] *not mind* [drinking dirty water]?"—"*It* [a fly] *is dead, why?*"

The rest of the questions about animals are either finalistic, or else those "whys" about special fortuitous circumstances or about anomalies for which the child wishes to find a reason.

"*Why is it* [a pigeon] *like an eagle, why?*"—"*If they* [snakes] *are not dangerous, why have they got those things* [fangs]?"—"*Why has a cockchafer always got these things* [antennæ]?"—"*It [an insect] sticks to you, why?*"—[Looking at an ant]: "*I can see green and red, why?*"—"*It [a cockchafer] can't go as far as the sun, why?*"—[Del draws a whale with the bones sticking out of its skin]. "You shouldn't see the bones, they don't stick out.— "*Why, would it die?*"

Some of these questions mean something, others (those about the pigeon, the ant, etc.) do not. That is because in the second case we bring in chance by way of explanation. If our idea of chance is really due to the impotence of our explanation, then this distinction is naturally not one that can be made a priori. The child, therefore, can have no knowledge of these shades of difference; hence his habit of asking questions in season and out of season. Shall we adopt Groos' view that curiosity is the play of attention, and interpret all these questions as the outcome of invention? But this would not explain their contents. If childish questions strike us as uncouth, it is because for the child, everything can a priori be connected with everything else. Once the notion of chance, which is a derivative notion, is discarded, there is no reason for choosing one question rather than another. On the contrary, if everything is connected with everything else it is probable that everything has an end, and an anthropomorphic end at that. Consequently no question is absurd in itself.

Questions referring to the human body will help us to understand more clearly this relation between finalism and those "whys" which are the negation of chance. Here is an example of a definitely finalistic "why" where we would have expected a purely causal one: Del asks in connexion with negroes: "*If I stayed out there for only one day, would I get black all over?*" (This question without being a "why" appears to be definitely causal. The sequel shows that it is nothing of the kind)—No—*Why are they made to be* [exist] *like that?* Although too much stress must not be laid on the expression "are they made to," it obviously points to a latent finalism. There is therefore every likelihood that the following questions will be of the same order:

> "*Why have you got little ones* [ears] *and I have big ones although I am small?*" and "*Why is my daddy bigger than you although he is young?*"—"*Why do ladies not have beards?*"—"*Why have I got a bump* [on the wrist]?"—"*Why was I not born like that* [dumb]?"— "*Caterpillars turn into butterflies, then shall I turn into a little girl?*"—No—*Why?*—"*Why has it* [a dead caterpillar] *grown quite small? When I die shall I also grow quite small?*"[1]

Now here again, most of the questions are put as though the child were incapable of giving himself the answer: "By chance." At this stage, therefore, the idea of the fortuitous does not exist; causality presupposes a "maker," God, the parents, etc., and the questions refer to the intentions which he may have had. Even those of the preceding questions which come nearest to causality presuppose a more or less definite finalism. Organic life is,

---

[1] These last two questions correspond to two spontaneous ideas of childhood which are well known to psycho-analysts: that it is possible to change one's sex, and that after death one becomes a child again.

for the child, a sort of story, well regulated according to the wishes and intentions of its inventor.

We can now see what is the part played by questions about death and accidents. If the child is at this stage puzzled by the problem of death, it is precisely because in his conception of things death is inexplicable. Apart from theological ideas, which the child of 6 or 7 has not yet incorporated into his mentality, death is the fortuitous and mysterious phenomenon *par excellence*. And in the questions about plants, animals, and the human body, it is those which refer to death which will cause the child to leave behind him the stage of pure finalism, and to acquire the notion of statistical causality or chance.

This distinction between the causal order and the order of ends is undoubtedly a subtle one if each case be examined in detail, but we believe that the general conclusions which can be drawn from it hold good. Del has a tendency to ask questions about everything indiscriminately, because he inclines to believe that everything has an aim. The result is, that the idea of the fortuitous eludes him. But the very fact that it eludes him leads him to a preference for questions about anything accidental or inexplicable, because accident is more of a problem for him than for us. Sometimes, therefore, he tries to do away with the accidental element as such, and to account for it by an end, sometimes he fails in this attempt, and then, recognizing the fortuitous element for what it is, he tries to explain it causally. When, therefore, we are faced with a child's question that appears to be causal, we must be on our guard against any hasty conclusion, and see by careful examination whether the finalistic interpretation is excluded. It is not always possible to come to a conclusion, and out of the 81 "whys" referring to nature, only one-tenth can be said to be definitely causal. This is very little. Classification of the questions by their contents cannot therefore correspond term for term with a formal classification: the interest shown in natural objects does not constitute a direct proof of interest in mechanical or physical causality.

Before enquiring any further into the nature of childish causality, let us examine the "whys" that relate to the *technical appliances* of human beings, we mean machines or manufactured articles. Out of 22 such questions, two-thirds are simply about the intention of the maker: *"Why are the funnels* [of a boat] *slanting?"*—*"Why have two holes been made in this whistle?"* These are the questions which are continuous with the "whys of motivation," but easily distinguishable from them, since the question refers to the manufactured object. Only in a few cases can there be any doubt as to the particular shade of meaning. For example, before a picture of a woman handing a cabbage to a little girl: *"Why does it always stay like that?"* Does Del wish to know the psychological intention of the artist or of the woman, or is he asking why the drawing represents movement by fixing a single position into immobility?

The other "whys" are more interesting: they refer to the actual working of the machines, or to the properties of the raw materials that are used:

> *"Why has it* [a crane] *got wheels?"*—*"There are lamps in our attic at home. When there's a thunderstorm the electricity can't be mended. Why?"* After leaning too heavily with his pencil on a sheet of paper: *"Why can you see through?"* He traces a penny: *"Why is this one all right and not the other one?"* His name had been written in pencil on his wooden gun. The next day it did not show any more: *"Why do wood and iron rub out pencil marks?"* While he is painting: *"When I mix red and orange it makes brown, why?"*

Several of these questions do seem to call for a causal explanation. But here, as in the questions about nature, the definitely causal questions are concerned almost exclusively with the element of accident, whereas those which refer to a customary event [the question about the crane or about the colours] seem as much concerned with utility or motive as with cause. At any rate, we have not found one indisputably causal question, even among those concerning the working of machines. In this respect, therefore, the questions of this group confirm our previous findings.

§ 3. STRUCTURE OF THE "WHYS OF EXPLANATION."—The reader can now see for himself how complex is the problem of causality in the child, and how much a classification based on the contents of the questions differs from a formal classification, i.e., one relating to the structure of "whys" and to the different types of causality. We should like to be able to give such a formal classification which would be homogeneous with the rest of our work. Unfortunately, the present conditions of knowledge render this impossible. To carry out such a scheme, it would have been necessary to examine Del in detail on all the natural phenomena about which he had asked questions, and thus establish a parallel between his questions and the types of explanation which he gave. An enquiry which has since been set on foot, and is now being carried out with the collaboration of Mlle Guex, will perhaps yield the desired result. In the meantime, and pending the establishment of formal types of "whys of explanation," let us content ourselves with bringing some system into the preceding considerations, and let us try to indicate what is the general structure of Del's "whys of explanation."

There are five principal types of adult explanation. First of all there is *causal explanation* properly so-called, or *mechanical explanation*: "the chain of a bicycle revolves because the pedals set the gearwheel in motion." This is causation by spatial contact. Then there is *statistical explanation*, in a sense a special case of the former, but relating to the sum of these phenomena which are directly or indirectly subject to the laws of chance. *Finalistic explanation* is used by common sense in connexion with the phenomena of life: "Animals have legs to walk with." *Psychological explanation*, or explanation by *motive*, accounts for purposive actions: "I read this book because I wished to know its author." Finally, *logical explanation*, or *justification*, accounts for the reason of an assertion: "x_1 larger than y_1, because all x's are larger than y's." These various types naturally encroach upon each other's territory, but in the main they are distinct in adult thought and even in ordinary common sense.

Now what we purpose to show is that in the child before the age of 7 or 8, these types of explanation are, if not completely undifferentiated, at any rate far more similar to each other than they are with us. Causal explanation and logical justification in particular are still entirely identified with motivation; because causation in the child's mind takes on the character of finalism and psychological motivation far rather than that of spatial contact, and because, moreover, logical justification hardly ever exists in an unadulterated form, but always tends to reduce itself to psychological motivation. We shall designate by the name of *precausality* this primitive relation in which causation still bears the marks of a quasi-psychological motivation. One of the forms taken by this precausality is the anthropomorphic explanation of nature. In this case, the causes of phenomena are always confused with the intentions of the Creator or with those of men, who are the makers of mountains and rivers. But even if no "intention" can be detected in this anthropomorphic form, the "reason" which the child tries to give for phenomena is far more in the nature of a utilitarian reason or of a motive than of spatial contact.

It will be easier to understand the nature of this precausality if we explain it at once by means of one of the most important phenomena of the mental life of the child between the years of 3 and 7; we mean that which was discovered by specialists in the drawings of children, and which has been most successfully characterized by M. Luquet as "logical realism," or, as he now calls it, "intellectual realism." The child, as we all know, begins by drawing only what he sees around him—men, houses, etc. In this sense, he is a realist. But instead of drawing them as he sees them, he reduces them to a fixed schematic type; in a word, he draws them as he knows them to be. In this sense, his realism is not visual, but intellectual. The logic of this primitive draughtsmanship is childish but entirely rational, since it consists, for instance, in adding a second eye to a face seen in profile, or rooms to a house seen from the outside. Now this intellectual realism has a significance which, as we have shown elsewhere,[1] extends beyond the sphere of drawing. The child thinks and observes as he draws. His mind attaches itself to things, to the contents of a chain of thought rather than to its form. In deductive reasoning he examines only the practical bearing of the premises, and is incapable of arguing as we do, vi formae, on any given "data." He does not share the point of view of his interlocutor (see in this connexion Vol. II where we shall meet again with the child's incapacity for formal ratiocination). He contradicts himself rather than lose his hold on reality. In this sense, he is a realist. But, on the other hand, this reality to which he clings so continuously is the outcome of his own mental construction rather than the fruit of pure observation. The child sees only what he knows and what he anticipates. If his powers of observation seem good, it is because his trains of thought, which are very different from ours, cause him to see things which do not interest us, and which it therefore astonishes us that he should have noticed. But on closer observation one is struck by the extent to which his vision is distorted by his ideas. If a child believes that rivers flow backwards, he will see the Seine or the Rhone flowing upwards towards their sources; if he believes the sun to be alive, he will see it

[1] Journal de Psychologie, 1922, pp. 223, 256–257, etc.

walking about in the sky; if he believes it to be inanimate, he will see it always motionless, etc. In a word, the child observes and thinks as he draws: his thought is realistic, but intellectually so.

The structure of childish precausality will now be clear. Children's "whys" are realistic in the sense that in Del's language, as we shall see in § 4, there are no genuine "whys of logical justification." Curiosity is concentrated always on the causes of phenomena (or actions), and not logical deductions. But this causation is not visual or mechanical, since spatial contact plays in it only a very restricted part. Everything happens as though nature were the outcome, or rather the reflexion of a mental activity whose reasons or intentions the child is always trying to find out.

This does not mean that the whole of nature is, for the child, the work of a God or of men. These reasons and intentions are no more referred to one single mental activity than they are in the prelogical mentality of primitive races. What is meant is that instead of looking for an explanation in spatial contact (visual realism) or in logical deduction of laws and concepts (intellectualism), the child reasons, as he draws, according to a sort of "internal model," similar to nature, but reconstructed by his intelligence, and henceforth pictured in such a fashion that everything in it can be explained psychologically, and that everything in it can be justified or accounted for (intellectual realism). Thus the child invokes as the causes of phenomena, sometimes motives or intentions (finalism), sometimes pseudo-logical reasons which are of the nature of a sort of ethical necessity hanging over everything ("it always must be so"). It is in this sense that the explanations of children point to intellectual realism and are as yet neither causal (spatial contact) nor logical (deduction), but precausal. For the child, an event leading to an event, a motive leading to an action, and an idea leading to an idea are all one and the same thing; or rather, the physical world is still confused with the intellectual or psychical world. This is a result which we shall frequently meet with in our subsequent investigations.

Three independent groups of facts seem to confirm our analysis of precausality in the child. The first is the rareness of "whys" of pure causation and of "whys" of justification or logical reason properly so-called. We showed in the last paragraph that out of 103 "whys of causal explanation" only about 13, i.e., an eighth or a seventh, could be interpreted as "whys" of causation properly so-called, or of mechanical causation. We shall show elsewhere, in § 4, that "whys of logical reason" are even rarer. Thus childish thought is ignorant both of mechanical causality and of logical justification. It must therefore hover between the two in the realm of simple motivation, whence arises the notion of precausality.

In addition to this, what was said about the notion of chance and the element of fortuitousness also favours the hypothesis of precausality. The child asks questions as if the answer were always possible, and as if chance never intervened in the course of events. The child cannot grasp the idea of the "given," and he refuses to admit that experience contains fortuitous concurrences which simply happen without being accounted for. Thus there is in the child a tendency towards justification at all costs, a spontaneous belief that everything is connected with everything else, and that everything can be explained by everything else. Such a mentality necessarily involves a use of causality which is other than mechanical, which tends to justification as much as to explanation, and thus once more gives rise to the notion of precausality.

It should be remembered, however, that this tendency to justify, though it is an essential factor in the precausal explanation, is dependent in its turn upon a wider phenomenon which we studied in the last chapter under the name of "syncretism." The incapacity for conceiving of the fortuitous as such, or of the "given" in experience is reflected in the verbal intelligence of the child. We have shown elsewhere[1] that up till the age of about 11, the child cannot keep to a formal chain of argument, i.e., to a deduction based on given premises, precisely because he does not admit the premises as given. He wants to justify them at all costs, and if he does not succeed, he refuses to pursue the argument or to take up the interlocutor's point of view. Then, whenever he does argue, instead of confining himself to the data, he connects the most heterogeneous statements, and always contrives to justify any sort of connexion. In a word, he has a tendency, both in verbal intelligence and in perceptive intelligence (and the tendency lasts longer in the former than in the latter type of mental activity), to look for a justification at any cost of what is either simply a fortuitous concurrence or a mere "datum." Now in verbal intelligence this tendency to justify at any cost is connected with the fact that the child thinks in personal, vague and unanalysed schemas (syncretism). He does not adapt himself to the details of the sentence, but retains only a general image of it which is more or less adequate. These schemas connect with one another all the more easily owing to their vague and therefore more plastic character. In this way, the syncretism of verbal thought implies a tendency to connect everything with everything else, and to justify everything. Exactly the same thing happens in perceptive intelligence. If the precausal questions of the child have a tendency to justify everything and connect everything with everything else, it is because perceptive intelligence is syncretistic, at any rate before the age of 7 or 8. In view of this, intellectual realism can be thought of as necessarily connected with syncretism by a relation of mutual dependence. Syncretism, as we have already shown, is the characteristic of confused perception which takes in objects as a whole, and jumbles them together without order.[2] The result of this is that since objects are perceived in a lump and constitute general schemas,

[1] Loc. cit., Journ. Psych., 1922, p. 249, sq. et passim.
[2] Claparède, Psychologie de l'Enfant, Geneva, 7th ed., p. 522 (1916).

instead of being diffused and discontinuous, childish realism can only be intellectual and not visual. For lack of an adequate vision of detail, and in particular of spatial and mechanical contacts, syncretistic perception is bound to make the child connect things together by thought alone. Or, conversely, it can be maintained that it is because the child's realism is intellectual and not visual, that his perception is syncretistic. Be that as it may, there is a relation of solidarity between syncretism and intellectual realism, and enough has been said to show how deeply rooted is the childish tendency to precausal explanation, and to the negation of anything fortuitous or "given."

Finally, a third group of facts compels us to adopt the hypothesis of precausality. A great number of "whys" of causal explanation seem to demand nothing but an interpretation of the statements made. When Del, for example, asks: "*Daddy says that it* [lightning] *makes itself by itself in the sky. Why?*" it looks as though we were asking: "Why does Daddy say that?" Or, when he asks why the lake does not reach as far as Bern, it may seem that Del is simply looking for the reasons which may exist for making this assertion. As a matter of fact, this is far from being the case. Del cares very little whether statements put forward are proved or not. What he wants to know is something quite different. When he asks: "*Why is it* [a pigeon] *like an eagle?*" or "*Why do I see* [on an insect] *red and green colours?*" the question, though it has the same form, can obviously not receive the same interpretation. Sully and his commentators will help us to understand cases of this kind. This author has rightly pointed out that if the questions of children frequently relate to new and unexpected subjects, it is very often because the child wants to know whether things are really as he sees them, whether the new elements can be made to fit into the old framework, whether there is a "rule."[1] But what

---

[1] See for example Bühler, *Die geistige Entwicklung des Kindes*, 2nd ed. Jena, 1921, p. 388 *et seq.*

should be especially noticed is, that this rule is not merely factual: it is accompanied by a sort of ethical necessity. The child feels about each assertion that "it must be so," even though he is unable precisely to find any definite justification for it. Thus at a certain stage of development (from 5 to 6), a boy who is beginning to understand the mechanism of a bicycle, does not concern himself with the contact of the different pieces of the machine, but declares them all to be necessary, and all equally necessary. It is as though he said to himself: "it is necessary since it is there." The feeling of necessity precedes the explanation.[1] Its meaning is just and as finalistic as it is causal, just as ethical as it is logical. As a general rule, moreover, the child confuses human necessity (moral and social, the "decus") with physical necessity. (The idea of law has long retained the traces of this complex origin). A great many of the "whys" of children, therefore, do no more than appeal to this feeling of necessity. It is probable that the answer to the last few "whys" we have quoted is not only "because it always is so" but also "because it should be, because it must be so." The connexion will now be seen between this type of explanation and precausality, which is precisely the result of a confusion between the psychical or intellectual world, or the world of ethical or logical necessity and the world of mechanical necessity.

§ 4. "WHYS OF MOTIVATION."—We have shown that among the "whys" relating to nature and manufactured articles there are several which are not really "whys" of causal explanation properly so-called, but questions connected more or less with motives, and therefore leading back to the present category. This category therefore predominates in Del's questions, numbering altogether 183/360 of the total.

Many of these questions are concerned only with the motive

---

[1] J. Piaget, "Pour l'étude des explications d'enfants" L'Educateur, Lausanne and Geneva, 1922, pp. 33–39.

of a chance action or of an indifferent phrase, and are not, therefore, particularly interesting. Here are some examples:

"Are you having lunch here?—No, I can't to-day—Why?"—"Does this caterpillar bite?—No—Then why did Anita tell me it did? Horrid of her!"—"What is your drawing supposed to be?—You want to know everything. That's greedy of you. Why do you want to know everything, teacher? Do you think I am doing silly things?"—"Why is she frightened?" etc.

It is in this category that we find the earliest "whys" of indirect interrogation: *"Do you know why I would rather you didn't come this afternoon?"*

Other "whys of motivation" relate less to purely momentary intentions than to psychological explanation properly so-called. It is in such cases as these that the term "motive" takes on its full meaning, both causal and finalistic, for to explain an action psychologically is really to consider its motive both as its cause and as its aim. We can extend this meaning of "why of motivation" to cover all questions concerning the cause of an unintentional act or psychological event. For example: *"Why do you never make a mistake?"* Between a motive and the cause of a psychological action there are numerous transitional stages. We can talk of the motive of a fear as well as of its cause, and though we may not be able to speak of the motive of an involuntary error, we can do so in the case of one that is semi-intentional. In a word, short of making them definitely separate, we shall agree to place among the "whys of motivation" all questions relating to psychological explanation, even when it is causal. Here are some examples:

"Why do you teach me to count?"—"Why does Daddy not know [what day of the month it is], *he is a grownup."—"And does my Mummy* [love the Lord Jesus]?—Yes, I think so—*Why are you not sure?" "Why shall I be able to defend you even if I don't take it*

[an iron bar]? *Because I am a boy?*"—"*Why are angels always kind to people? Is it because angels don't have to learn to read and do very nasty things? Are there people who are wicked because they are hungry?*"—"*Why can I do it quickly and well now, and before I did it quickly and badly?*"

In all these cases we can see that the cause of the actions referred to in the "why" is inextricably bound up with their aim and with the intention which has directed them. The phenomenon is the same as in the "whys" relating to nature, but in this case it is justified, since these "whys" relate to human actions. We may therefore assert that among all the questions of the child, "whys of motivation" are those which are the most correctly expressed and the least removed from our own manner of thinking.

Between these "whys" and those relating to momentary intentions there is naturally every intermediate shade of meaning. For instance: "I like men who swim that way.—*Why?*"—"*Why are you not pleased that I should have killed him?*" Thus it would appear possible to establish two sub-categories among the "whys of motivation," one relating to momentary intentions, the other to psychological states of a more lasting character. The distinction, however, is unimportant. What would be more interesting would be to bring greater precision into the relation between "whys of motivation" and "whys of justification." At times, it seems as though the explanation required by the child as an answer to his "why" were something between logical explanation (one idea bringing another idea in its wake) and psychological explanation (a motive bringing about an action). For example: "*Do you like mice best, or rats?—Why?—Because they are not so fierce and because you are weak.*" Cases like these help us to understand how "whys of logical justification," which we shall study presently, have gradually separated themselves from "whys of motivation."

To the "whys of motivation" must also be added a fairly

abundant group of "whys" (34 out of 183): we mean those which the child expresses simply in order to contradict a statement or a command which annoys him. If these questions are taken literally and seriously, they would seem to constitute "whys of motivation" properly so-called, and at times even "whys of logical justification" in the sense we have just instanced. But, as a matter of fact, we are dealing here, not with genuine questions as before, but with affirmations, or rather disguised negations, which assume the form of questions only as a matter of politeness. The proof of this is, that the child does not wait for an answer. Here are some examples: "*Anita wouldn't, so I hit her*—You should never hit a lady—*Why?* She isn't a lady . . . " etc.—"Up to here—*Why?*"—"Draw me a watch.—*Why not cannons,* etc." The child is apparently asking: "Why do you say this?" or "Why do you want this?" etc. As a matter of fact the question simply amounts to saying: "That's not true" or "I don't want to." But it goes without saying that between "whys" of contradiction and those relating to intentions there is a whole series of transitional types.

Finally, mention must be made of a class of "whys" which hover between "whys of motivation" and "whys of causal explanation," and which may be called *whys of invention.* In these the child tells stories, or personifies in play the objects which surround him, and it is in connexion with this romancing, that he asks questions which, incidentally, do not admit of any possible answer: "*Why do you do that* [rub with an india-rubber] *to the poor little table? Is it still old?*" "*Do you know why I don't kill you? It's because I don't want to hurt you.*"

§ 5. "WHYS OF JUSTIFICATION."—"Whys of justification" are interesting in many connexions. They are a sign of the child's curiosity about a whole set of customs and rules which are imposed from outside, without motive, and for which he would like to find a justification. This justification is not a causal, nor even a strictly finalistic explanation. It is more like the motivation of the last group which we described, but is to be distinguished from it by the following characteristic: what the child looks for under the rules is not so much a psychological motive as a reason which will satisfy his intelligence. If, therefore, we place the "whys" of this category in a special group, it is because they form the germ which after the age of 7 or 8 will develop into "whys of logical reason." In the case of Del we can even see this gradual formation taking place.

Del's "whys of justification" can be divided into three subgroups easily distinguishable from one another. They are "whys" relating 1° to social rules and customs, 2° to rules appertaining to lessons learnt in school (language, spelling), and 3° to definitions. Of these three, the third alone contains "whys of logical reason." The first is still closely connected to pychological motivation, the second constitutes an intermediate group.

Out of the "74 whys of justification," 14 relate to social customs. Among these, some point simply to psychological curiosity and might just as well be classed under "whys of motivation." For example: "*Why in some churches are the gowns black, and* [in] *others they are coloured?*" Others come nearer to the idea of a rule: "*Why is it forbidden* [to open letters]? *Would he* [the postman] *be sent to prison?*" etc.

This first group, as may be seen, is hardly in the right place among "whys of justification." If we have classified it in this way, it is simply because it is connected through a chain of intermediate links with the "whys" relating to scholastic rules. Here is a transitional case: "*Why not 'in'* [in Alain]," or in connexion with the spelling of "quatre": "*k?—No—Who said not, was it the grown-ups in Paris?*"—The "grown-ups" who settle the spelling of words are thus more or less on the same level as those who make police regulations and send postmen to prison.

The "whys" genuinely relating to scholastic rules (55 out of 74) are much further removed from the "whys" of psychological motivation. Here are some examples:

"*Why* [are proper names spelt with capitals]? *I want to know*"—"You must always put a 'd' at the end of 'grand'— *Why, what would happen if you didn't put any?*"—"*Why is it* ['bonsoir'] *not spelt with a 'c,' that makes coi*"—"You don't have to put a dot on a capital I.—*Why?*"—"*Why do you put full-stops here* [at the end of sentences], *and not here* [at the end of words]? *Funny!*"

It is well known that in spelling and in grammar children are more logical than we are. The large number of "whys of justification" furnishes additional proof of this. They are the exact parallel of the "whys of causal explanation" with which we have already dealt. Language, like nature, is full of freaks and accidents, and the explanation of these must be *sui generis* and must take into account the fortuitous character of all historical development. The child, devoid alike of the notion of chance and of the notion of historical development, wants to justify everything immediately, or is surprised at his inability to do so.

If we lay stress once more upon this rather trivial fact, it is because these "whys of justification," added to the already abundant "whys of causal explanation," and showing the same tendency to justify at any cost, make it all the more extraordinary that Del's questions should be so poor in "whys of logical reason." One would have thought that since Del and the children of his age are inclined to justify everything, their language would be full of deductive arguments, of the frequent use of "because" and "why" connecting one idea to another, and not a fact to an idea or a fact to a fact. But this is not in the least what happens. Out of the 74 "whys of justification," only 5 are "whys of logical justification or reason." It is needless to repeat the reason for this paradox: the child is not an intellectualist, he is an intellectual realist.

Let us rather try to analyse the nature of this logical justification, and find out how it differs from other "whys." "Whys" relating to language furnish us with several transitional cases along the path leading to the true logical "why." These are the etymological "whys": "*Why do you say 'strayed' when it means lost?*"— "*Why are there lots of words with several names, the lake of Geneva, Lake Leman*"—"*Why is it* [a park in Geneva] *called Mon Repos*"—"*Why 'black coffee,' all coffee is black?*" Just at first, it looks as though these were genuine "whys of logical justification," connecting a definition to an idea which serves as a reason for it. This is true of the last of these "whys," which we shall therefore class along with four subsequent examples under logical justification. But the others aim chiefly at the psychological intention. They are, moreover, still tainted with intellectual realism. It is well known that, for the child, the name is still closely bound up with the thing; to explain an etymology is to explain the thing itself. Del's slip, "words with several names" is significant in this connexion.[1] Therefore we cannot talk here about one idea being connected to another: the ideas are connected to the objects themselves.

The only cases, then, in which one can say that there is logical justification are cases of pure definition, and cases of demonstration, in which the mind tries to establish a proof in such a way as to render strict deductions possible.

In definition, the question falls under the following schema: "If you call all objects having such-and-such characteristics x, why do you call this object x?" Here the connexion is really between one idea and another, or, to speak more accurately, between one judgment recognized as such (an x is . . . etc.) and another (I call such-and-such an object x), and not between one thing and another. This distinction, however subtle it may

[1] A child of whom we asked: "Have words any strength?" answered that they had if they denoted things that had strength, not otherwise. We asked for an example. He mentioned the word "boxing." "Why has it got strength"—"*Oh no! I was wrong,*" he answered, "*I thought it was the word that hit!*"

appear, is of the greatest importance from the point of view of genetic psychology. Up till now, the mind has dealt solely with things and their relations, without being conscious of itself, and above all without being conscious of deducing. In logical justification, thought becomes conscious of its own independence, of its possible mistakes, and of its conventions, it no longer seeks to justify the things in themselves, but its own personal judgments about them. Such a process as this appears late in the psychological evolution of the child. The earlier chapters have led us not to expect it before the age of 7 or 8. The small number of "whys of logical justification" asked by Del confirms our previous treatment of the subject.

Similarly, in all demonstration the connexion holding between "because" and "why" relates to judgments and not to things. In the following example:—"Why does the water of the Rhone not flow upwards?" if an explanation is expected the answer must be: "Because the weight of the water drags it along in the direction of the slope." But if a demonstration is expected, the answer must be: "Because experience shows that it does" or "Because all rivers flow downwards." In the first case the connexion connects the direction of the water to the downward slope, it relates to the actual things themselves and is causal. In the second case the connexion relates to the judgments as such, and is logical. Therefore all "whys" of demonstrations are "logical whys." But demonstration rarely operates before the age of 7 or 8. The first two chapters showed us that in their arguments, children abstained from any attempt to check or demonstrate their statements.

In short, "logical whys" can by rights relate to anything, since they include all "whys" which refer to definitions or demonstrations. Here are the only questions of Del's which can be said to belong to this group (in addition to the example about the black coffee which we have just recalled):

> "*Why* [do you say 'tom cat']? *A she-cat is a mummy cat. A cat is a baby cat. ... I want to write 'a daddy cat'*"—"They are torrents—*Why not rivers?*"—"That isn't a bone, it's a bump—*Why? If I was killed, would it burst?*"—"*Is that snow?* [question of classification]—No, it is rocks—*Then why is it white?*"

The last of these "whys" is ambiguous; it is probably an elliptical form, meaning: "why do you say it is rocks, since it is white?" At the same time, it may very well be a simple "why of causal explanation." There are therefore only four authentic "whys of logical reason." They can be recognized by the fact that under the interrogative word itself the phrase "why do you assert that . . . " can be understood; and this is never so in the other categories. In a word, *"whys of logical justification" look for the reason of a judgment which is recognised as such, and not of the thing to which the judgment relates.* "Whys" of this kind are therefore very rare before the age of 7 or 8. The child, while he tries to justify everything, yet neglects to use the one legitimate justification, that of opinions and judgments as such. After the age of 7 or 8, however, these questions will probably be more frequent. We have fixed at 11–12 the age where formal thought first makes its appearance, i.e., thought relating to hypotheses which are held as such, and only seeking to ascertain whether the conclusions drawn from these hypotheses are justified or not, simply from the point of view of deduction and without any reference to reality.[1] Between the period of pure intellectual realism (up till 7 or 8) and the beginnings of formal thought there must therefore be an intermediate stage, in which children try to justify judgments as such, yet without for that matter being able to share the interlocutor's point of view nor, consequently, to handle formal deduction. The presence of "whys of logical justification" must correspond to this intermediary stage.

[1] J. Piaget, "Essai sur la multiplication logique et les débuts de la pensée formelle chez l'enfant. Journ. Psych., 1922, pp. 222–261.

In conclusion, the results of this section confirm those reached in our study of the "why of causal explanation." In the case of Del, there are no more "whys of logical reason" than there are "whys" of pure causality. Consequently, Del's mind must have interests which are intermediate between mechanical explanation and logical deduction. It is in this failure to distinguish between the causal and the logical point of view, both of which are also confused with the point of view of intention or of psychological motive, that we see the chief characteristic of childish precausality.

Finally, it may be of interest to point out a curious phenomenon which supports the hypothesis that the child often confuses notions which in our minds are perfectly distinct. The peculiarity we are speaking of is that Del occasionally takes the word "why" in the sense of "because," and thus uses the same word to express the relation of reason to consequence and that of consequence to reason.[1] Here is an example which happens precisely to be concerned with a logical "why" or "because": "Rain water is good—*Is it why* (= because) *it is a spring?*" Now, this is a phenomenon which we have already noticed in connexion with explanations between one child and another (chapter 3, § 5), and which we shall meet with again in our study of the conjunctions of causality (Vol. II). It occurs frequently in ordinary life in children from 3 to 6. We remember in particular a little Greek boy of 5 years old who learnt French very well, but systematically used the word "why" instead of the word "because" which is absent from his vocabulary: "Why does the boat stay on top of the water?"—"*Why* (= because) *it is light,*" etc. As a matter of fact this phenomenon indicates only a confusion of words. But this confusion shows how hard it is for a child to distinguish between relations which language has differentiated.

[1] This confusion of why and because is easier to understand in the case of French children. There is a certain degree of assonance between "pourquoi" and "parce que." [Translator's note.]

§ 6. CONCLUSIONS.—The complexity of Del's "whys" will now be apparent, as will also the necessity for classifying them partly according to material, since it is impossible to say straight away to which type of relation (strictly causal, finalistic or logical explanation, etc.) they refer. The frequencies obtained out of our 360 "whys" are summed up in the following table:

			Numbers (roughly)	
Whys of causal explanation (in the wide sense)	Physical objects	26		
	Plants	10		
	Animals	29		
	Human body	16		
	Natural objects	—	81	22%
	Manufactured objects		22	6%
	Total		103	29%
Whys of psychological motivation	Properly so-called	143		
	Contradiction	34		
	Invention	6		
	Total	—	183	50%
Whys of justification	Social Rules	14		
	Scholastic Rules	55		
	Rules	—	69	19%
	Logical reason or justification		5	1%
	Total		74	21%

Thus the "whys of motivation" outnumber all the others. Does this preponderance indicate that the other types of "why" radiate from this group as from a common centre? This would seem to be the case, for the "whys of causal explanation" are connected with motivation through a whole series of anthropomorphic "whys," finalistic "whys," and "whys" which reveal precausality itself. The "whys of justification," on their side, are connected with those of motivation by the series of "whys" relating to social usage and to rules conceived of as obeying psychological motives. The relations between the two groups of causal explanation and justification are not so close. The idea of precausality certainly presupposes a confusion between causal explanation and logical justification, but this confusion is only possible owing to the fact that both are, as yet, insufficiently differentiated from psychological motivation. In a word, the source of Del's "whys" does seem to be motivation, the search for an intention underlying every action and every event. From this source there would seem to arise two divergent currents, one formed of "whys" which try to interpret nature as a thing of intentions, the other formed of those which relate to customs and to the rules associated with them. Between those finalistic "whys" and the "whys" of justification interaction would naturally be possible. Finally, causality proper would emerge from the "whys" of precausality, and true logical justification from the "whys" of justification. Such, approximately, would be the genealogy of the whys asked by Del. We shall try to sum it up in a table.

Is such a systematization as this the result of an individual mentality of a particular type, or does it mark the general character of child thought before 7 or 8 years of age? The answer to this question will have to be supplied by other monographs. What we know of other lines of research leads us to believe that the schema is a very general one, but this supposition must serve for the present only as a working hypothesis.

GENETIC TABLE—DEL'S WHYS

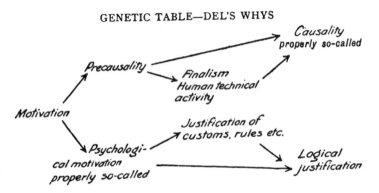

II. QUESTIONS NOT EXPRESSED UNDER THE FORM OF "WHY"

Let us now approach the whole problem presented by Del's questions. The "whys" served as an introduction, forming as they did a clearly defined, partly homogeneous group, and capable of being classified in a schema. The moment has now come to verify this schema and to complete it with any information which may be supplied by Del's other questions.

§ 7. CLASSIFICATION OF DEL'S QUESTIONS NOT EXPRESSED UNDER THE FORM "WHY."—It is even more difficult than in the previous case to classify Del's questions simply according to the material which is the object of the child's curiosity. The same object, say, a physical phenomenon, can give rise to questions too widely different from one another: "When did it happen." "How?" "Is it true that . . . " "What is it that . . . " We shall therefore have to use a mixed classification, which will partly coincide with and partly extend beyond that which we adopted in connexion with the "whys." The important thing to remember now is that for every "why" there may be a corresponding question of another form having the same meaning, but that the converse does not hold.

A first group is formed by *questions of causal explanation*, these words being used in exactly the same sense as above. Here are some examples: "[Talking of a marble which is rolling down a slope] *What is making it go?"*—*"What makes the lake run?"*—*"Do you have to have a fire to make india-rubber?"* To these will probably have to be added questions of the following form: "What is he for?" [a greyhound], given the close connexion between finalism and causal explanation in the child's mind. Some of these questions are therefore exactly analogous to "whys," others are asked from a different point of view, but always referring to explanation, either causal, precausal, or finalistic.

A second group, also very important and earlier in appearance than the former (at least as regards questions of place), is that which we shall call *questions of reality and history*. These questions do not relate to the explanation of a fact or of an event, but to its reality or to the circumstances of time and place in which it appeared, independently of their explanation. It is not: "What is the cause of *x*?" but "Did *x* happen, or will it happen?" or "When did or will *x* happen?" or again "Where did *x* happen?" etc. Such a class of questions obviously has no equivalent among "whys," since the function of these is to relate to the motive or the reason of facts and events, and never simply to their history or their existence. Here are a few examples: *"Does he* [the fish] *find food?"*—*"Are there really any* [men who cut up children]*?"*—*"How soon is Christmas?"*—*"Is Schafthausen in Switzerland?"* As will be seen, this type of question can have a great many different shades of meaning—history, time, place, existence, but the central function remains obvious. The criterion for determining whether a question belongs to this group is therefore as follows. Whenever a question relates to an object, a fact, or an event other than a person or a human action, and whenever the child asks for neither the cause, the class, nor the name of this object, the question belongs to the present category.

A third group resembles the last two in form, and probably constitutes their common source; it is the sum of questions asked about personal activities, and about persons themselves, excluding those about their names or about social or scholastic rules. These are therefore *questions relating to human actions and intentions*. At first it might seem as though one could subdivide this group into two smaller groups, one including questions about the causes of actions and corresponding to "whys" of motivation, the other including questions about the actions themselves, independently of their cause, and corresponding to the last group of questions (reality and history). But as a matter of fact these two points of view merge imperceptibly into one another, and cannot be made too rigidly separate. On the other hand, it is useful to put in a class apart everything that concerns human actions, and thus to separate the questions we are now dealing with from those discussed in the last section. Here are some examples: "*Did you want to sit here this morning?*"—Yes—"*Because it isn't fine to-day?*"—"*Will you come?*—Perhaps"—"*May I eat this pear?*"—"*Would you rather have an ugly face or a pretty face?*" It is clear that the first of these questions is exactly analogous to a "why of motivation"; the others depart from psychological explanation, and concern themselves more closely with matters of fact, without any thought of cause. Nevertheless, the group is quite homogeneous.

A fourth group is that which corresponds to certain of the "whys of justification"; these are all *questions relating to rules and usage*: "*How is it* [a name] *written?*" etc.

We can also distinguish a category of *arithmetical questions*, but its number is very small. The form which these questions take is, for example: "*How much is 9 and 9?*"

Finally, there is a whole group of *questions of classification and valuation*, relating to the names of objects, to their value, to the classes to which they belong, and to comparisons between them. We have placed in this group questions implying judgments of value (evaluation), for between the class referred to, in "Is it big?" and the value in "Is it pretty?" we can find a whole series of intermediate cases. Here are examples: "*Is that a bee?*"—"*Is that mountains?*"—"*What are those balls with 1* [quavers]?"—"*What is a cup?*"—"*That's pretty, isn't it?*" etc. This group of questions raises certain borderland problems. It is occasionally hard to decide whether a question should be classed in this group or among the questions of reality or history, in spite of the fact that in principle the criteria are quite definite. There are, moreover, many transitional cases between rules about names and classification, so that the distinction between this group and the preceding one is sometimes a very delicate matter.

In the main, however, these groups correspond to certain fundamental functions of the mind, which are distinct from one another, and for which when we come to examine them in greater detail, we shall find it quite possible to establish reliable criteria.

§ 8. QUESTIONS OF CAUSAL EXPLANATION.—Let us try to verify by means of these questions the results obtained from the corresponding "whys"—such as artificialism and finalism of questions relating to natural objects, absence of any purely causal relations, etc.

We give from among the questions asked about physical objects, those which seem to us the least ambiguous:

[Del sees a marble rolling down a sloping piece of ground]. "*What is making it go?*"—It is because the ground is not flat, it is sloping and goes down—[a moment later] "*It* [the marble rolling in the direction of Mlle V.] *knows that you are down there?*"—[A few seconds later]: "*It is on a slope, isn't it?*" (This question ought to be placed among questions of reality, were it not for its obviously causal significance).

"*What makes the Rhone go so fast?*"—"*But what makes the lake run?*"—[A few months later] "*It's funny, the ground* [here] *is quite flat, how can it* [the water] *go down?*"

"*How do you make one* [a river source]"—"*Do you also have to have a spade to make a source?*"—"*But how is the rain made up in the sky? Are there pipes, or running torrents?*"—"[after the explanation] *Then it comes unstuck? Then when it falls, it is rain?*"—"*After that it* [the river] *becomes a glacier?*"—"*But it* [the glacier] *melts, all of a sudden you don't see it any more?*"—"*Then clouds often drop down* [on to the mountains]?"

"[Talking about a magnet] *I would like to know how it happens?*"—"*Look, it attracts it* [a key]. *What makes it move forward?*"

> *"But what does the snow do when we go tobagganing? Instead of melting, it stays nice and flat?"*

Thus the only questions of a truly causal nature are those relating to phenomena for which a mechanistic explanation has already been given to Del (function of the slope, etc.). Now Del had put quite a different interpretation upon these phenomena, as is shown by his questions before the explanation. The last two questions can indeed be regarded as instances of mechanical causality, but with the following reservations. In the first place, the verbal form "to do" (what does the snow do) should be noticed. Psychologists have often been struck by it, M. Bühler, for instance, rightly concluding from the frequent occurrence of the verb *machen* that the child attributes anthropomorphic activity to ordinary objects.[1] But this may be a mere aftermath of earlier stages, since verbal forms always evolve more slowly than actual understanding. What is more singular is that in both cases (questions about the magnet and about the snow) the child seems to be looking for the explanation in some internal force residing in the object, and not in any mechanical contact. Del may say that the magnet attracts the key, this does not really satisfy him. Similarly, there is surely a latent idea of force in the fact that the snow does not melt. If these questions are causal, it is obvious that the causality they invoke is more dynamic than mechanical.

This dynamism is strikingly expressed in the question about the marble: "Does it know that you are down there?" The minimum hypothesis, so to speak, is that we have here a question of romancing: Del personifies the marble in play, just as, in his games, he will lend life to a stone or a piece of wood. But to say "romancing" takes us nowhere. We may well ask, in a problem of this kind, whether the child could do anything but invent. This

---

[1] K. Bühler, *Die geistige Entwicklung des Kindes*, Jena. 1921, 2nd ed. p. 387.

leads us to the maximum hypothesis: Does not Del attribute to the marble a force analogous to that of a living being? A very curious question about dead leaves will presently show us that for Del, life and spontaneous movement are still one and the same thing.[1] There is therefore nothing surprising in the fact that the same question should arise in connexion with a marble, the "why" of whose movements is not yet understood by Del. Even if Del is romancing about the marble itself, the fact that he should ask the question in this form and with apparent serious-ness is an index of the child's lack of interest in mechanical causality and of his inability to be satisfied by it. A case like this takes us to the very root of precausal explanation. The child confuses moving cause and motive because for him, phenomena are animated with real life or with a dynamic character derived from life.

Other questions endow men or gods with the power of making river sources, rain, etc., by means of purely human contrivances. Whether this "artificialism" as M. Brunschwicg has called it, is earlier than the last-mentioned type of causality or is derived from it is a question which we do not wish to settle here, and one which, incidentally, is outside the range of our subject. We will content ourselves with pointing out that Del does not generally try to find out exactly who is the manu-facturer of such-and-such a phenomenon (with the exception of river sources and the Rhone). Most of the corresponding whys should therefore be interpreted as simply looking for an intention in phenomena, without this intention being attributed to a given being. Which brings us once again to precausal explanation and the confusion of motive and mechan-ical cause. From this point of view, it is possible to suppose that animism preceded artificialism, both in the child and in the race.

[1] A recent enquiry, of which we are not yet able to publish the results, shows that Geneva boys up to the age of 7–8 look upon stars, fire, wind, and eventu-ally water, etc., as alive and conscious, because they move by themselves.

In short, these questions about physical objects, of which only a very few admit of a genuinely causal interpretation, confirm and define our hypothesis of precausality by linking it up with the well-known phenomenon of animism among very young children. It may be thought that we are dealing too summarily with these various types of childish explanations and their affiliations, and that they require to be more searchingly analysed, and compared with materials from other sources. But our aim, be it said once more, is not the analysis of causality, but the study of child logic, and from that point of view it is sufficient for our purposes to know that logical implication and physical causation are as yet undifferentiated, and that this identification constitutes the notion of precausality.

The childish conception according to which moving objects are endowed with an activity of their own gives a special importance to Del's questions about life and death. The reader will remember the result of our study of "whys" relating to animals and plants. It was that since chance does not exist for the child, and all phenomena appear to be regulated by order and "decus," life is a perfectly normal phenomenon, without any elements of surprise in it, up till the moment when the child takes cognizance of the difference between life and death. From this moment, the idea of death sets the child's curiosity in action, precisely because, if every cause is coupled with a motive, then death calls for a special explanation. The child will therefore look for the distinguishing criteria of life and of death, and this will lead him in a certain measure to replace precausal explanation and even at moments the search for motives by a conscious realization of the accidental element in the world.

"*Are they dead* [those leaves]?—Yes—*But they move with the wind*"—"*Is it* [a leaf which Del has just cut off] *still alive now? . . .*" [He puts it back on the branch] "*Is it alive now?*"—"*If it is put in water?*—It will last longer—*Another day, and then?*—It will dry up—*Will it die?*—Yes—*Poor little leaf!*—*If it* [a leaf] *was planted in blood, would it die* [too]?"

"*Was that* [a tree] *planted, or did it grow by itself?*"—"*What makes the flowers grow in summer?*" "*Daddy told me that wystaria grows two seasons, spring and summer. Then does it grow twice?*"

The first of these questions shows us the confusion between movement and life. This confusion is of very great importance in understanding the precausal mind. It enables us to see how, for the child, every activity is comparable to that of life. Henceforth, to appeal to a motive cause is at the same time to appeal to a living cause, i.e., to one mentally based on a model endowed with spontaneity if not with intentions. We can now understand how a return shock will give rise to curiosity about death, since the fact of death is an obstacle to these habits of thought; and to curiosity about the causes of life (later questions quoted above) since the course of life can be disturbed by death.

Questions about animals point to the same preoccupations, likewise those about their powers and intentions.

"*If you kill him* [a pigeon] *at this little corner of his wing, will he die?*"—"*Does it* [a caterpillar] *know it has got to die if it becomes a butterfly?*" (*cf.* "*Doesn't it* [id.] *know it has to die very soon?*"), etc.

"[Reindeers draw sledges] *Are they persons, so that they can hear what people say to them?*"—"[A moment later]: *How are horses driven?*"—"*What is a greyhound for?*" etc.

The human body gives rise to analogous questions[1]:

---

[1] Cf. "*Is he dead*" (a Geneva statue: Cartaret)—Yes—"*Shall I be dead too?*" etc.

> *"Do you die* [of eating a chestnut]*?"—"If you breathe poison,*
> *do you die?"* etc.—*"Who makes those little spots, how* [freckles on
> the arms]*?"*

We need press the point no further. All these questions show that the order of causality imagined by the child is hardly mechanical at all, but anthropomorphic or finalistic.

Finally, we should mention here a group of questions about manufactured objects which is analogous to the corresponding group of "whys."

> *"What are rails for?"—"Is that machine there* [which is sifting
> sand] *not of any use to that one* [a crane]*?"—"If I have a boat and*
> *it is dipped in water and put in the sun, it will stick again won't*
> *it?"—"If you fire a cannon on to a fire-work . . . the shell will go on*
> *to the fire and it will burst, won't it?"*

In conclusion, this section may be said to verify the hypothesis advanced in connexion with "whys of causal explanation," in particular as concerns the rareness of strictly causal questions.

§ 9. QUESTIONS OF REALITY AND HISTORY.—Questions of this category are, by definition, those which relate to facts and events, without relating to their cause or to their causal structure. This criterion is not an easy one to apply, and this group of questions merges into the last by a whole series of intermediate stages. There is nothing in this that need surprise us, since the very notion of reality comes into being thanks only to the relations of causality which the mind weaves between the facts of experience. Still, as we are in need of reliable classifications about which every one can agree, we shall have to adopt a criterion—arbitrary, we admit, but definite.

When the question which has been asked calls for a causal answer, i.e., one beginning with the causal "because," or consisting of the phrase: "It was by God" or "by man," then this question is undoubtedly causal. But we have tacked on to this group such questions as: "If you breathe poison do you die?" or "Does the marble know you are down there?" which seem to be questions of fact. In such cases, the criterion is more subtle. These questions certainly do touch on causality, since they amount to asking whether poison does or does not cause one to die, whether the marble rolls in a certain direction because it is conscious, or for any other reason, etc. Whereas a question of pure fact like this one: "Are there also little fishes round the edge?" does not involve any search for the causal relation, nor any use of it. We shall therefore adopt the following convention for lack of a better one. When the relation between the terms referred to in the question implies a movement, an activity, or an intention, the question is causal; when the relation is purely static (existence, description, or place) or simply temporal, the question is not causal.

It is only by applying them, that we shall find out whether these arbitrary distinctions are of any use. If, for example, by applying them to several children of different ages, one discovers a law of development, or finds a means of distinguishing between different types of inquisitive children, then the schema will be worth preserving. Otherwise, it will share the fate of the classifications of the grammarians and old logicians. For the problems which occupy us here, problems of general and not of individual psychology, the schema is of no importance whatsoever.

Questions of reality and history should, moreover, be divided into various categories of which the first alone is in any way likely to be confused with questions of causal explanation. We mean the questions about facts or events.

> "*Is it* [this pool] *very deep?*"—"*I can see myself in your eyes, can you?*"—"*Are there also little fishes round the edge?*"—"*Do they* [rockets] *go up as high as the sky?*" (This question can also be

classed as about place)—"[Are the clouds] *much, much higher than our roof?—yes—I can't believe it!*" (id.): "*What is in there* [in a box]?"—"*Are there whales* [in the lake]?" [Looking at a geographical map with the lake Zoug which he takes for a hole]: "*Are there holes?*"—"*Are its* [a snail's] *horns outside?*"—"*Are there blue and green flies?*" etc.

This first group merges by a series of intermediate stages into a second category which relates more especially to place:

"*Where do the big boats land?*"—"*Where is German Switzerland?*"—"*Where is the Saint Bernard*"—"*Then Zermatt is not in Switzerland?*" etc.

A third category consists of questions about time:

"*How long is it till Christmas?*"—"*Will my birthday be on Monday? I think it is Monday. Is it really?*—I don't know—*I thought grown-up people could think about these things*" [Note that the idea of "thinking about a thing" is confused with that of "knowing," a mistake frequently made by children].

A fourth group is made up of questions of modality, i.e., of those relating, not to facts and events, but to their degree of reality. Between this group and the others, there are naturally many intervening shades of stages, but it is interesting, all the same, to consider it by itself.

"*Are there really any?* [men who cut up little children]?"—"*Is it true* [that it is poison]?"—"*Isn't that a story?*" etc. Along with these questions of modality, mention may be made of the following statement uttered by Del, which is none the less suggestive for having undoubtedly been prompted by the tendency to romance: "*Jean* [a friend] *does not exist, because I don't like him!*"

Finally comes the whole group of questions of imagination or invention relating to facts and events which Del knows to be untrue.

> "*Is the little girl burnt up, now?*"—"*That Mr J.* [the capital letter J] *has eaten a lot, hasn't he?*"—"*Are the waves on the lake unkind?*" [Is this romancing, or does Del mean "are they dangerous?"]

These are the five categories into which it is possible to divide Del's questions of reality and history. As such, these questions tell us little that we do not already know. Their chief value is that they partly enable us to enquire into the nature of childish assumptions. Meinong, it will be remembered, described as assumptions those propositions about which the subject reasons, although he does not believe them. He showed that assumption originated in the "if" of childish games, in the affirmation which the child chooses to take as the basis of imaginary deductions.

Now these assumptions give rise to a very serious problem: what is the degree of reality which the child attributes to them? The adult has, amongst others, two kinds of assumptions at his disposal—physical and logical. Physical assumption is that which assumes a fact as such, and deduces from it a relation between one fact and another. "If the sun were to disappear, we should not see any more," for instance, means that between one given fact (disappearance of the sun) and another fact (night) there is a relation of causality. Logical assumption, on the other hand, simply assumes a judgment as such, and deduces another judgment from it: "If all winged vertebrates are to be called birds, then the bat is a bird." Here the relation is no longer between two facts but between two judgments.

Now, of all the assumptions made by Del, not one is logical. We have already given instances of assumptions in questions of causal explanation ("*If you breathe in poison, do you die?*") Others refer to psychological motivation ("*Would your mother be sorry if they rang her up and told her you were dead?*—Yes, she would come and fetch you. . . . etc.—*And if I had gone away?*—She would tell the police—*And if the police did not find me?*—They would find you—*But if they didn't . . .* etc.") Others refer to social usages ("*Do the policemen forbid it* [tobogganing in the streets]?—Yes.—*If I were a judge could I do it?*") For the most part they are questions of reality and history, in which the child alters reality at will, to see what would happen in such-and-such conditions. They are "experiments just to see," the work of imagination such as Baldwin describes it, whose function it is to loosen the spirit from the bonds of reality, leaving it free to build up its ideas into a world of their own. For example:

> "*If I was an angel, and had wings, and was flying in the fir-tree, would I see the squirrels or would they run away?*"
>
> "*If there was a tree in the middle of the lake, what would it do?*"—But there isn't one.—"*I know there isn't, but if there was . . .* (id)."
>
> "*But then supposing it* [the round of the seasons] *stopped one day?*"
>
> "*If I was to put a dragon and a bear together which would win?*— . . . *And if I put a baby dragon?*"

All these assumptions, it will be seen, are physical; they are, in the words of Mach and Rignano, "mental experiments." This therefore confirms our hypotheses that before the age of 7–8 children do not care to deal with logical relations. But it does more than this. Childish assumptions point to a confusion between the logical and the real order of things, just as precausality confuses logical implication and causal explanation. In other words, the child, thanks to the notion of precausality, conceives the world as more logical than it really is. This makes him believe it possible to connect everything and to foresee everything, and the assumptions which he makes are endowed in his eyes with a richness in possible deductions which our adult logic could never allow them to possess.

Indeed, the outstanding characteristic of children's assumptions is that for us they contain no definite conclusion, such as they should contain for the children themselves. We do not know what would happen "if I were an angel," or "if I was to put a dragon and a bear together." Del would like to know. He thinks it possible to reason where we deem it impossible, for lack of data. Since everything in nature seems to him constructed, intentional, and coherent, what more natural than that there should be an answer to every "if"? The structure of childish assumptions therefore is probably analogous to that of precausality—confusion of the causal or physical order (the real) with the logical or human order (motivation).

The real, as we have seen, can in the last resort be deformed at will by Del ("*Jean does not exist because I don't like him*"). Thus childish assumptions deal with a reality which is far more fluctuating than ours, one which is perpetually shifting its level from the plane of observation to that of play, and vice versa. In this respect, reality is for the child both more arbitrary and better regulated than for us. It is more arbitrary, because nothing is impossible, and nothing obeys causal laws. But whatever may happen, it can always be accounted for, for behind the most fantastic events which he believes in, the child will always discover motives which are sufficient to justify them; just as the world of the primitive races is peopled with a wealth of arbitrary intentions, but is devoid of chance.

The result of this is that the idea of the possible is far less precise in the child than in the adult. For the adult, the possible is from one point of view simply a degree of reality (physical possibility), and from another point of view, the sum of all logical assumptions (hypotheses forming the basis of logical deduction).

Thus the adult will be able to make an indefinite number of deductions in the realm of the possible, or of hypothesis, so long as he is able to conform to the rules of logical deduction. But any illusion he may have of building up reality in this way will disappear the moment he remembers that the world of hypotheses is subject to the world of observation. The child, on the other hand, never makes logical assumptions, so that for him the possible, or the world of hypotheses is not one that is inferior to the real world, not a mere degree of being, but a special world of its own, analogous to the world of play. Just as the real is crammed with motives and intentions, the possible is the world where those intentions are laid bare, the world where one can play with them unhindered and unchecked. Hence those chains of suppositions which we saw above: "If . . . yes, but if . . . yes, but if . . . " etc.

The possible is therefore not a lower degree of being, it is a world apart, as real as the other, and an assumption does not differ from a simple induction made about the real world.

For the rest—and this is the last point to be borne in mind—Del's deduction, like that of all children of his age, is not pure (formal deduction), but is still deeply tinged with intellectual realism. What constitutes the validity of adult deductions based on assumptions (and this applies to all demonstration) is that deduction confines itself to connecting judgments to judgments. In order to demonstrate the judgment already quoted. "If the sun disappeared we should not see any more," one must perforce resort to logical assumptions and deductions of this kind: If (you allow that) daylight is not due to the sun, then (you will have to admit that) there must be daylight after sunset, because . . . etc." Del, on the other hand, never attempts to demonstrate. He never makes logical assumptions to see where they would lead; he reasons directly on the imaginary model which he has made, and which he regards as real.

In conclusion, these questions about reality corroborate what we learnt from the questions of causal explanation. The child shows signs of a perpetual intellectual realism: he is too much of a realist to be a logician, and too much of an intellectualist to be a pure observer. The physical world and the world of ideas still constitute for him an undifferentiated complex; causality and motivation are still thought of as one and the same. Adults too, with the exception of metaphysicians and naïve realists, regard the connexion of events and that of ideas as one, in the sense that logic and reality constitute two series inextricably bound up with each other. But the adult is sufficiently detached from his ego and from his ideas to be an objective observer, and sufficiently detached from external things to be able to reason about assumptions or hypotheses held as such. This brings about a twofold liberation and a twofold adaptation of the mind. The child's ideas, on the other hand, hinder his observations, and his observations hinder his ideas, whence his equal and correlative ignorance of both reality and logic.

§ 10. QUESTIONS ABOUT HUMAN ACTIONS AND QUESTIONS ABOUT RULES.—Like the corresponding "whys," questions about human actions relate sometimes to psychological explanation properly so-called, sometimes to purely momentary actions. Here are some examples.

"Who do you love best, me or mummy?—You—You shouldn't say that. It's a little bit naughty"—"Does every one love Jesus—Yes—Do you?—Yes—If he was unkind, would he punish us?"—"Would you be a little bit funky [climbing up a tree]?" etc.

And the whole set of questions of the form: "What do you think I am going to do, jump [or not jump]?"—"Then do grown-up people make mistakes also? I thought grown-up people could think about these things?" (already quoted in connexion with a question about time), etc.

The only thing about these questions which is of interest for our subject is the omniscience which the child ascribes to adults. This circumstance is not without influence in forming the child's anthropomorphic view of nature. If the adult knows everything, foresees everything, can answer everything if he only chooses to, it must be because everything is harmoniously ordained, and because everything can be justified. The child's increasing scepticism towards adult thought is of the greatest importance in this connexion, for this it is which will give rise to the idea of the given as such, of chance. Questions such as we have given should therefore be very carefully studied if we wish to be aware of the moment when scepticism is first acquired by the child. At the period when the questions were asked, faith in the adult was still considerable. At the end of the year during which we studied Del (7; 2) this faith had ceased to exist: "*Then Daddy can't know everything either, nor me neither?*"

As to questions about usages and rules, they are continuous with those we have already discussed. It is worth while, however, treating them separately; in the first place, because they correspond to a parallel group of "whys," and secondly, because they in turn merge into the questions of classification proper, which constitute a very important group. In spite of this, however, the necessity for making a separate class of "questions about rules" may be questioned.

These questions therefore begin by being simply psychological, but relating to social usages: "*It is always ladies who begin at games and parties, isn't it?*" etc. But immediately there is a transition to school rules: "*Who said not [to spell 'quatre' with a k] Was it the grown-ups in Paris?*"

Then comes a set of questions about rules as such: "*How do you spell [a name]?*"—"*Should there be an acute accent?*"—"*Is that right?*" etc. These questions show no new features, and we have already pointed out their affiliation with the corresponding "whys."

§ 11. QUESTIONS OF CLASSIFICATION AND CALCULATION.—How does the transition occur from the interest taken in rules, in "one does," or "one must" to the logical interest, or search for a reason which will cause a judgment to be adopted or rejected? We have seen that Del's earliest "whys" were connected with definition, and therefore seemed to arise out of "whys about rules" relating to language. The following questions will confirm this affiliation.

There is a category half-way between questions about rules and questions about classification, which is probably the root from which both have sprung. We mean the collection of questions about names. Sometimes it is simply the search for the meaning of an unknown word, sometimes it is an etymological analysis:

> "What does year-end mean?"—"What does hob-nobbing mean?"—"Who is Rodolphe?"—"What are rivers called that run between mountains?"—"Pric [He is reading], yes does it prick?"—"What does 'mar' [the first half of the word 'Mardi'] mean?"

There is a definite progression from these questions about names to questions of classification. Questions of classification are those which in face of a new object no longer ask "what is it called?" but "what is it." They also look for the definition of an already familiar object.

> "What is that, a pond?"—"What is that, a cockchafer?"
> "What is a cup"—" . . . a table-cloth?"—" . . . a home," etc.
> (the name as such being already known).

It is easy, therefore, to establish the genealogy of these questions. As Sully and Compayré have said, children believe that every object has received a primordial and absolute name, which is somehow part of its being.[1] When very young children ask about an unknown object "what is it?", it is the name of the object they are enquiring for, and this name plays the part not only of a symbol, but of a definition and even of an explanation. Among the questions of rule and classification it is therefore the question of name which comes first in point of time. But since this question of name is both normative and classificatory, it is easy to understand how it can give birth to questions so different from one another as those of rules, of classification, and finally of logical reason. One can, indeed, conceive of all the successive stages, passing from nominal realism to intellectual realism, and from intellectual realism to logical justification.

Finally, we must add to classification questions of evaluation (judgments of value): "Is it pretty?"—"Isn't that fair?"—"Isn't that right?" etc.

Questions of calculation, on the other hand, must be put in a class apart. In Del's case their number is very small owing to the age of the child and the individual type to which he belongs: "My daddy told me that 1,000 was 10 times 100?—Yes—And to make 10,000?—10 times 1,000—And to make 100,000?"

III. CONCLUSIONS

We must now bring forward some of the general results obtained from Del's questions from the statistical point of view, from the point of view of age, and from the point of view of the psychology of child thought in general.

§ 12. STATISTICAL RESULTS.—For the purpose of comparing Del's questions with each other from the point of view of constancy and age, we divided them up into three lots of 250 successive questions, including, of course, all the "whys." These are

[1] M. Rougier has suggested calling this phenomenon "nominal realism" in the theory of knowledge.

questions 201 to 405 (September to November 3, 1921), 481 to 730 (March 3 to March 24, 1992), and 744 to 993 (June 3 to June 23, 1922). In this way we obtained the following table:—

	I.	II.	III.
I. *Questions of causal explanation*—			
Physics	13	16	8
Plants	6	3	3
Animals	14	5	17
Human body	8	3	3
Natural phenomena	(41)	(27)	(31)
Manufacture	14	5	17
Total	(55)	(32)	(48)
II. *Questions of reality and history*—			
Facts and events	24	19	50
Place	2	8	9
Time	1	10	7
Modality	3	1	1
Invented history	26	8	1
Total	(56)	(46)	(68)
Total of explanation and of reality	(111)	(78)	(116)
III. *Questions on actions and intentions*	(68)	(97)	(71)
IV. *Questions on rules*—			
Social rules	6	3	0
School rules	17	9	14
Total	(23)	(12)	(14)
Total of actions and rules	(91)	(109)	(85)
V. *Questions of classification*—			
Name	18	3	19
Logical reason	2	1	3
Classification	25	52	23
Total	(45)	(56)	(45)
VI. *Questions of calculation*	3	7	4
Total of calculation and classification	48	63	49
	250	250	250

Here are the results obtained with the same three series from the verbal point of view:

Simple Questions	Why?	How?	Is?	What is?	Who is?	Who?	Where?	When?	How many?
I.	95	91	7	28	27	...	...	...	3	...
II.	122	53	13	18	21	5	4	7	3	6
III.	143	41	18	21	29	...	1	...	...	4
	360	185	28	67	77	5	5	7	6	10

These tables extend over a period of ten months, each series being separated from the succeeding one by an interval of two months. They enable us to form a certain number of conclusions.

To begin with, there is the relative constancy shown by the three big groups—first by the questions of explanation and reality (111, 78, 116), then by the questions relating to human actions and rules (91, 109, 85), and thirdly by the questions of classification and calculation (48, 63, 49). This constancy is rather interesting if it proves to be verifiable in subsequent research. The development undergone by the questions follows perhaps a law analogous to that which governs the development of language. It is a well-known fact that while a subject's vocabulary will grow considerably richer with increasing age, the proportions of its various categories of words to each other, are always subject to fairly rigid laws. And the constancy of our big groups of questions over the space of ten months remains pretty much the same, in spite of very definite fluctuations within each group.

The fluctuation which first attracts our attention is the diminution of "whys" and the corresponding increase of questions without any interrogative expression: 91, 53 and 41; and 95, 122 and 143. This must, of course, be considered in relation to the diminution of questions of causal explanation in comparison with the questions of reality and history, which tend to increase in number. Finally—and this seems to contradict the last two facts—"whys," although they are diminishing relatively to the number of questions (which does not mean that they are diminishing absolutely), take on a more and more causal character in the widest sense of the term. To make quite sure of this, we cut out from questions 200 to 1,125 three sections, each consisting of 60 successive "whys," at a period when the questions were all being taken down. Here is the result:

	I	II	III
Whys of causal explanation	15	21	30
Whys of motivation	28	27	25
Whys of justification	17	12	5

These figures may of course be the result of changes in Del's particular interests, and they may be peculiar to the year during which they were collected. We therefore do not wish to establish general laws on such a slender foundation. It may, nevertheless, be interesting to see whether those three kinds of fluctuations are independent of one another, or whether there is not a certain solidarity between them. If the problem be stated in this way, it will admit of a more generalized treatment, even with the special data collected from Del.

Thus, on the one hand, the relative frequency of "whys" diminishes; on the other hand, there is an increase of questions of reality and history in comparison to those of explanation; finally, the sense of the "whys" becomes increasingly causal. These movements seem to us to be closely connected with one another. It is true that statistics can be made to prove anything, but in this case statistical induction corresponds with the results of qualitative analysis and clinical examination.

For one thing, if the frequency of "whys" diminishes in proportion to the bulk of the questions, this is because between the years of 3 and 7 "why" is really a question which is used for every purpose, which demands a reason for everything indiscriminately, even when there is no reason present except through a confusion of the psychological and the physical order of things. It is therefore quite natural that when these two orders come to be differentiated, and when the idea of chance or of "the given" first makes its appearance, a large number of questions should break away from the "why" form. They will then take on the form of "how" or of simple questions without any interrogative words in them, and will concern themselves as much with the consequences and inner mechanism of phenomena as with their "reason." The decrease of "whys" would thus be an index of a weakening of precausality. This weakening, it seems to us, can also be seen in the increase of simple questions in so far as these show signs, as compared to "whys," of a desire for supplementary information.

Furthermore, the increase of "whys" of causal explanation in comparison with other "whys" is probably due to the same reason. It is because precausality, or rather the tendency to justify everything, is on the decline that Del's curiosity is less eager in seeking a justification for rules in which no such motivation is involved. It is because "whys" have become specialized that the "why" of explanation predominates. This, incidentally, does not mean that the "whys of logical justification" are condemned to grow less, for these only make their appearance after the age of 7 or 8, and they do so in connexion with any kind of demonstration. In order to prove these assertions one would, of course, have to separate the "whys" of precausality from those of causality proper, and then take the percentages. But since it would be impossible to carry this out without making very arbitrary judgments, we must needs content ourselves with suppositions. The diminution of "whys" concerning the justification of rules, moreover, is certainly an index in favour of the hypothesis that Del is losing his desire to justify things at any price, and that, consequently, precausality is giving way to a wish for a more strictly causal explanation of phenomena.

From this point of view we are also enabled to understand why questions of reality and history increase in comparison to questions of explanation, always assuming that this increase is not due to the arbitrary character of the classification. If questions about facts and circumstances are multiplied, it is because the child gives up the attempt to account for phenomena which are simply given, and tries to gain a more detailed knowledge of the historical circumstances in which they appeared, of their conditions, and of their consequences.

These results recall very clearly those obtained by M. Groos in the fine work he has done on provoked questions. By presenting children with any proposition whatsoever, and then noting down the question which it calls forth, M. Groos has shown that whatever the age of the subject, from 12 to 17, questions of causality taken in the widest sense of the term constitute a more or less constant percentage (40%). But these causal questions can be divided into regressive (cause), and progressive (consequence). Now progressive questions increase quite regularly with age. This result has been roughly confirmed by the experiments carried out at the Institut Rousseau on children under 12 (and above 9).[1] Therefore, the transformation of causal questions into questions relating to consequences does not prove that the general interest in causality has in any way weakened; it merely indicates that this interest is no longer confined to the "why" pure and simple, but now attaches itself to the details of the mechanism itself.

With regard to Del, our statistics enable us to conclude that he has gradually lost his interest in precausality. The hypothesis can therefore be put forward that the decline of precausality takes place between the ages of 7 and 8. Now our earlier chapters have already shown the importance of this age from the point of view of the decline of ego-centrism, from the point of view of the

---

[1] Intermédiaire des Educateurs, 2nd year, 1913–14, p. 132 et seq.

understanding between children, and above all from the point of view of the mental habits involved in genuine argument and collaboration in abstract thought. This synchronizing is probably an index of important correlations. Before attempting to establish these, let us first see whether we cannot verify the statement that, as Del approaches the age of 7 or 8, precausality tends to give place to true causality.

§ 13. THE DECLINE OF PRECAUSALITY.—There is a very simple method of measuring Del's evolution in connexion with precausality; that is, after a little time, to ask him his own questions, or at least those whose form clearly bring out their precausal character. We chose 50 questions of causal explanation, etc., for this purpose, and submitted them to Del himself when he was 7 years and 8 months, telling him they were the questions of a little boy of his age. Now the first point to note is that Del had not the slightest idea that they were his own questions. (It will be remembered that he never noticed that all his questions were taken down). Not only that, but he actually interspersed his answers with remarks like these: "It's silly to ask that when it's so easy. It's silly. It doesn't go together. It's so [silly] that I don't understand a word of it." But this in itself is not conclusive. A child's thought at 6 or 7 is still so undirected, so unsystematized, in other words, it is still so subconscious in the Freudian sense of the word, that the fact of his forgetting questions asked by him a few months ago and of his being incapable of answering them does not prove much in the way of any change of mentality. On the other hand, there is a very definite hiatus between the type of answer and the actual form of the question, a hiatus at times so strange that we felt it incumbent upon us to make sure that the questions which were asked really had a precausal significance. We therefore tested them by submitting them to ten children of 7 years old. Some of them answered us in the definitely precausal manner which the Del of 6 to 7 expected when he asked the questions. Others answered us like the Del of

7; 2, thus showing that they too had got beyond the precausal stage.[1]

Here are some of Del's answers:

"Why is there a Little Salève and a Great Salève?—*Because there are two. There were two mountains stuck close together, so people said that one was to be the great Salève, and the other the little Salève.*"

"Why are they [negroes] made to be like that?—*It is the sun, because in the negroes' country it is very hot, much hotter than here.*"

"What makes it go [the marble]?—*It's because it is going down-hill*—Does it know you are down there?—*No, but it goes down to where you are.*"

"What makes the Rhone go so fast?—*Why! because it goes down-hill a little.*"

"A little boy wrote his name on some wood. The next day the name had gone. He asked: 'Why do wood and iron rub out pencil marks?'—*Because you put your hands on it and rub, and then it goes away. Is that right? He made a mistake, because if you make pencil marks on paper and take some wood and iron and rub, it doesn't go away.*" Del has obviously not understood his own question.

"The lake does not go as far as Bern, why?—*Because Bern is far away and the lake is quite small. But the lake of Geneva is big, but it doesn't go as far as Bern. If it was the sea, it might, but it is not that country, that is not what it is called.*"

---

[1] It may be objected that Del has passed from the precausal stage to a more advanced mental state because he has remembered the answers given by the adult to the questions which he used to ask. This goes without saying, but it is no explanation. The problem still remains to be solved, why the child has accepted these answers and above all why he has assimilated them without distorting them. It is of this capacity for assimilating causal or natural explanations that we speak when we say that Del has entered upon a new stage of development.

"What makes the lake run?—*The Rhone.*"

"Was it [a tree] planted or did it grow by itself?—*It was planted. A few flowers can grow by themselves.*"

"When I put red and orange together, it makes brown, why?—*I don't know. My daddy couldn't know everything, so neither can I.*" Here we see the signs of scepticism in Del. He would not have answered in this way at six-and-a-half.

"If they are not dangerous, why do they have those things (poisonous fangs)?—*Because they live as we do. We have nails and they aren't of any use.*"

Reading those answers, we begin to doubt whether such a thing as precausality exists. It looks as though Del had never had any but the most positive explanations in mind, and as though any appearance to the contrary were due simply to the clumsiness of his style. But if this were the case he would never have asked one of these questions. The explanation given by Del of the fact that adders are not dangerous is significant in this connexion. It amounts to saying that the question should not be put, or is badly put. The same applies to the answer about the size of the lake, and, in a certain measure, to the answer about the two Salèves, while the refusal to explain why red and orange make brown is highly characteristic. In short, in all these cases, if Del had expected the same answer as he gives himself at 7; 2 he would not have asked the question. With regard to the questions about the negroes and the swiftness of the Rhone, it is obvious that the very positive answers given by Del at 7; 2 must not deceive us as to the anthropomorphic and artificialistic character of the questions when he was 6, otherwise the verbal form employed would be incomprehensible. We shall presently have occasion to verify these statements when we come to examine the way in which other children answered the same questions.

There is, therefore, a complete discord between the questions asked by Del and the manner in which he answers them a few months later, and this seems to indicate that the child has partly given up the use of precausal explanations. The questions were originally put as though a precausal explanation were possible, as though everything in nature could be accounted for, as though everything were animated by intentions, so that the looked-for cause of phenomena could be identified with a psychological motive or a moral reason. The answer given at 7; 2 shows, on the contrary, that in his mind the distinction is being formed between strictly causal explanation, psychological motivation, and logical justification. Not only does he give up the attempt to account for everything, but the answers which he gives are sometimes causal explanations properly so-called, sometimes logical justifications. For instance he explains the current of the Rhone by the slope, the colour of the negroes by the sun (causal explanation). The answers to the question about the two Salèves and to that about the size of the lake began in both cases with a simple logical justification (because there are two Salèves, because Bern is far away from the lake). Precausality would therefore seem to be on the wane in Del's mentality, and the distinction to be growing between strictly causal explanation and other types of relations.

Too much emphasis, however, must not be laid on the contrast between Del's mentality at six-and-a-half and at 7; 2. Even in the few answers which have been reproduced here, neither causality nor logical justification are present in an unadulterated form. The answer to the question about the size of the lake is still very confused in this respect. It amounts to ascribing to the lake or withholding from it certain powers, just us though it were not exactly a body endowed with spontaneous activity (such as the wind and sun appear to be to the child), but a big river, which goes where it chooses. The lake could go to Bern if it were the sea, but it is not called (i.e. it is not) the same as the sea, therefore it cannot.

We decided to test these results by asking 10 children of 7 to 8 those same questions of Del's. This procedure showed in the first place that the questions were interpreted as requests for pre-causal explanation, at least by most of the children, who can be regarded as only slightly backward in comparison to Del; and in the second place, that between 7 and 8 many of the answers are already more or less causal or logical as the case may be, just as those of Del at 7; 2.

Here are some examples of precausal answers:

"Why is there a great and a little Salève?—*For children, and the great one for grown-ups* (Au). *Because there is one for little children and the other for big ones* (De). *Because of people who want to go into the little one or the great one* (Gia). *The little one is to go on to, and so is the great one* (Ru)."

"My daddy told me that thunder made itself by itself in the sky. Why?—*It was God who made it* (Ri). *Because God made it* (Au)."

"Why are they (negroes) made to be like that?—*Because God punished them. They were naughty when they were little* (Au). *Because they are dirty* (Ga). *God did it* (Go). *Because they were born like that* (Gia)," etc.

"What makes the Rhone go so fast? *The water* (Ru, Ant, etc.), *the boats* (Ri)."

"What makes the lake run?—*The machines* [the locks] (Ri), *God* (Ru, Go, etc.), *the rocks* (Au)," etc.

"The lake does not go as far as Bern, why?—*It is shut* (Ru). *Because it is stopped. There is a big wall* (Go). *Because it isn't so big. There is another lake at Bern. There's a lake in every country* (Au). *Because the lake of Bern is another lake* (De). *Because they are not all the same lakes* (Ant). *Because it is too far* (Gia)."

These answers are probably all precausal. But they also show the polymorphism of precausality, and we cannot possibly at this point enter upon an analysis of these childish explanations. That will be the work of later enquiries. We must therefore limit ourselves to the one conclusion which is of any value to the study of logical reasoning in the child, viz., that precausality points to a confusion between the psychical and the physical order of things. The result is that in the child logical justification will never appear in unadulterated form, but will continually oscillate between justification and psychological motivation.

§ 14. CONCLUSION. CATEGORIES OF THOUGHT OR LOGICAL FUNCTIONS IN THE CHILD OF SEVEN.—A question, says Claparède, "Is the conscious realization of a problem or of the difficulty of solving it, i.e., of the direction in which to seek for its solution. To search effectually, one must know what it is one is searching for, one must have asked oneself a question. The nature of this question will determine the whole orientation of subsequent research. Thus the function of the question is quite clear: it is an incitement to mental activity, in a certain direction in view of readjustment . . .

" . . . Logicians have tried to catalogue . . . [different kinds of questions], or rather the different kinds of judgments which constitute their appropriate answers, and they have given the name of category to the various classes observed in this way. This enumeration of different sorts of questions is of very little interest to psychology. The number of questions that can be asked is infinite, they are as many as the different ways of being unadapted; and the question of whether they can be grouped under certain headings is only one of secondary interest.

"It is more interesting to enquire into the biological origin of these various types of questions. How did the individual ever come to ask questions about cause, aim, or place, etc. This problem of origins is the same as that of knowing how the individual gradually came to interest himself in the cause, the aim, and the place of things, etc. And there is good reason for believing that his interest was only directed to these 'categories' when his action was unadapted to one of them. Need creates consciousness, and the consciousness of cause (or of aim, or of place, etc.), only arose in the mind when the need was felt for adaptation in relation to the cause (or the aim, etc.).

"When adaptation is purely instinctive, the mind is not conscious of these categories, even though the instinct in question acts as if it were; the action here is automatic, and its execution presents the mind with no problems; there is no failure to adapt, therefore there is no felt need, and consequently no consciousness of any such need in the direction which would lead to its satisfaction.

"We may note in passing how greatly our conception of 'categories' differs from that of philosophers. According to the Faculty Psychology the categories are the result of some sort of primitive mental intuition. But observation shows that those categories only come into being through some defect in adaptation. According to Associationism, the categories are the result of reiterated associations which have become inseparable. But observation shows that precisely when association reaches its highest degree of automatism (instinct, habit), the individual is not conscious of the categories, because, not having failed to adapt himself, he has no need to ask any questions."[1]

We have quoted this remarkable passage because, having reached the end of this book, we can do no more than express our complete agreement with it. In a sense, we have gone further along the path of functional psychology in asserting that the fact of becoming conscious of a category will alter its actual nature. If, therefore, we accept the formula: "The child is cause long before having any idea of cause" it must be remembered that we do so only for the sake of convenience. It is only as a concession to language (and one which if we are not careful will involve us in a thoroughly realistic theory of knowledge entirely outside the scope of psychology) that we can talk of "causality" as a relation entirely independent of the consciousness which may

[1] Ed. Claparède, "La Psychologie de l'intelligence," *Scientia* 1917, pp. 361–3.

be had of it. As a matter of fact, there are as many types of causality as there are types and degrees of becoming conscious of it. When the child "is cause," or acts as though he knew one thing was cause of another, this, even though he has not consciously realized causality, is an early type of causality, and, if one wishes, the functional equivalent of causality. Then, when the same child becomes conscious of the relation in question, this realization, just because it depends upon the needs and interests of the moment, is capable of assuming a number of different types—animistic causality, artificialistic, finalistic, mechanistic (by contact), or dynamic (force), etc. The list of types can never be considered complete, and the types of relation used nowadays by adults and scientists are probably only as provisional as those which have been used by the child and the savage.

The study of categories is, as M. Claparède rightly maintains, a study of functional psychology, and vast new horizons are opened to it by the law of conscious realization. Here the psychologist meets on common ground with the historian of science and the modern logician. Traditional logic, whether we take the realism of the Schools or Kant's apriorism, regarded the categories as fixed, and imposed on the mind and on things once and for all, and in a definite form. This hypothesis is psychologically false, and has been brilliantly attacked by William James at a period when logicians themselves had begun to abandon it. Renouvier and Cournot have given to the theory of categories a turn which it is no exaggeration to characterize as psychological, since the task they have set themselves is to define the categories according to their genesis in the history of thought and to their progressive use in the history of the sciences. This is the point of view which Messrs Höffding,[1] Brunschvicg[2] and Lalande[3]

---

[1] *La pensée humaine.*

[2] *Les étapes de la philosophie mathématique.*

[3] *Bulletins de la Sociéte française de philosophie,* passim.

have since very elaborately developed. From this angle the problem of categories must therefore be formulated in connexion with the intellectual development of the child himself. The genetician will therefore have to note the appearance and use of these categories at every stage of intelligence traversed by the child, and to bring these facts under the functional laws of thought.

It is in this spirit that we should like to build up out of Del's questions a table which, though only approximately correct, might still serve to orientate subsequent research. To do this we need only transcribe the classifications we adopted, and consider them from the genetic point of view.

In the first place, what relations can we allow to exist between our classification of questions and our attempted genealogy of whys? Questions of the form "what is . . . ?" and "when?" are admittedly earlier than "whys" (Stern, Mlle. Descœudres). But it can be definitely stated that at the moment when "whys" first make their appearance, a reorganization of values takes place in the child's mind, which enables us to see more clearly the relations uniting the different categories of questions. We shall therefore occupy ourselves only with the period extending from the age of 3 to that of 7–8, i.e., with what Stern has called the second questioning age.

In what circumstances do the first "whys" appear? Approximately at the same age as the three following fundamental phenomena: 1° The formation of two distinct planes of reality. Up till the age of 3, the real may be said to be simply what is desired. There is, indeed, after 1; 9 or 2 a yes and a no, a real and an unreal, but without any further shade of difference. At about 3, on the other hand, the imagined is something distinct from the real. According to Stern, this is the age when we first meet with such words as "perhaps,"[1] etc., which are precisely those which

---

[1] In the lists given by Mlle Descœudres (*Le Développement de l'enfant de deux à sept ans*, Neuchatel, 1922) "perhaps" occurs only in the language of the child of 5, but we have ourselves noted it at 3.

mark a divergence between the imagined and the real. Again, to quote Stern, there appear at the same date such verbs as "to think," "to believe,"[1] etc. As we take it, the advent of these words, whatever may be said to the contrary, in no way indicates a distinction between the psychical and the physical, or between thought and thing, but a distinction between what is imagined and what is perceived. 2° It is at about the same period (2; 9 and 3; 10) that Scupin detected the earliest lies, or, as P. Janet has so excellently described them, "beliefs about the future" as opposed to beliefs about the present. 3° Finally, it is also at about the age of three that grammatical accident makes its first appearance. Cases and tenses of a certain complexity, the simpler forms of subordinate prepositions—in a word, the whole necessary apparatus for the beginnings of formulated reasoning begins to be incorporated into the language of the subject. Now the function of this reasoning is to construct, over and above the immediate world of sensation, a reality supposedly deeper than the merely given world. And all these transformations have this fundamental trait in common, that they indicate an act of conscious realization. From now onwards the child distinguishes between the real as it appears immediately to his senses, and something which precedes events and underlies all phenomena. Let us describe this something by the very comprehensive term—intention. The intentions of people and of things sometimes conform to the wishes of the child, sometimes they do not; hence the distinction between the imagined or desired and the real. Hence, also, the resistance put up by reality which necessitates lying. Intentions can sometimes be detected at once, and fit in spontaneously with the events; at other times they cannot, whence the necessity of reconstructing them, of supposing their presence behind things, in a word, of reasoning instead of simply looking on.

[1] According to the same authority "to think" is noted at 2; 9, "to believe" at 5.

These changes, contemporaneous with the earliest "whys," are not altogether unrelated to this type of question. Up till this age, reality coincided almost entirely with desire, and existed on a single plane, so to speak, without the child having ever become clearly conscious of intentions contrary to its own, or definitely independent of them. The questions asked relate simply to the names of objects and to the place which they occupied after they have disappeared. Roughly speaking, at about three years old the child takes cognizance of the resistance set up by things and people; there is discord between desire and its realization. For a mentality that has not yet learnt to distinguish between thought and things, between animate and inanimate, between ego and non-ego, this discord can only be conceived as an intentional resistance on the part of people and things. The real, henceforth, becomes crowded with intentions ascribed first to other people, then to things, whether these things are thought of as autonomous or dependent upon persons. Thus the whole world becomes peopled in various degrees—not, it is true, with personified spirits, because at this age the child is still unconscious of its own personal unity, and does not think of ascribing intentions to definite "I's"—but of intentions that are impersonal, so to speak, or at any rate improperly localized and multiform. Hence the earliest "whys," "why" being the specific question for seeking the intention hidden behind an action or an event.

The earliest "whys" are generally asked in connexion with human actions. The first "why" noted by Scupin in the case of "Bubi" is of this order. The child's mother was lying on the ground. The boy wants to get her up: "*Du bis ya nicht tot warum stehste nicht immersu auf?*" The second one appears when the child is forbidden to pull the petals off flowers. "*Warum denn?*" But even where children begin with a "why of explanation," it is difficult not to see in the expected explanation not only a precausal explanation, but one in which precausality is almost entirely confused with psychological or intentional causality. *"Why do trees have leaves?"*

It is these intentions ascribed to people and to things which will give rise to the types of question corresponding to the principal categories of child thought. These categories will therefore have an intentionalistic origin, i.e., they will arise from the conscious realization of psychological operations relative to intentions, and not from a mere observation of the world given in perception. Moreover, the earlier categories of name and place, etc., will join themselves to these categories of intention, and together with them will form a single whole.

This intentionalism gives rise to two fundamental categories or primitive functions of thought: the *explicatory function* and the *implicatory function*. These do not represent two separate departments of the mind, but describe two moments which are present in all mental activity. The explicatory function is the centrifugal moment, in which the mind turns to the external world; the implicatory function is the centripetal, in which the mind turns inwards to the analysis of intentions and of their relations.

The explicatory functions arise out of the need felt by the child, as soon as he becomes conscious of intentions, to project these into the world around him. On the one hand, he finds himself surrounded by people whose actions can be foreseen and whose motives can be detected; on the other hand, he is faced by a world of phenomena and events which up till now have never resisted his thought and therefore required no explanation, but which have now become as great obstacles to his fantasy as are people themselves. This duality has to be abolished; since there is a "why" to human actions, the same treatment must be applied to everything which presents itself. Hence this universal desire for precausal explanation which comes from confusing psychological intentionalism with physical causality. Thus the explicatory function has two poles—psychological explanation and material explanation. These two poles are close together at first and not easily distinguishable, but as time goes on they grow more and more distinct, though always held together by the fact that both are rooted in one and the same desire for explanation.

Owing to the fact, moreover, that the idea of intention first appears through the resistance of reality, and in particular through the resistance of persons, everything seems to the child to obey some sort of necessity which is both moral and physical. Everything seems to him to be as it should be. So that the child's tendency will be, not only to project intentions into every object so as to explain events, but also to seek to account for everything, to justify every event, and to look for the connexions existing between intentions. Hence the implicatory function. The explicatory function was centrifugal in this sense, that from the intention it sought to draw out the material consequence, the resultant act or event. The direction of the implicatory function is, on the contrary, centripetal, in the sense that from the intention it seeks to trace its way back to the directing motive or idea. The explicatory function tends towards things, the implicatory function tends towards ideas or judgments. And child thought, being at its origin equally removed from things and from thought, occupies an intermediate position between the two.

Thus the implicatory function also has two poles. First a psychological pole in common with that of the explicatory function and which causes the child to ask: "Why do people do so? etc." The "whys of justification" which we collected from Del are naturally of a much later date than these primitive questions, although they constitute a special case of the "whys" concerning what ought to be. The other pole is made up of questions about names, definitions, the reason for judgments, in a word, about everything concerning logical justification. Just as between psychological and physical explanation there are innumerable transitional cases, so also between the implication of psychological actions (justification) and the implication of names, classes and later on of numbers, there is every type of intermediate example. Thus the pole which is common to both functions, i.e., the psychological pole (psychological justification and explanation) serves both as a starting point and as a point of divergence for the two functions, explicatory and implicatory, which are at first confused and then grow more and more distinct. We shall call mixed, that function of psychological justification and explanation which partakes of the nature of explication and implication.

This schema may be thought to apply only to "whys," but it is obvious that other types of question, even of earlier date, such as those of place ("where is . . . ?" etc.) and of name ("who is . . . ?") are more or less in corporated in it. As the explicatory function develops, questions of place come more and more to resemble the great group of questions of reality and history, to which the desire for explanation gives its chief impetus. Questions about names are originally independent, and belong as such neither to the desire for explanation nor to that for justification or implication; but their function is modified concomitantly with the development of the implicatory function. The child finds that names which originally were bound up in his mind with the object can be subjected to an increasingly logical justification (childish etymologies). This in itself tightens the bond between questions of names and the implicatory function. The same thing happens to questions of classification and definition, definitions being at first, as is well known, purely utilitarian, and then becoming increasingly logical.

The main categories of child thought between the years of 3 and 7–8 are therefore represented by the following table:

Explicatory function	. .	Causality. Reality, time and place.
Mixed function	. . .	Motivation of actions. Justification of rules.
Implicatory function	. .	Classification. Names. Number. Logical relations.

To bring this chapter to an end, we must now try very briefly to connect the results we have obtained with the factors established in the earlier chapters, and particularly with the ego-centrism of child thought.

In this chapter special stress has been laid on the importance of precausality and consequently of intellectual realism; in other words, we have emphasized the paradoxical fact that child thought is equally removed from dealing with strictly causal explanation as it is from dealing with logical justification properly so-called. The whole mechanism of children's questions, as we have studied it, can be accounted for by this fundamental fact.

What relation could there be between this fact and the ego-centrism of child thought? A fairly close one of mutual dependence, since (see § 12) precausality tends to disappear at the same age as ego-centrism, viz., between 7 and 8. In every strictly causal explanation there is, after all, an effort to adapt oneself to the external world, an effort to objectify, and, one might almost say, to depersonalize one's thought. Without this effort, the mind tends to project intentions into everything, or connect everything together by means of relations not based on observation, as is apparent from the childish habit of justifying everything and of conceiving nothing as fortuitous. Now ego-centrism certainly hinders this effort towards the adaptation and depersonalization of thought. It interferes with it directly, in the first place, because the more the ego is made the centre of interests, the less will the mind be able to depersonalize its thought, and to get rid of the idea that in all things are intentions either favourable or hostile (animism, artificialism, etc.). But ego-centrism is also an indirect hindrance, for in so far as he is ego-centric, the child will not trouble to pit his own ideas against those of others, and thus prove what he has come to believe. He will therefore give way to the primitive impulse of all thought, i.e., he will substitute for things as they are, a fragmentary world of his own making in which everything has an aim, and in which everything can be justified. But there is also in the logical habit an effort towards internal coherence and direction of thought, which is not spontaneously given to the primitive mind, but is a gradual conquest of reason. Here again, ego-centrism is a real obstacle to the acquisition of this desire for implication or logical systematization. It is a direct obstacle, because all ego-centrism is designed by its structure to stand half-way between autistic thought which is "undirected," i.e., which as in day-dreaming hovers about at the mercy of every whim, and "directed" intelligence. Ego-centrism is therefore obedient to the self's good pleasure and not to the dictates of impersonal logic. It is also an indirect obstacle, because only the habits of discussion and social life will lead to the logical point of view, and ego-centrism is precisely what renders these habits impossible.

We can now see that ego-centrism, while it does not exactly explain the child's incapacity for true causal explanation and logical justification, is nevertheless closely connected with it. And we can understand how, as a result of this, the child's mind is always hovering between these two convergent paths, and is also equally removed from both. This it is that gives rise to the phenomena of precausality and intellectual realism, both of which bear witness to this intermediate position. And this it is also that gives rise to that tendency in children to justify things at any price, or to connect everything with everything else, which we have dealt with at length in the course of this chapter.

usual meaning and not the conventional one that we had adopted. This in particular explains Charlotte Bühler's opposition. An American author has even gone so far as to take as a criterion of ego-centrism the use of the words "I" or "me," etc., as though one could not speak of oneself in a perfectly socially adapted manner and nevertheless remain ego-centric, i.e., confusing one's own point of view with that of others, and at the same time not speak of one's *self*!

Secondly, results, as is to be expected, vary in different school surroundings; the child's speech will be more or less influenced according to the amount of freedom to speak and the nature of the occupation or the intervention of the teacher.

Thirdly, there remains above all an important problem, that of verbal relationship between the child and the adult. In their work *Conversations with Children*,[1] D. and R. Katz give us an example of two children who are very slightly ego-centric with each other and perfectly "socialized" in their conversation with an adult. The 154 dialogues that have been written down are very clear on this second point. As to conversation between the two children themselves, the authors admit (p. 8) that this is less developed and poorer, without actually being ego-centric. In short, these children's speech, according to Katz, while not ego-centric, is more "socialized" with their parents than with each other.

Faced with the results of this analysis, which contradict those obtained by us at the *Maison des Petits*, Mme A. Leuzinger-Schuler set herself the task of solving the problem on her own account by observing her own son, then aged 3 years, and three other children of from 3 to 4 years old. The two questions which had to be answered may be stated as follows: 1. Does verbal ego-centrism show itself on an average more forcefully in the presence of an adult or in the presence of other children?

---

[1] D. and R. Katz, *Conversations with Children*, London, 1928.

2. What modification do these two types of social relationship undergo in relation to each other during the course of the child's fourth year? In short, is it with the adult or is it with his fellows that the child begins to socialize his thought in the sense of exchange and co-operation?

Mme Leuzinger-Schuler has tried to solve these problems by a statistical analysis identical with the one which we have used in this book. The point needs emphasizing. It does indeed seem to us difficult to compare purely qualitative results, such as those given by Katz, with conclusions based on both statistics and direct analysis. When Katz merely assures us that their children, when left to themselves, never presented the same phenomena of verbal ego-centrism as the children of the Maison des Petits, one cannot help thinking that in 500 or 1,000 successive statements, taken down at random, one would have found at least a small fraction of ego-centric phrases.

§ 1. Hans' Remarks during the Course of his Fourth Year.—At the beginning, in the middle and at the end of her son Hans' fourth year, Mme Leuzinger-Schuler wrote down several hundreds of this child's remarks, making a careful distinction between remarks made only in the presence of an adult and those made in the presence of his small friends. It should be stated that Hans, an only child, attended a private school run by Mme Leuzinger herself, in a town in German Switzerland. Hans' questioners are therefore schoolmates and in a school organized on the pattern of the Maison des Petits, which makes the results easy to compare with those obtained in Geneva.

The most important conclusion reached by Mme Leuzinger-Schuler is that Hans made use of more socialized language in the presence of his own kind than in the presence of an adult, especially that of his mother. Moreover, this clear-cut opposition, which is obvious at the beginning of the fourth year, lessens and tends to be reversed as the child gradually gets into the habit of questioning the adult. Here are the figures obtained (the coefficients have been determined according to the method described in chapter 1):

Age	3; 1	3; 6	4—4; 1
Coefficient of ego-centrism in the presence of an adult	71.2%	50.3%	43.5%

Age	3; 4	3; 8	3; 11—4; 0
Coefficient of ego-centrism in the presence of other children	56.2%	43.2%	46%

A result such as this one deserves careful study. Our notes show, in fact, that at the beginning of his fourth year the child's speech shows a greater coefficient of ego-centrism (i.e., it is less socialized in character) in intercourse with adults than in that with children of his own age (71.2% against 56.2%). From the beginning to the end of the year the coefficient of ego-centrism becomes manifestly less in the child's relationship with the adult (from 71 to 43%, i.e., a lowering of 28%), whereas in his intercourse with children this lessening is not so marked (10%). On the total result, i.e., without distinction between intercourse with adults and intercourse with children, the coefficient of ego-centrism in the course of the fourth year changes from 63.7% to 44.7%.

Let us now examine the quality of these data beginning with ego-centric speech. It can immediately be observed that with Hans, the longest and purest monologues show themselves in the language of child to adult, the child uninterruptedly following the thread of his imagination whereas monologues spoken in the presence of other children are broken into by questions of all kinds and constantly affected by interruptions relevantly related to the incidents of the game.

Here are examples of these monologues in the presence of the adult:

At 3; 1 (while building): (124) "'m making a house for the Chinese, 'm making a house, a very big house. I've made a house for the Chinese. (125) Up high, the bedrooms. On the top I put the roof, the ceiling. There. That's right, the ceiling. (126) Now the beds. I put the beds, a bed like that for the Chinese, a bed for the Chinese. The beds on top of one another. (127) There. The Chinese sleep up there, near God. They are asleep. I have put them just there, near God. (128) There is God. (He puts a block in place.) Here he has head, his little head. (129) Look (he speaks to himself): God is up there, on the roof."

(While drawing at 3; 1) (318) "want another paper. (319) I must finish the steeple. Here are the bells that go with the string. (320) I put it there (the paper). (321) You've still got to make something else (he speaks to himself), make a chest. I make . . . there . . . the legs. (322) It's only a table. (323) There, I'm drawing on this sheet. (324) I'm making a funny man. (325) What am I doing? (speaks to himself) It's a waterworks. Here I must draw the water. Now the water. (326) I'll make a boat too. A little boat and an Indian, a man and a woman, two men and a woman. Two men and an Indian. (327) They've fallen in the water, you see (to himself). (328) There's a waterworks. Here's the boat, the Indians and a man and a woman. Must put them inside. (329) Now 'm making an animal."

These long monologues are very typical of ego-centric language in a child's intercourse with an adult. On the one hand this is undoubtedly a case of social relationship. The child loves to know that he is near his mother. He feels that he is close to her in each of his acts and thoughts. What he says does not seem to him to be addressed to himself but is enveloped with the feeling of a presence, so that to speak of himself or to speak to his mother appear to him to be one and the same thing. His activity is thus bathed in an atmosphere of communion or syntonization, one might almost speak of "the life of union" to use the terms of mysticism, and this atmosphere excludes all consciousness of ego-centrism. But, on the other hand, one cannot but be struck by the soliloquistic character of these same remarks. The child does not ask questions and expects no answer, neither does he attempt to give any definite information to his mother who is present. He does not ask himself whether she is listening or not. He speaks for himself just as an adult does when he speaks within himself. But here again in such a case the adult has the impression of being alone or, on the contrary, of arguing as in real life with fictitious questioners, whereas, there is no doubt that the child, when speaking, experiences neither of these impressions. We are thus in the presence either of a *maximum* of social communion, the ego being united to another, or of a *maximum* absorption of another in the ego. The truth is not between these two, it is in the simultaneous affirmation of both points of view. The first is true from the inner point of view, that is to say from the point of view of the actual consciousness of the child. The second is true from the point of view of the observer. It is this lack of differentiation between another and the ego that characterizes ego-centrism.

It will serve no purpose here to give examples of verbal ego-centrism in Hans' social intercourse with his playmates. They are similar to those of the *Maison des Petits* but with this shade of difference. In the case of relationship between children themselves one cannot speak of so intimate a communion. The difference, or simply the distinction, between the ego and another is more clearly felt than with parents. As we have maintained from the very beginning of our enquiry, it could no doubt in one sense be said that in intercourse between children of from 3 to 5 years old, who live together constantly, "the individual life and the social life are undifferentiated."[1]

Thus, on the one hand, the child is less individualized

---

[1] See pp. 48–9.

than the adult in that he gives way to all suggestions and his personality is not strong enough to resist the currents of imitation which flow through a group. But, on the other hand, the child is less socialized than the adult in that he refers everything to his own point of view. It is in this sense that one may consider ego-centric language between children as indicating a relative lack of differentiation between what is individual and what is social. But this condition, while reminiscent of the child's monologue in his mother's presence, nevertheless lends itself much more to socialization. Thus, the small child receives from the adult the double impression of being dominated by a mind far superior to his own and at the same time of being completely understood by this mind with which he shares everything. The relationship is therefore primarily one of identification, which is of course followed by disappointments, revolts and returns to obedience and thus reidentification; but, broadly speaking, the child absorbs into himself all that he finds in his parents and offers to his parents all that he feels within himself. This is truly the "life of union." The playmate is, on the contrary, his fellow (as against a superior and alien), hence the need for more highly developed differentiation.

This is what we shall now see as we examine socialized language. In doing this let us distinguish between a first group of remarks made up of dialogues, discussions, information, criticism, orders, etc. (we shall call them simply dialogues), and a second group made up of questions.

Here first is the evolution of the forms of dialogue during Hans' third year. The figures in parentheses thus contain all this child's socialized speech, apart from questions and answers, but including adapted information.[1] We have added separately and in parentheses the figures belonging only to adapted information since they make up the most specific form of socialized speech:

---

[1] For the definition of these terms see chapter 1.

Age	3; 1	3; 6	4–4; 1
Dialogues with the adult	16%	17%	19%
(Information given to the adult)	(10%)	(10.3%)	(14.7%)

Age	3; 4	3; 8	3; 11–4
Dialogue with children	23.2%	32.8%	35%
(Information given to children)	(13.8%)	(22.7%)	(26.4%)

This table clearly shows first that dialogue and adapted information are considerably better represented in conversation with children than in conversation with the adult. Thus between 3; 1 and 3; 4 dialogue with children is 23% as against 16% with the adult, which is to be expected as the coefficient of ego-centrism at this age is 71% with the adult and 56% with children. But, at the end of the year (3; 11–4; 1) when the coefficients of ego-centrism with the adult and with children have become practically equal (43.5 and 46%), dialogue is found to represent only 19% of speech with the adult whereas it rises to 35% with children! At the end of the year, dialogue with children is therefore nearly twice as important as dialogue with the adult. This point is significant and we must try to work out the reason for this. The matter could be expressed otherwise: during the year, dialogue has only slightly increased in importance (16 to 19%) whereas real conversation with other children has increased considerably (23 to 35%).

Let us pass on to the qualitative examination of this collected information or dialogues. In the remarks noted down by Mme Leuzinger-Schuler, what strikes one most is that not only are those with information more numerous between children but the information is of a more evolved type. The first of the more sophisticated examples of information, in which statements are no longer merely static or descriptive but form part of discussions or of active collaboration, are to be found in conversation between children. Everything happens as though the conflict of opinions and of different intentions had finally opened up a channel for discussion on a higher plane.

Here first are the best examples of dialogues with an adult or of information given to the adult:

At 3; 1 Mother says "I've looked to see if it's hot or cold."— Answer: (73) *The barometer's hot too.* (91) *Mummy there's still a light in the little room. (92) I can't shut the door by myself, I'm too stupid.* (510) *Mummy, that, you can't eat it* (an over-ripe banana), *it's rotten.* (594) *Mummy the larder door is shut.*

At 3; 6: "Look, the arm is a bit broken too." (60) *It's broken, it's spoilt* (the indiarubber). (230) *That's a little berry there, on the ground.* No discussion in 500 remarks.

At 4; 1. Discussion becomes more frequent but does not go very far. (3) "Who's Irma?—That's what Aunt Irma is called.— (4) *No, it's not what she's called.* (46) "D'you hear them talking (the soldiers)?—No, they're singing,—(47) *No, they're talking. Why are those soldiers singing?*" (167) *What is Edward?* It is a name. *No it isn't a name. It's only to call* "Edward, come in, come in, come in at once." (196) "Why am I a big boy?—Because you are older.—(197) *No, I'm not old, not old, I'm young, I'm quite young.*"

Here now are examples of discussion in Hans' speech with other children:

I. At 3; 4: "Ruth, (also 3; 4) look up there [on the rocks of Glaris] is the railway that goes to heaven.—(257) *No, there aren't any railways up there.* But there are railway lines. (258) *No, there aren't any railway lines up there. There are no railway lines in heaven. God doesn't need any railway lines.* Yes he does. (259) *No, God doesn't need any railway lines nor any trains.*—But there must be a railway line for a train."—Or again: (222) "It's my jug (he seizes it),—No, I want it.—(223) *No, it's me to pour. Please, give me the jug.*— (224) *I've got to put a leaf into it—there, now you can have it.*"

II. At 3; 8: (Barbara 4; 1) "I want to make a fire (goes near the stove).—(141) *No, Barbara, you mustn't make a fire because we have central heating.*"—Yes, I will.—(142) *No, mustn't make a fire because it's already warm with the central heating.* Another example: (500) "*Yesterday, I had to have tea all alone.* (Barbara), Why, all alone?—(501) *Because of you, you weren't there.* No, because there were visitors." Here is another discussion taking place at 3; 8 and in which the logic of relations occurs: (272) "*Barbara, somebody's got your aunt on the telephone*—No, they haven't got her, she's my aunt just now. When I am far away, in Paris, she'll be your aunt again.—(273) *Not yours?*—Yours *and* mine, like that—isn't that right?" One can see that Barbara and Hans have difficulty in distinguishing *meum* and *tuum*, although both long for conciliation.

III. At 4; 0: (Sotti 6; 8) "I've only got three trucks and you've got four.—(195) *You've got four.*—No, you've got four and I've only got three—(196) *No, that one there makes four, there's one.*—No you've got four, I've got three.—(197) "*Look, it's four trucks—like that, it makes four.* (Sotti's) *But a train that long* (H. J.'s) *it's not four it's more like a little bit three.*"

Note this qualitative evaluation of H.J.'s, as opposed to the exact numbering by his senior.

Obviously these discussions between children are still strangely "primitive." Sometimes the questioners are not speaking about the same thing (discussion on railway lines between Ruth and Hans). Sometimes their knowledge of the terms of relationship is not sufficient to establish reciprocity in points of view (discussion with Barbara on "your" aunt), sometimes they have different numbering-systems (discussion with Sotti). But, functionally the usefulness of these exchanges cannot be overestimated just because they show an effort towards mutual understanding and the sharing of view-points. Thus, if there is still ego-centrism structurally, co-operation is already present functionally.

Discussions with the adult, when compared with all this, certainly present the same phenomenon, but in a less developed form. The child also tries to compare his opinion or his point of view with that of others and in this the discussion remains excellent. But as the questioner in this particular case is a powerful and wise being, there can only be acceptance of a superior judgment or refusal to give in. In the discussion about the soldiers singing, for example, Hans without seeming to do so gives in, whereas, in the argument about the names of Irma and Edward or about his age he sticks to his opinion without justification. Can it then be said that Hans' mother might have continued the conversation? She certainly could have done so, but if she refrained from this it was just because she did not wish to impose her way of looking at things, which the child would eventually be able to discover for himself.

On the other hand, or just on that account, the true function of conversation between children and adults is questioning. If we now pass on to the analysis of questions, we shall, in fact, notice that the true reason for this decrease in the coefficient of ego-centrism between Hans and the adult is the considerable increase in the number of questions.

Here first is a statistical table:

Age	3; 1	3; 6	4—4; 1
Questions put to an adult	12.8%	29.6%	35.2%

Age	3; 4	3; 8	3; 11—4
Questions put to children	13.6%	14.8%	12%

In considering this table it becomes at once obvious that the number of questions put to other children remains more or less stationary throughout the year, whereas the number of questions put to an adult has nearly trebled. Taking into account only speech between child and adult, questions have risen from 12 to 35%. It is this increase which almost of itself explains the decrease in the coefficient of ego-centrism in remarks made in the presence of an adult. In other words, in the case of Hans it is this progress in questioning that almost entirely accounts for socialization.

Moreover, it is interesting to note the qualitative difference between questions put to adults and questions put to other children. The first contain a considerable proportion of questions related to causality and explanation, whereas in the second this element is almost completely absent.

Here are examples of questions put to an adult:

> At 3; 4: "*Why has the cloud gone away?—Why has the wind sent it away?—Why does the sun hide behind the clouds?—Why does the transformer make such a noise?*"
>
> At 3; 6: "*Why has the cave got to be so dark? Why are there berries just there?*"
>
> "*Why does the roof break if we throw stones?*"
>
> At 4 years old: "*The radiator is cold. Why? Why does water make a hole in the stone?—Why do teeth break if I bite stones? What did God do to make cherries so big?—What are chains for?—Why must they hold weights?—Why must the glue stay liquid?*"

As to questions put to children, these are similar to those we have already quoted (see chapter 1). They relate to daily and immediate activity and not to problems involving theoretical explanation, whereas these abound in questions put to adults. That the latter remain "precausal" and permeated with an infantile mental approach to things is quite clear and it would serve no purpose to demonstrate this again here. As N. Isaacs has insisted upon with so much subtlety, a question such as "Why has the cave got to be so dark?" may well show, from the functional point of view, the surprise of a mind accustomed to a rule in the presence of an exceptional fact, which goes against this rule (for instance, natural hiding places are not usually dark; why then should this cave be so dark?). It remains nevertheless clear that the rule is conceived as a kind of moral as well as a physical obligation: Why "has it be" so dark? But what interests us here is the following fact, which we had already noted in the past: as long as the orientation of the child's mind is in the main precausal he constantly has recourse to the adult as a dispenser of readymade truth and not to other children who know no more than he does himself. Later, on the contrary, as his explanations gradually become positive, he will like to discuss them with his equals just as he already talks to them about games and general activities.

From this point of view it is therefore easy to understand why, during Hans' fourth year, dialogue with the adult shows little increase whereas questions put to the adult have nearly trebled; and why questions to children show little increase, whereas information and discussion have nearly doubled. This is because the child's attitude towards other children and his attitude towards the adult are essentially different: the first is made up of co-operation: the second is made up of intellectual submission and as such remains at the surface of the bonds of true co-operation or of reciprocity.

§ 2. THE REACTIONS OF THREE OTHER CHILDREN.—The process of evolution in Hans' language during his fourth year is thus clearly defined. On the one hand, at the beginning of the year, the coefficient of ego-centrism is weaker in the presence of other children than in the presence of an adult. On the other hand, at the end of the year the coefficients tend to become equal: but this is because questions to the adult have almost trebled, whereas discussion with other children continues to exceed discussion with the adult and in relation to this may even sometimes attain the proportion of nearly two to one. The problem that naturally arises is whether Hans' case is a special one, or whether all children react in the same way and become socialized in each other's company in a different way from when in the presence of the adult. As the results published by Katz contradict those of Mme Leuzinger, it is clear that Hans' case cannot be considered as universal, and that the question of development is here complicated by that of differing types and surroundings. We have therefore to consider the part played by different types of education, i.e., types of social relationship, as well as varying individual types of children. In other words, the problem is one of knowing whether Hans' relations with his mother are representative of all relations of children to adults. We have to ask ourselves, on the one hand, if other children would react in the same way towards Mme Leuzinger and, on the other hand, if their reactions towards other adults would be the same. We shall therefore begin by analysing the behaviour of other children who belong to the little group in Mme Leuzinger's school. Then, in the light of these facts we shall examine the results obtained by Katz (see § 3).

Mme Leuzinger has studied the language of three other children of 3 to 4 years old. She has used the same procedure: i.e., taking down some hundreds of remarks of each child, made sometimes in the presence of other children, sometimes only in her presence. These children were perfectly acquainted with their observer because they spent their time at her school; playing, drawing, building and talking. One cannot attribute the following results to a school atmosphere because the school in question was one only in name and consisted of a big family in which the children were perfectly free to occupy themselves as they pleased. We should also remember that we are dealing with children of 3 years old who, therefore, have not yet learned to distinguish between pedagogues and other human beings. This having been stated, we find the coefficient of ego-centrism in the three subjects to be as follows:

Name and Age	Rob 3; 6	Sli 3; 8	Wer 3; 11–4
Coefficient of ego-centrism in the presence of an adult	61.5%	38.1%	47.8%
Coefficient of ego-centrism in the presence of other children	46.3%	36.7%	41.2%

It is interesting to note that all three children's reactions to their observer are similar to those of Hans to his own mother, i.e., all three are less socialized with an adult than with their playmates. Naturally, this does not mean that they speak less to an adult than to their friends, but that their remarks to an adult are more ego-centric. In Rob and Wer there is a marked difference between their speech to an adult and speech with other children. With Sli, on the other hand, the disparity is slight enough to be attributed to chance. But, as we shall see, this child practises questioning on a large scale, hence his highly socialized speech with the adult. Moreover, he is, generally speaking, the least ego-centric of the three subjects under observation.

If, in broad lines, these statistics confirm those obtained with Hans, we can see that the individual type of each child will have to be taken into consideration. The relatively exceptional case of Sli is a proof of this and needs to be carefully examined. We shall be meeting a second problem of type in comparing Rob's reactions to those of the two other children from the point of view of discussion and adapted information.

It would be no use to give new examples of ego-centric language here; they would only serve the same purpose as those of Hans; let us, however, take up the paradoxical case of Rob. This child's language is considerably less ego-centric with his contemporaries than in the presence only of an adult: 46.3 as against 61.5. Rob, however, speaks German very badly and is considerably hampered by this in communicating with his friends, whereas he speaks French with Mme Leuzinger. Nevertheless, when he speaks to his fellows, his speech is better adapted to the others' than when he uses his mother tongue in the presence of an adult! This is another point in favour of our hypothesis that an exchange of thought between equals is of a different type of socialization from exchanges with the adult alone.

Let us pass on to questions which, as we have seen with Hans, form the essential part of socialized speech between the child and the adult. Here is the table of statistics:

Name and Age	Rob 3; 6	Sli 3; 8	Wer 3; 11–4
Questions put to the adult	18.5%	47%	38%
Questions put to children	7.6%	22.5%	20.5%

The meaning of this table is clear.[1] It signifies that questions put to the adult are relatively far more numerous than questions put to children. The proportion is, on the average, two to one. Moreover, questions of a causal nature, which in the great majority of cases are "precausal," are almost entirely put to the adult. This fact indicates that the child speaks to the adult above all as the source of truth and not as either an opponent or a collaborator with equal intellectual rights. In this respect one is struck by the percentage of questions put to the adult, not, as in the table, in proportion to the sum total of speech used, but merely in proportion to socialized speech. With Rob 48%, with Sli 75% and with Wer 72% of socialized remarks to the adult are questions!

This last remark explains the differences in the coefficient of ego-centrism of our three subjects in their relationship with the adult. It may thus be said that the less a child is ego-centric with the adult the more he is given to questioning; his verbal socialization as regards the adult consists almost entirely in asking questions. The following small table will show what we mean:

[1] This table should be read like the corresponding table of Hans Jorg. 18.5% of Rob's speech with the adult is made up of questions, and so also is 7.6% of his speech with children, etc.

Name	Sli	Wer	Rob
Ego-centric speech addressed to the adult	38.1%	47.8%	61.5%
Questions put to the adult	47%	38%	18.5%
Total	85.1%	85.8%	80%

1°. It can easily be seen that the percentage of questions is in inverse relation to the percentage of ego-centric speech.

2°. That questions, plus ego-centric speech, make up almost all speech addressed to the adult with the exception of 15% or 20% given over to dialogue or information, etc., to which we will refer again later.

It is true that there is also an inverse relation between questions put to playmates and the percentage of ego-centric speech addressed to other children. This indicates that, in all situations, questioning is correlated with socialization. But in speech between children, questions play only a small part and the sum total of questions and of ego-centric speech only slightly exceeds half the total speech. We need not therefore insist on this point, whereas it is important to understand that socialization in connexion with the adult is of a very special type which, in its most essential part, is based on questioning.

Finally, let us pass on to forms of dialogue, to adapted information, etc. (not including answers to another's questioning, which are devoid of interest and which, moreover, make up only 2 or 3% of all speech). What is most striking is that here again the results obtained from Rob, Sli and Wer confirm those obtained from the analysis of Hans' speech, i.e., truly socialized speech, once questions and answers have been eliminated, is much more frequent between children than between the child and the adult.

Here is the table of statistics:

Name and Age	Rob 3;6	Sli 3;8	Wer 3;11—4
Dialogue with the adult	16.7%	12.3%	11.2%
(Information given to the adult)	(15.5%)	(9.3%)	(9.6%)
Dialogue with children	33.3%	30.3%	27%
(Information given to children)	(16%)	(21%)	(20%)

These results clearly confirm those which the analysis of Hans' speech had given. In all three cases, of Rob, Sli and Wer, the amount of socialized speech addressed to children is as great as, or even more than double, that of socialized speech addressed to the adult. This conforms so completely to all that has been said that there is no need to quote further examples.

Just one point, however, requires to be explained: it is the percentage of "adapted information" which we have put in parenthesis, and which is, moreover, included in our global figures, which are not in parenthesis. With Sli and Wer the adapted information given to adults does not amount to half as much as information included in speech from one child to another. This is only natural when we consider the overall figures. On the other hand, with Rob information to the adult reaches the same percentage as information to children, in contrast to all other data on the socialized speech of this subject. To what can this be due? According to Mme Leuzinger it is a matter of education. Rob asks few questions, as compared with his friends, but is constantly parading his knowledge of words, picked up in conversation with his parents. In other words, this is a case of a child who is being pushed and constantly taught more than he can assimilate, instead of being allowed to develop naturally and have his intellectual spontaneity respected. Here again, as with Sli, the type of individual or the kind of education given to the child are factors which make the problem more complex and obviously prevent the assessment of general averages. Sometimes the multiplicity of questions gives rise to a strong percentage of socialized speech with the adult, as is the case with Sli. Sometimes education in speech may produce a slightly higher percentage of dialogue with the adult, as is the case with Rob.

But, allowing for these very natural complications, we do find, in Mme Leuzinger's observation of Rob, Sli and Wer, confirmation of the results obtained from the analysis of Hans' language. We can now attempt to draw some conclusions by comparing her data with that previously obtained at the *Maison des Petits*.

§ 3. THE EGO-CENTRISM OF CHILDISH SPEECH.—The first lesson to be learned from the preceding data is that, in surroundings where children are free to act spontaneously, ego-centric speech, similar to the one observed at the *Maison des Petits*, does in fact exist. No doubt this form of speech does not ever affect the whole of the child's speech. It probably only acts at all ages, as a more or less important fringe of speech, which, from the outset, is socialized and made up of commands or requests, of word-sentences or of sentences expressing desire and, later, questions and statements. But, with a child of three, like Hans, and in the presence of his mother, this fringe still makes up 71.2% of the total of spontaneous speech. It may, therefore, be presumed, and this is immediately evident in observing children of one to two years, that, in the beginnings of speech, only a few definite requests or commands may be considered as truly spoken to another, all other utterances are a soliloquy in the course of which the child speaks as much to himself as to those around him.

But we need not here concern ourselves with these questions of origin. We shall confine ourselves to including Mme Leuzinger's results in the table which gives those we had previously obtained. If we take the average of the coefficients of ego-centrism in Hans at 3 and 4 years old, and in Rob, Sli and Wer, we get the following figures: 0.52 and 0.44; 0.55; 0.37 and

by Mme Leuzinger. It is that the child's socialization operates in two different channels, corresponding to the opposing attitudes which he adopts towards the adult and towards his fellows.

The adult is at one and the same time far superior to the child and very near to him. He dominates everything, but at the same time penetrates into the intimacy of every wish and every thought. So that the child fluctuates between question and request (or prayer) and soliloquy accompanied by a feeling of communion. Sometimes—and this is the last case mentioned—he reacts towards him as a glorified omnipresent *alter ego*. All that the child does he shares with his mother and, from his point of view, there is no frontier separating his ego from her superior ego. In such a case the child's ego-centric speech is greater with the adult than with other children. Sometimes on the contrary—and this is the first case mentioned—the child speaks to his parents as to all powerful wills or as to superior intellects. The child's thought is then able to distinguish between himself and another and becomes socialized, but the relationship thus created is one of inferior to superior, and the spiritual authority of the adult presses with all its weight on the thought of the child.

The playfellow, on the other hand, both resembles and is very different from the child's ego. He is like him because he is his equal in what he can do and in what he knows. But he is very different just because, being on the same level with him, he cannot enter into his most intimate desires or personal point of view as a friendly adult would. The child thus becomes socialized with his contemporaries in quite another way than as with the adult. He fluctuates between two poles: the monologue—individual or collective—and discussion or genuine exchange of ideas, and that is why the child's socialization with his fellows is greater than, or at least different to, his socialization with the adult alone. Where the superiority of the adult prevents discussion and co-operation, the playfellow provides the opportunity for such social conduct as will determine the true socialization of the intelligence. Conversely, where equality between play-mates prevents questions and interrogation, the adult is there to supply an answer.

There are therefore two quite distinct processes of socialization. From the point of view of thought, one is of far greater importance than the other. As the child grows older, his respect for the superiority of the adult diminishes or at least alters in character. The adult ceases to represent unquestioned or even unquestionable Truth and interrogation becomes discussion. It is then that all that makes up a socialized attitude towards others, developed in the give and take of exchanges with contemporaries, prevails over a feeling of intellectual submission and thus constitutes that instrument so essential to the individual, of which he will make ever-increasing use and which will serve him throughout his life.

Now, if the process of socialization really varies according as it arises through relationship with the adult or through intercourse between children, it is obvious that the statistical records and in particular the percentage of socialized speech will vary not only in respect of the child but also in a considerable degree in respect of the adult. If the adult makes a rule of keeping to the indispensable minimum of interference, the child, in his intercourse with him, will fluctuate between soliloquy and interrogation, interspersed, no doubt, with a small amount of adapted information or embryonic discussion. But, if the adult constantly intervenes, it will be up to him to reduce the child's soliloquy to a satisfactory proportion and to develop dialogue. The resulting discussions will be fundamental so far as number goes. But will their quality be comparable with that of spontaneous discussions prompted by the child's own needs? This raises all the questions relating to "active" education and education based on authority.

We refer to this point in order to explain why results as divergent as those of Mme Leuzinger and those of Katz may be quite compatible. In the book entitled *Conversations with Children*, the latter describes two children devoid of ego-centrism with each other and especially when with their parents. The 154 recorded conversations are quite clearly adapted dialogue. But can such facts be looked upon as applicable generally? We repeat that, in the absence of statistical data, and of exact records of conversations held consecutively for several days in succession, it is difficult to judge whether these children *never* used collective dialogue when speaking to each other. Our two girls, who were as united as if they had been sisters, and were able to collaborate and have discussions, gave us, on the contrary, an example of children who, for a long time, fluctuated between dual mono-logue and true dialogue before the latter predominated.[1] It seems to us difficult to deny the presence of some such reaction in all children.

As to the interesting conversations with parents which Katz has taken down, it is impossible, on reading them, not to become aware of the contrasting attitudes of the adult towards Hans Leuzinger and towards Theodor and Julius Katz. Without necessarily describing the differences between teaching methods which these conversations illustrate, we note that most of these exchanges quoted by D. and R. Katz are carried on under the guidance of the adult himself. A great number of these dialogues are examinations of conscience or moral confessions during which, at the end of the day, the child is asked if he has been good, if he has been disobedient, etc. The children are so accustomed to this imposed scheme of conversation that they themselves ask to be questioned about their faults: Ask me if I have been naughty (p. 106)—Moreover, when the children ask questions of a purely intellectual nature, the tendency is to give them an immediate answer, rather than allow them to try and find one for themselves or discuss the matter with them as on an equal footing. In short, if, as we have already tried to do

[1] See La Formation du Symbole chez l'Enfant.

elsewhere, we make a distinction between unilateral respect and mutual respect, it may be said that these conversations are impregnated with the former type of respect, as much from the intellectual as from the moral point of view.

Now, it is clear that such interventionism on the part of the adult transforms the child's conversation. The great interest of Katz's book lies in showing us how much the child has adapted himself to this type of dialogue. But, from our point of view, this is but one particular type of relationship between children and adults, of which there are other possible types. Mme Leuzinger's data were collected under very different conditions and it is only natural that they should give results which differ from those now being discussed. The lesson to be learned from this apparent contradiction is that the child's language does not depend only on the child's development but, as the evidence shows, on the type of relationship which he maintains with the adult.

The verbal ego-centrism of the child cannot, therefore, give us the exact measure of his intellectual ego-centrism but is merely a more or less apparent and mobile indication of deeper attitudes which are both social and epistemic. There must be no uncertainty on this point.

What then is the verbal ego-centrism of a child? When two normal adults converse together because they have something to tell each other, their conversation has two correlated characteristics. In the first place each one tries to influence the other; whether it be a question, a request, a command, or information, the object in view is always to modify the other speaker's conduct or thought. Secondly, and just because of this, each one distinguishes between his own point of view and the other man's. One's speech is a function of what the other speaker either ignores or already knows; we thus put ourselves in his place and, even when we speak only of ourselves, while seeming to speak of others or of general principles (which constitutes the conscious and even hypocritical ego-centrism of the adult, in the generally accepted meaning of the word), we do so with the firm purpose of influencing another (although to our own advantage) and knowing full well what is his frame of mind, so as to judge of the effect produced. Now the child is in some degree capable of all this when still quite young, and "socialized" speech comes no doubt as early as speech itself: when still in its infancy the child shows the greatest skill (moreover an almost unconscious skill) in trying to get what he wants from others. But, besides this characteristic, childish speech shows us another, of which the adult equivalent is only to be found in some exceptional cases such as, among others, the mystical soliloquies in which the filial relationship of the child reappears. Two aspects of this ego-centric speech make it recognizable. In the first place the child may speak without trying to influence the other speaker. For instance, when the child is playing and working in the presence of adults or even of his own friends, he sometimes talks without a pause so that it is impossible to decide whether he is speaking to someone else or to himself. In §§ 1 and 2, we have given some new examples of this phenomenon and noted that the child, while he mentally turns to the *alter ego*— i.e., the adult or the companion—is trying not so much to instruct or to question him as to rouse himself to action in which the other has a share. Secondly, and because of this, it is impossible for one engaged in such talking to make a distinction between his own point of view and someone else's. When he soliloquizes in communion with the adult, the child does not differentiate between his own thought and his hearer's any more than the mystic distinguishes between his own thought and that in which he is plunged. And for the small child of 2 or 3 years old who is using monologue in the presence of those he knows, the question does not even arise.

There can therefore, in general, be little doubt about the close relationship of this phenomenon with social and intellectual ego-centrism, although, as we have already said, verbal ego-centrism is much more variable just because it depends more on external social factors. If ego-centrism is an absorption of the ego in things and in persons, without differentiation between one's own point of view and other people's, this clearly shows that the child's use of speech, in what we call ego-centric language, is a particular case of this general phenomenon and may, in this respect, serve as a guide in analysing its evolution as a function of age. But it will only be a clue and external circumstances will affect the child's use of speech, and in consequence the evolution of the coefficient of ego-centrism, far more rapidly than his deeper mode of thought or epistemic attitude, to which we shall refer again later, and which cannot be directly observed.

Thus we cannot subscribe to Stern's opinion. In the 4th edition of his *Psychologie der frühen Kindheit*, Stern admits that the originality of the child's ego-centric speech, when compared with adult speech, shows "that the child's personality has quite a different structure."[1] But in the 5th edition of this work, in view of the different results put forward by Katz, Stern declares that the child's ego-centric speech does not involve all the consequences attributed to it by us. Nevertheless, although Stern is a great authority on the subject, what seems more important to us is not so much the extent to which verbal ego-centrism may be reduced by social environment and education, but how much of it is revealed when the child is left to himself. If ego-centrism is merely a sign and not a first cause, it would seem fitting to determine the exact connection of this sign with deeper realities of which it is a manifestation, before taking stock of its variations in order to throw doubt on its meaning. Take, for instance, the examination of a zoological species which one wishes to compare with a neighbouring species. It is more important to know that in surroundings A, the first will produce a morphosis

---

[1] Miss Muchow, in Hamburg, had, in fact, found results equivalent to ours at the *Maison des Petits* in Geneva.

or special variety which the second does not produce, than to know that the first reacts in the same way as the second in different surroundings B. Likewise, the fact that at the *Maison des Petits* at Geneva or in the Kindergarten at Hamburg, the child's percentage of ego-centrism is very high, tells us far more about his spontaneous tendencies than we should know if we were told that his socialized speech may reach the same proportion as that of an adult in other social surroundings: in fact, if in some circumstances the child is able entirely to abstain from ego-centric speech, for the normal adult, it would be impossible to adopt such speech.

True, A. Luria, in his writings published in Russian, compares ego-centric speech in the child to the inner language of the adult. This comparison is excellent from the functional point of view or, as Luria tells us, using Dewey's language, from the "instrumental" point of view. But it does not seem to us to do away with differences of structure. We find a similar case in the symbolic game when it simply reproduces an interesting reality. In such cases the child seems to reproduce plastically events which we merely re-enact in our minds. Functionally one may therefore also say that the symbolic game corresponds to some form of adult thought. But if from this we proceed to structural analysis, the opposing factors at once become obvious. In both cases the essential difference is as follows: the child's speech and thought are externalized by him, as it were made "objective"; while in ours there would be a feeling of inwardness and subjectivity. For instance, what engages the child's mind in the imaginative game is projected on to the very things themselves and they are thus symbolically incarnated into external reality: instead of merely recalling in her mind the scenes of mealtime, the child identifies herself with her dolls and even transforms sticks and blades of grass into food which she uses to represent their meals. In the same way ego-centric speech exteriorizes under the form of conversation with a real or fictitious social group what we would merely say to ourselves. In both cases identity of function does not exclude structural difference, and in both cases there is ego-centrism because the subject does not sufficiently differentiate between himself and the outer world but projects into that world the content of his own subjectivity.

This close relationship between verbal ego-centrism and the symbolic game—another form of ego-centric assimilation which lessens as the child's age increases[1]—allows us to reach the following conclusions.

In the first place it would seem, in view of our previous work and of Mme Leuzinger's recent research, that in a well-defined and homogeneous centre, such as the one of spontaneous work at the *Maison des Petits*, the coefficient of ego-centrism decreases with more or less regularity as the child grows older. This is a fact of importance, which remains so quite apart from any connexion with possibly differing environments. Let us now suppose that a series of measures of the coefficient as a function of age has been made in an environment where, on an average and at corresponding ages, the coefficient of ego-centrism is less strong than at Geneva (for example at the Hamburg centre, of which Miss Muchow has made a study); if, in such an environment, the coefficient of ego-centrism also decreases with age—and this on an average is proved—then its interest as an indication of the law of evolution of verbal ego-centrism will not be affected by the sum total of variations between one environment and another.

Secondly, if we compare the different environments under review, we note that verbal ego-centrism does not vary in a haphazard way but in relation to causes which are not difficult to discern. These causes may be related to the children's activity or to the child's reactions to his surroundings.

[1] See our work on *La Formation du Symbole chez l'Enfant* (Delachaux et Niéstlé).

As regards the child's activity, generally speaking, one may say that the coefficient of ego-centrism is higher in so far as activity tends to consist mainly of play and in particular of play that is physical exercise and imaginative play (the symbolic game): it is on the contrary weaker in so far as activity approximates to real work. This would seem to explain the differences between centres such as the *Maison des Petits*, the Kindergarten at Hamburg and the Malting House at Cambridge. At the *Maison des Petits* in Geneva or at Mme Leuzinger's school in Glaris, the children have at their disposal material for educational games (Lotto for sums and reading, ball games, building bricks, records, etc.) which they are quite free to use as they like, so that action starts as a pure game either of movement or of symbol, and only gradually tends to become intellectual enquiry. In such an environment it is thus impossible to establish a clear division between play and work. Now it is precisely in such an environment that ego-centric speech appears to be most highly developed. At the other extreme of these three centres of which we have just spoken is the Malting House, which is so organized that the child is constantly experimenting and dealing with problems of a scientific nature. In this environment ego-centric speech is found to be much weaker. Mrs. Isaacs has herself noted that the frequency of monologue, whether private or collective, has always been in proportion to that of imaginative play, and that it tends to be excluded from experimental enquiry and is then accompanied by adapted speech. In the Kindergarten at Hamburg which stands halfway as regards the coefficient of ego-centrism, we find there also the same proportion of work and play.

Now the connexion between these two poles, the pole of play in the child's activity, and the pole of ego-centrism, becomes obvious when one realizes that symbolic thought, which is common to the imaginative game, to dreams and to day dreaming, is itself always an assimilation of reality to the ego, rather than an objective adaptation of the mind to things. As to the convergence of the socialized pole of language with the pole of organized activity (work, games with rules, etc.), this also is self-evident if adaptation to others is parallel to adaptation to the outer physical world. Let us not forget that the younger the child, the less clear will be the dividing line between play and work. I find it therefore difficult to agree with Mrs. Isaacs when she concludes that there is nothing ego-centric about a child's intellectual activity, as though work and imagination were always clearly distinguishable.

The child's social environment will also naturally have a bearing on variations in the coefficient of ego-centrism. But here things are complicated by the fact that we have two types of relationship to consider: relationship with contemporaries and relationship with adults. Speaking generally, one may say that two factors contribute to lessen the coefficient of ego-centrism although they do so in very different ways: community of interests of the child with his friends, and adult interventionism. The first of these factors is present when brothers and sisters are together or in surroundings such as the Malting House, when an enquiry pursued in common leads to united effort; it then naturally produces socialized speech and directs the mind towards co-operation. The adult's authority may also produce socialized speech, but in a different way, as Mme Leuzinger's and Katz's observations have shown us. In non-interventionist surroundings, where the children's work may either be diverted according to individual choice or concentrated on some special kind of enquiry, speech is, on the contrary, more ego-centric: this is the case at the *Maison des Petits*. Here again Miss Muchow's observations show an intermediate result because conditions there are also of an intermediate nature. The children at the Kindergarten in Hamburg are grouped in small family units and are so to speak halfway between the conditions at the *Maison des Petits* and the collaboration between children at the Malting House or as observed by Katz.

§ 4. The Child's Intellectual Ego-Centrism.—In our first studies of the child's thought, we used the word ego-centrism for lack of a better one, to denote an orientation of the mind, which seemed to us important at the outset of the individual's intellectual development, and which survives in adults in all circumstances where they are still dominated by spontaneous, naïve and consequently infantile attitudes. Since our use of this word has given rise to some misunderstanding,[1] we think it will be useful once again to make its meaning clear before determining how far verbal or social ego-centrism is related to intellectual ego-centrism.

In the first place we must notice that what specifically characterizes the child's ego-centrism is not to be found in the social or moral sphere nor in the child's awareness of his own self, but definitely in the intellectual field. Childish ego-centrism is a feature of his knowledge; we might even say that it is an epistemic phenomenon if one could speak of comparative epistemology in regard to the psychology of the child's intelligence. It is undoubtedly because we began by describing the social and verbal ego-centrism of the child before we described this

[1] Because of the usual meaning of this word. Practice does, however, override such ambiguity: there is, for instance, as much difference between the meaning of what in common use is called "realism" and that given to it in the language of philosophy, as there is between the generally accepted meaning of the word "ego-centrism" and the one which we have adopted by convention. "Realism" in ordinary language signifies taking only facts into account, as opposed to the ideas or feelings of the subject; philosophical realism, on the contrary, consists in assuming the existence of things such as they appear to be, i.e., in confounding the subjective with the objective. Similarly, in daily speech, ego-centrism means referring everything back to oneself, i.e., to a conscious self, whereas, when we use the term ego-centrism, we mean the inability to differentiate between one's own point of view and other people's or between one's own activity and changes in the object. We adopted this word by analogy with anthropocentrism, but the child's anthropocentrism is as yet only adjusted to his own individual activity as opposed to the activity of men in general.

epistemic ego-centrism—the only important one from our point of view—that people have objected to some of our conclusions and shifted the discussion from its source to related but different ground.

What then is intellectual ego-centrism in the child? It is the assemblage of all the different precritical and consequently pre-objective cognitive attitudes of the child's mind; whether these attitudes relate to nature, to others or to himself matters little. Fundamentally, ego-centrism is thus neither a conscious phenomenon (ego-centrism, when self-conscious, is no longer ego-centrism), nor a phenomenon of social behaviour (behaviour is an indirect manifestation of ego-centrism but does not constitute it) but a kind of systematic and unconscious illusion, an illusion of perspective.

An illustration will help to make this clear. Let us picture a simple ignorant man, who has lived since his birth in a small corner at the foot of mountains of which he has a good view but which he has never explored. From the point of view of physical knowledge, this observer will obviously fall a prey to all sorts of illusions: he will not only reckon that a neighbouring mountain is higher than a more distant one but will imagine that the source of a river is in a mountain from which it appears to flow, whereas this is not the case. He will see the world as a system of which he occupies the centre and all the mountains and valleys grouped in relation to the place in which he lives. Similar illusions will colour his knowledge of other people: the traveller coming from a neighbouring town will be taken for a foreigner from across the frontier; the intellectual, enjoying a holiday, will be looked upon as a lazy *rentier*. Everybody else's activity will thus be measured only in terms of his own. Finally, as regards knowledge of his ego, the man we are considering, whom we suppose has never defined his physical position (because he has not travelled his own country, is unable to locate it in relation to others) nor his moral position (to judge others objectively), will lack the necessary systems of reference for knowing himself. He will, of course, know that he is Joseph and different from Peter, James or John. But in his own opinion he will be wiser than the foreigner visiting his country and more industrious than the writer who has come to it in order to describe it.

Now this man will not appear ego-centric to himself and perhaps not to others. So far as he himself is concerned, he has obviously no idea of how changed his outlook would be if it were broadened by gradually increasing his knowledge of the neighbourhood, especially if it went beyond the limits of his present horizon, just because this new outlook would not merely add to the type of knowledge he already possesses but would bring about a kind of readjustment, i.e., a recasting of his system of perspectives and values. He is thus ego-centric without being aware of it and consciousness of his ego-centrism would either lessen or eliminate it. In his conversation with others he speaks of the same mountains, the same valleys, the same work and the same events as everyone else, which makes it difficult to detect the restricted and always personal way in which he makes use of ideas that are common property. Only a close observer will be able from time to time to discover, from some naïve remark, in what way his view of the world differs from that of the man who has been able to leave his small homestead and can see himself in relation to others.

To what then can the ego-centrism of the subject we have just described be attributed? In the first place, to a combination of external circumstances: absence of knowledge, the fact of being riveted to one particular small place and social group, etc. But does ignorance explain everything? Certainly not; for, should the subject go beyond his primitive horizon and gradually discover the surrounding country and get to know different kinds of men and social groups, he will be adding more than a few facts to those he already knows: he will be changing the system of his interpretation of things; what for him had been an absolute or a central group of ideas will become merely a point of view as against other points of view. There is thus a second factor to be considered in initial ego-centrism: as a mode of spontaneous apperception, which is common to every individual and as such needs no preliminary explanation, ego-centrism consists of a kind of primary adjustment of thought, an "intellectual simplicity of mind" in the sense of absence of all intellectual relatively and any rational system of reference. Now, such a mode of apperception cannot consist of a quality, susceptible of isolation, which can be observed either externally or by introspection; it remains nevertheless an essential feature of the intellect, conditioning a person's behaviour as well as his conscience, although it is on a different plane from them.

Let us now return to the child. From the double point of view of knowledge of the physical world and knowledge of others or of himself, the child's position is the same as that of the man whose case we have been considering. He finds himself in a physical and social universe, which he has never explored, he cannot therefore escape from making his own the particular view of things created by the circumstances in which he is placed. As to the epistemic attitude, which forms his response to this external situation, it could only be even more "innocent," since, during the first weeks of his existence, the child is unaware of himself as capable of thought or even as a living and conscious being, to such an extent that he is entirely absorbed in the things he sees, and knows nothing of critical distinction between the ego and the outside world.

What then is intellectual ego-centrism? It is a spontaneous attitude which, at the beginning, rules the child's psychical activity and which persists throughout life during periods of mental inertia. From a negative point of view, such an attitude runs counter to a comprehensive view of the universe and to the co-ordination of different points of view, in short, to any impersonal activity of the mind. From the positive point of view this attitude consists in the ego being absorbed in things and in the social group: but this absorption is such that the subject, while thinking that he has knowledge of people and things as they are, in reality attributes to them not only their objective characteristics but also qualities which come from his own ego or from the particular aspect of things of which he is aware at the time. For the subject, release from his ego-centrism will therefore consist not so much in acquiring new knowledge about things or his social group, nor even in turning more closely to the object qua external, but in uncentring himself and in being able to dissociate the subject or the object: in becoming aware of what is subjective in himself, in being able to find his true place in all possible circumstances and thereby to establish between things, people and his own self a system of common and reciprocal relationship. Ego-centrism is thus in opposition with objectivity in so far as objectivity signifies relativity on the physical plane and reciprocity on the social plane.

To say that the child is ego-centric as regards knowledge of the physical world is thus merely to state that the child's conception of things is at one and the same time what they appear to be (phenomenalism) and endowed with qualities similar to those which he possesses (intentionality, force and life, binding laws, etc.). For example, the moon is following us (phenomenalism) and it does so "in order to" give us light, watch us, or anything else you may choose (finalism due to lack of dissociation between subjective and objective). How will the child correct this double illusion? In exactly the same way as when, during his first year, he ceased to believe in the changing size of things and attributed to them one that remained constant; just as Copernicus ceased to believe in geocentrism and Einstein in Newtonian absolutes; by seeing himself in relation to a system of objective relationships, which, as a complementary effect, eliminates phenomenalism in favour of a rational sense of reality and reduces previous subjective links (finality, force, intentionality, etc.) by dissociating subject from object. The example of the moon, however clear it may be, has no special privilege: in his interpretation of any movement, of any causal relation, etc., the child has an opportunity of linking the phenomenalism of the immediate data with false absolutes of subjective origin. One can thus see what initial ego-centrism of physical knowledge is; it is not an over-developed consciousness of the ego, which would lead the child to lose interest in the experience of external things; it is, on the contrary, pure "realism," i.e., an immediate taking possession of the object, but so immediate that the subject, who does not know himself, cannot manage to get outside himself in order to see himself in a universe of relations freed from subjective accretions.

We are now in a position to understand what children's social ego-centrism is and, in the light of this knowledge, what their logical ego-centrism is. Social ego-centrism may be recognized as a particular form of epistemic ego-centrism, just as the latter can be deduced from the former. In other words, the child discovers people in exactly the same way as he discovers things and he knows them both in the same way. He is a prey to the same illusory lack of perspective in considering the social group and the external world, and his ego is mingled with his picture of both people and material things.

In the first place, neither the child's social ego-centrism nor the ego-centrism of his knowledge of the physical world is a quality which can be observed within his self-consciousness or by watching his external behaviour. Social ego-centrism, as much as purely intellectual ego-centrism, is an epistemic attitude: it is a way of understanding others just as ego-centrism in general is a way of looking at things. A close watch on the child's language will no doubt show that it exists, as will careful observation of the child's spontaneous reactions to physical phenomena. But, considered as an epistemic attitude, ego-centrism can never be directly observed. Thus, as on the physical plane, the child turns entirely towards things and away from his own self as a subject of knowledge, so, on the social plane, the child turns completely towards others and thus finds himself at the antipodes of what in common language is called ego-centrism, i.e., constant and conscious preoccupation with self. Nevertheless, just as on the physical plane he only sees things imbued with certain qualities which are personal to him, so, on the social plane, he sees others only in a symbiosis (unconscious of itself) between himself and those around him.

We can therefore from the start brush aside an objection often raised by the best of authors and which, to our mind, is due to a mere misunderstanding; ego-centrism would seem to be irreconcilable with the established fact that the child is a fundamentally sociable creature, "syntonizing" not only with human beings but with all living things and even with the entire universe. For example, Grünbaum, in a stimulating essay,[1] believes that what characterizes the child's mentality is this universal sympathy, this need of a sense of community with things themselves. As a point in support of his thesis Grünbaum remarks that, in our explanations, which are based on the ego-centrism of the child, we have to admit that this ego-centrism is unconscious of itself. Grünbaum thus seems to make an antithesis of the child's ego-centrism and his "*Gemeindschaftsbindung*"—Mrs. Buhler[2] likewise refuses to admit the existence of ego-centrism in children because of the sociability of those she has studied. We find similar views expressed by Katz and by Isaacs.

Now, from our point of view, an argument such as this is based on a confusion of words. If we give the word ego-centrism its generally accepted meaning, that of conscious self-

[1] A. A. Grünbaum, "Die Struktur der Kinderpsyche," *Zeitschr. f. Pädag. Psychol.*, Oct. 1927, p. 446 ff.

[2] From *Birth to Maturity*, London (Kegan Paul).

preoccupation, which precludes a feeling for the community, the word is clearly being given contradictory meanings. But if we use this word ego-centrism to describe something purely epistemic, to denote the confusion of subject with object during the act of acquiring knowledge, in which the subject does not know himself and, in turning towards the object, is unable to uncentre himself, then, ego-centrism and a sense of community are so little opposed to each other that they often constitute one and the same phenomenon. Thus, on the physical plane, Grünbaum gives as examples of social feeling those very attitudes of which we made use to illustrate ego-centrism. The balloons go up in the air "because they love the air" declares a child of 6½ years old. The child, we said, is ego-centric, hence he sees the balloon as being like himself and endows it with purpose and finality. Grünbaum answers that the child personifies things in so far as he is in communion with them. But, who would not see that the two explanations come to the same thing? Not realizing that he is himself a subject, it is because the child projects his inner qualities into the thing, that he is in communion with it!

Exactly the same thing happens on the social plane. Here the child is drawn towards others as he is towards things. He dislikes being alone, and, even when he is alone, he feels in communion with his own usual group. Nevertheless, in his understanding of others as in his intellectual and moral relationship with others, which is maintained by means of speech, he cannot, as yet, completely dissociate his ego from another's: between himself and another there is identification, even confusion rather than differentiation and reciprocity. Thus, according to one's point of view, the child may simultaneously appear to be very ego-centric and completely absorbed in others.

An example will help us to understand the unity of these two characters, as well as the union of social and intellectual ego-centrism. As we have said elsewhere, a boy of 6 to 7 years old is ready to declare that he has a brother but that this brother has himself no brother. On the other hand, as Brunschvicg has rightly remarked, a child, when trying to count up the number of people in a room, will not include himself: as a subject who is doing the counting, he does not notice himself and does not put himself among those to be counted. The paradox is evident: in the first of these two examples the child is dominated by his own ego to such an extent that he is unable to see things from his brother's point of view, and in the second example he forgets himself entirely! But, in reality, we have here only one and the same phenomenon. In both cases the personal view is looked upon as the only possible one, and this is because the thinking subject does not recognize himself as a subject; but, according to whether one focuses one's attention on the ego's perspective, or on the subject's self-forgetfulness, the child will appear to be ego-centric or to be entirely extroverted.

We can now see that social ego-centrism, as well as physical ego-centrism, is as much a matter of external circumstances which affect the child's position as a ready and spontaneous attitude of mind. Launched into a world of social reactions, of feelings, beliefs, intellectual relationship and linguistic expressions, which are in every way beyond him, it is very natural that the child should be unable to assimilate this world without first having discovered it, except from the narrow and limited angle of his particular view of it. But, on this point as on the question of physical ego-centrism, absence of knowledge does not provide a full explanation. Let us quote from a very subtle analysis of our hypotheses by Charles Blondel. He writes, for example: "A customer cannot make a carpenter understand what he wants; this need not be exclusively due to the autism of his thought. Language is similar to many other movements, which we have to master and begin by making badly and by using in the wrong way. Take a young man at his first dance. He does not keep time with the music, he steps on his partner's toes, he bumps into other couples, he dances as if he were alone. This need not give rise to making a distinction between an ego-centric dance and one that is well-directed."[1] Farther on, Blondel compares a dilettante in modern physics discoursing on the subject of relativity with a scientist to a child speaking with adults about things which he only half understands. Now, it is a fact that in collective monologue with those around him, the child's lack of information plays an important part. There is, however, a great difference between the case of the child who, because of his ignorance, relates everything to his own point of view, and the position of the adult whose incompetence prevents any adapted conduct in relation with his interlocutor or companion. The adult who does not understand carpentry, dancing or the theory of relativity is aware of his ignorance and, because of his competence in other fields, is able to put himself in the place of those with whom he is dealing: that is just why there is no need to speak of an ego-centric dance to describe the faltering efforts of a young man at his first dance, whereas the word could be applied if the young man imagined that he was dancing like everyone else. The child's inexperience is, on the contrary, so complete that his knowledge of it can only be very approximate and he thinks he is in communion with the whole group, even when he soliloquizes in a way which is incomprehensible to others.

It may be briefly stated that in the make-up of childish ego-centrism, both on the social and on the physical plane, absence of knowledge is a factor of secondary importance. A factor of primary importance is that spontaneous attitude of the individual mind in which thought turns directly towards the object without first being aware of its own point of view. This is why sociability and ego-centrism in no way exclude each other. The ego-centric mind is, in fact, far more susceptible to suggestions

[1] *Revue d'hist. et de phil. relig.*, Strasburg, 1924, 473.

from outside and to the influence of the group than a mind which has been disciplined by co-operation; in so far as it does not know itself, the ego-centric mind cannot become conscious of its own personality. Thus we find that the child shows a maximum of suggestibility at the same ages as a maximum of ego-centrism and that these two characteristics diminish as the individual becomes truly socialized.

How does this socialization operate? We can see here again a striking parallel between the physical and social planes of the child's behaviour; in both cases the decrease in ego-centrism can be explained not by the acquisition of new knowledge or new feelings but by a change in the subject's point of view so that, although he does not abandon his original point of view, he merely places it among the mass of other possible points of view. In other words, this means that for the understanding of other people as well as for the understanding of the outside world, two conditions are necessary: (1) consciousness of oneself as a subject, and the ability to detach subject from object so as not to attribute to the second the characteristics of the first; (2) to cease to look upon one's own point of view as the only possible one, and to co-ordinate it with that of others. Expressed in other terms this means that to adapt oneself to a social setting as well as to particular physical surroundings is to construct a group of relations and by an effort of co-ordination, which itself involves adjustment and reciprocity of points of view, to give oneself a place in that group.

Now it at once becomes evident that this double effort to relate oneself and reciprocate actually provides a definition of the process of co-operation or socialization between equals, of which one aspect was studied in §3, when we compared social intercourse between children with that between adults. From this point of view the study of co-operation will, in consequence, give us the best chance of analysing the true nature of the child's social ego-centrism.

Adults, we have seen, are both the child's superiors and close to him by their enveloping sympathy. In his approach to them, the child thus wavers between an attitude of prayer or request, and one of communion, which comes from his inability to distinguish the ego from another. In neither case does the child really emerge from his own view of things to co-ordinate it with that of others. Hence the predominance of ego-centric speech in children's intercourse with the adult, provided the latter does nothing to alter the relationship by imposing his authority. The playmate, on the contrary, in so far as he is himself an individual, who is both equal and different, presents a new problem: that of continually distinguishing the ego from the other person and the reciprocity of these two views. Hence the all-important part played by co-operation between equals, which, moreover, as a type of social relationship, is not entirely lacking between children and adults, provided both have been appropriately educated so that the factor of authority and superiority is kept in the background.

Thus, in the well-defined sense that we have just tried to analyse, social ego-centrism is completely on a parallel with intellectual ego-centrism, and childish ego-centrism in general cannot be qualified as presocial except in connexion with the actual process of co-operation.

Generally speaking, intellectual and social forms of ego-centrism are one and the same thing, because both are linked at their source to the conditions of initial activity and both vanish in correlation with one and the same factor: gradual co-ordination of actions, which is the common root both of the systematic operation of reason and of inter-individual co-operation, or the system of communal activities.

Thus, if we go back beyond thought to the actions from which it proceeds and in particular to that sensori-motory activity, which constitutes the foundation of symbolism and representation, we notice that the beginning of ego-centrism comes from the fact that initial actions are not well co-ordinated, ordinated, are irreversible and in consequence essentially adjusted towards reaching their goal or finishing point. On the plane of perception we already see that the most essential element in or the distortions or "illusions" of vision, touch, etc., is due to the unjustifiable part played by "centring" adjustments, whereas those uncentring adjustments which are inherent in perceptual activity have a regulating and co-ordinating effect.[1] On the plane of sensori-motory intelligence, i.e., of perception and habit rendered mobile, beginning to extend beyond their elementary field of action, we also find that the construction of the permanent object, of practical spacing, etc.,[2] is the result of an adjustment which reverses the aim of the original activity: thus, after having oriented the place of external things and their displacements merely in relation to his own movements, the baby finally locates his own body in the same practical space as contains the objects constructed by virtue of this co-ordination of the whole. When speech first begins by initiation into a system of collective signs and pictorial representation, with its individualistic symbolism, ego-centrism reappears in the form of intuitive centring linked with mentally imagined actions, which thus denote assimilation of what is real (physically or socially) to personal activity. It is on this level that our analysis of childish speech in this chapter and in chapter 1 should be placed.

Thus, at its starting point, ego-centrism clearly expresses the irreversibility of actions. One action cannot in fact be combined with other actions and it cannot be carried out in two directions in so far as it is centrally adjusted. And it is this initial central adjustment which simultaneously explains the phenomenon of

[1] On this subject, see our *The Psychology of Intelligence*, Chapter III (intellect and perception) (Routledge and Kegan Paul).

[2] See *The Origin of Intelligence in the Child*, and *The Child's Construction of Reality*, London (Routledge and Kegan Paul).

behaviour, the action's irreversibility and that illusory point of view which is ego-centrism or assimilation to personal activity. As A. R. Zazzo has rightly stated in a recent discussion of this point: "This is simply anthropomorphism."[1] But he demands an explanation of this idea from the psychologist. This author does not seem to have been fully aware of the indissoluble link between ego-centrism, which he hesitates to recognize, and the notion of primitive mental irreversibility, which he then unhesitatingly borrows from us.

Moreover, as the child's actions gradually become better co-ordinated, this co-ordination, which is both individual and social, is simultaneously shown by the reversible composition of the child's actions, which transforms them into operations and by the interindividual reciprocity of these operations which constitutes co-operation. It is also this double process which uncentres the individual as compared with his initial ego-centrism.

By being co-ordinated, actions are, in the first place, transformed into operations; an operation being a reversible action. Thus the most usual co-ordination of actions consists in establishing them in an order or rank based on systems which allow for a return to the starting point (reversibility) and for changes of direction or deviations (associativity) as well as for a combination into pairs (transitivity). These combined operational systems, of which the finished type corresponds to what mathematicians call "groups," show themselves in a simpler form in the field of classes and logical relations themselves (in such a case we would speak of "groupings"). Such groupings and groups are thus at the constructional starting point of logical and mathematical structures, and we have been able to show the essential part they play in the psychological elaboration of the logical forms of number, quantities, time, etc., not to mention

[1] A. R. Zazzo, *Le devenir de l'intelligence* (Paris, 1946, p. 39).

space, in which the influence of such a scheme has been revealed by H. Poincaré.

Now, from the fact that a grouping gives us that form of equilibrium achieved by the co-ordination of actions at the time of their becoming completely uncentred, it follows that we can measure intellectual ego-centrism by the irreversibility of thought and therefore by the absence of any groupings, and we can also determine the exact progress of reversibility by the gradual building up of such groupings. That is why, in our opinion, research, which is based on evidence as fragile as ego-centrism, should be replaced by an analysis of the actual operational mechanism of action and thought, i.e., of the inner source of intellectual development.

But, since in so far as they remain unco-ordinated the individual's actions are still centred on his personal activity, then, in so far as they are co-ordinated, this co-ordination implies reciprocity with the actions of others: obviously the individual could not act with any logical sequence without taking the actions of others into account. Operational systems or groupings and groups, which are the expression of co-ordinated operations, embody by their very organization this contact with the operations of others. More exactly, since the setting up of correspondence with others and of reciprocity, in itself constitutes the most important groupings, it follows that the operations of others and personal operations will necessarily combine to form a system of co-operation which is both logical and social. It is in this double sense of inter-individual co-operation and of intra-individual co-ordination that this system of operations constitutes a true instrument for adjustment, which will set the individual free from his initial ego-centrism.

APPENDIX

Fifty consecutive remarks made by Lev. (See chapter 1)

I. Repetition.
II. Monologue.
III. Collective monologue.
IV. Adapted information.

V. Criticism and derision.
VI. Orders and threats.
VII. Question.
VIII. Answer.

No.	TEXT	CAT.	REMARKS
1	Lev puts his pencil down Geo's neck. Geo cries out, "Lev!" *It doesn't matter.* Lev begins to draw his hat again. He shows his work:	IV	
2	*I look at things properly.* What are you looking at?	IV	This remark belongs to IV because it is part of a dialogue. It calls forth an answer and then remark 3.
3	*The hat.* Lev repeats some words which one of his companions is learning:	VIII	

No.	Text	Cat.	Remarks
4	*Luloid! celuloid!*	I	
	Turning his drawing upside down and addressing himself to no one:		
5	*I want to see how it looks.*	II	
	Ro brings some paper cigarettes. He distributes them. Lev asks for some:		
6	*How about me?*	VII	This is a request, but expressed in interrogative form; it therefore belongs to category VII.
	Lev goes back to his work. He points to the little ribs of straw on his hat and compares them with the drawing:		
7	*There are just those things like there ought to be, you see.* (No answer.)		7 Addresses himself to the community in general without expecting any response.
	To the other children:		
8	*You are moving the table.*	IV	8 Here Lev wants to make himself heard.
	He helps Go to play lotto. He takes a card which Go does not know where to put and places it:		
9	*I think it goes here.*	IV	9 Clear case.
	To Mlle L. To whom Go has shown a duplicate card:		
10	*Then if you lose one, there is one left.*	IV	
	Addressing himself to no one:		
11	*That is to make it hold together.*	II	
	Pointing to one of the paper cigarettes (without speaking to anyone in particular):		
12	*Look what Roger gave me. Roger gave me that.*	III	12 A doubtful case, but as he has spoken to the community in general, no one responds.
	To Go, speaking of the lotto cards:		
13	*You've got three of the same.*	V	
	To someone else, showing his cigarette:		
14	*It's like a cigarette, isn't it?*	VII	
	Geo is looking for the duplicate card; "Please, teacher, I can't find the one that there's two of."		
15	*No, I can see.*	IV	
	Talking to himself as he draws:		
16	*First I shall do the fingers, so as to make another round.*	II	16 Clear case.
	Has a hat got fingers?		

No.	TEXT	CAT.	REMARKS
17	They are the things that go below.	VIII	
	He shows his drawing:		
18	There is my hat—look at my hat. There now, isn't that like!	IV	18 Might be III, but has called forth a response on the part of a hearer.
	Not very.		
19	Still, it is just a little bit like.	IV	
20	Look at my hat, it twists round and round like a snail. The same here too.	III	20 Is addressed to no one in spite of the form "Look." A clear case.
	Geo asks the time. Lev, without moving from his work, mechanically repeats the question:		
21	What's the time?	I	
	Talking of his work:		
22	I have done one half properly, teacher.		22 Might be III.
	Mlle L. does not hear. Another child asks: "How is it a half?" Lev does not listen but goes on repeating:		
23	One half properly.	III	
	A silence.		
	"Now you must write."		
24	Write what?	VII	
	"What there is on the hat." A moment later Lev takes his hat and looks.		
25	It's something in English. I can't. It's "big."	III	
	Drawing attention to what he is doing:		
26	Please teacher, one half is right, yes, look.	IV	26 Might be III.
	Addresses himself to no one and returns to his former topic:		
27	I don't like that name in English.	II	
	Other children are building near the table where Lev is drawing. They are making a hut out of leaves. Lev looks on:		
28	I can make houses of leaves.	III	
	Ro is working with figures. Lev gets up and announces:		
29	I want to see.	III	
	He approves of what Ro is doing. Ro asks him nothing:		

No.	TEXT	CAT.	REMARKS
30	*Yes, it is 5.*	IV	30 Occupies himself here with the work of another.
	Ro makes a mistake. Lev:		
31	*You ought to count, down there.*	IV	
	Lev goes back to his place. He talks without being listened to by anyone:		
32	*I can make houses as big as trees, can't I, teacher.*	III	32 This is not a question.
33	*Mummy didn't give me a box, because she hadn't got a macaroni box.*	III	
	Lev looks on at Ro's work. Ro complains that he has lost a ticket.		
34	*And the 6 isn't there. In another box there is 6, 7, 8, 9.*	IV	
	Ro having followed this advice, and looked for the 6 in the other box, Lev returns to his drawing. He makes no attempt to explain what he is talking about. He is thinking aloud:		
35	*If I haven't took the things for making the roof. I shall have took them to-morrow.*	II	
	Ro, whose eyes are blind-folded, has to recognize by touch some figures cut out in wood. He makes a mistake. Lev who is at the same table cries out:		
36	*Wrong!*	V	
	Lev picks up a pencil which has been dropped and hands it to Bur:		
37	*Burny, take the pencil.*	VI	
	He takes some figures out of the box, puts them before Bur, and asks:		
38	*What are those?*	VII	
	Bur takes no notice, and does not answer. Lev announces:		
39	*I can do much more than Bur.*	V	
	He picks up a piece of wood, and makes it roll on the table:		
40	*Now then, the van is going to start—the van has arrived—the van is going to start.*	II	
	Another child looks at his drawing: "What's that?"		

No.	TEXT	CAT.	REMARKS
41	That's the ribbon that's come undone.	VIII	
	Lev is asked whether he won't put the date on his drawing.		
42	I'd rather put the name.	VIII	
43	He rises and leaves his place shouting:		43 Addresses himself to no one.
	I want to tell Mlle L. something.	III	
	Someone is going to write his name on his drawing. He looks on:		
44	You mustn't write Levane with an e. With an a it is Levana in Georgian, without a, e it's in French.	IV	
	Somebody tells Lev that he has seen him disobeying his father.		
45	Oh, no.	IV	
	By way of changing the subject:		
46	I shall write something else in Georgian for you.	IV	
	He looks to see what Bur is doing and asks:		
47	What is he doing?	VII	
48	To Bur:		
	Give me your pencil.	VI	
	No.		
	Yes.		
	No.		
49	"Yes" [in English]. That's all I know.	III	
	He leaves Bur and amuses himself by folding bits of paper.		
50	Look this is the way to do it.	III	
	(No answer.)		

INDEX

Routledge Classics
Get inside a great mind

The Psychology of Intelligence
Jean Piaget

'He found, to put it most succinctly, that children don't think like grown-ups. Einstein called it a discovery so simple that only a genius could have thought of it.'
Time

Piaget's theory of learning lies at the very heart of modern understanding of the human learning process, and he is celebrated as the founding father of child psychology. *The Psychology of Intelligence* is one of his most important works and contains a complete synthesis of his thoughts on the mechanisms of intellectual development. Given his significance, it is hardly surprising that *Psychology Today* pronounced Piaget the Best Psychologist of the Twentieth Century.

Pb: 0–415–25401–9

Modern Man in Search of a Soul
C. G. Jung

'He was more than a psychological or scientific phenomenon; he was to my mind one of the greatest religious phenomena the world has ever experienced.'
Laurens van der Post

Modern Man in Search of a Soul is the perfect introduction to the theories and concepts of one of the most original and influential religious thinkers of the twentieth century. Lively and insightful, it covers all his most significant themes, including man's need for a God and the mechanics of dream analysis. One of his most famous books, it perfectly captures the feelings of confusion that many sense today.

Hb: 0–415–25544–9   Pb: 0–415–25390–X

For these and other classic titles from Routledge, visit
www.routledgeclassics.com

Routledge Classics
Get inside a great mind

On the Nature of the Psyche
C. G. Jung

'Next to Freud, no psychiatrist of today has advanced our insight into the nature of the psyche more than Jung has.'
Hermann Hesse

Jung's discovery of the 'collective unconscious', a psychic inheritance common to all humankind, transformed the understanding of the self and the way we interpret the world. In *On the Nature of the Psyche* Jung describes this remarkable theory in his own words, and presents a masterly overview of his theories of the unconscious and its relation to the conscious mind. Also contained in this collection is *On Psychic Energy*, where Jung defends his interpretation of the libido, a key factor in the breakdown of his relations with Freud. For anyone seeking to understand Jung's insights into the human mind, this volume is essential reading.

Hb: 0–415–25545–7   Pb: 0–415–25391–8

Dreams
C. G. Jung

'He taught himself how to read the language of dreams as if they were the forgotten language of the gods themselves.'
Laurens van der Post

In this revolutionary work, the visionary thinker C. G. Jung examines the meaning and function of our dreams and argues that by paying proper attention to them and their significance we can better understand our inner selves. He believed that dreams are 'most common and most normal expression of the unconscious psyche' and therefore provide the 'bulk of the material for its investigation.' This edition comprises Jung's most important writings on dreams and offers an overall survey of the subject that is without parallel.

Hb: 0–415–26740–4   Pb: 0–415–26741–2

For these and other classic titles from Routledge, visit
www.routledgeclassics.com